Black Milk

ALSO BY ELIF SHAFAK

The Forty Rules of Love

The Bastard of Istanbul

The Saint of Incipient Insanities

The Gaze

The Flea Palace

Black Milk

ON WRITING, MOTHERHOOD,
AND THE HAREM WITHIN

ELIF SHAFAK

Translated by Hande Zapsu

Viking

VIKING
Published by the Penguin Group
Penguin Group (USA) Inc., 375 Hudson Street, New York, New York 10014, U.S.A. •
Penguin Group (Canada), 90 Eglinton Avenue East, Suite 700, Toronto, Ontario, Canada
M4P 2Y3 (a division of Pearson Penguin Canada Inc.) • Penguin Books Ltd, 80 Strand,
London WC2R 0RL, England • Penguin Ireland, 25 St. Stephen's Green, Dublin 2, Ireland
(a division of Penguin Books Ltd) • Penguin Books Australia Ltd, 250 Camberwell Road,
Camberwell, Victoria 3124, Australia (a division of Pearson Australia Group Pty Ltd) •
Penguin Books India Pvt Ltd, 11 Community Centre, Panchsheel Park, New Delhi—110 017,
India • Penguin Group (NZ), 67 Apollo Drive, Rosedale, Auckland 0632, New Zealand
(a division of Pearson New Zealand Ltd) • Penguin Books (South Africa) (Pty) Ltd,
24 Sturdee Avenue, Rosebank, Johannesburg 2196, South Africa

Penguin Books Ltd, Registered Offices:
80 Strand, London WC2R 0RL, England

First published in 2011 by Viking Penguin,
a member of Penguin Group (USA) Inc.

10 9 8 7 6 5 4 3 2 1

Copyright © Elif Shafak, 2007
Translation copyright © Penguin Group (USA) Inc., 2011
All rights reserved

Originally published in Turkish as *Siyah Sut* by Dogan Egmont Yayincilik ve Yapimcilik Tic,
A.S., Istanbul.

Library of Congress Cataloging-in-Publication Data
Shafak, Elif, 1971–
Black milk : on writing, motherhood, and the harem within / Elif Shafak ; translated by
Hande Zapsu.
p.   cm.
ISBN 978-0-670-02264-9
1. Shafak, Elif, 1971– 2. Authors, Turkish—21st century—Biography. I. Zapsu, Hande,
1983– II. Title.
PL248.S474Z46 2011
894'.3534—dc22
[B]   2010045818

Printed in the United States of America
Designed by Daniel Lagin

For three females,
Beyza, Aurora and Zelda

For seventy years I have been steadily lowering and lowering my opinion of women, and I must still lower it more. The woman question! How could there not be a woman question! Only not about how women should control life, but how they should stop ruining it.

—Tolstoy the Misogynist

The goal of our life should not be to find joy in marriage, but to bring more love and truth into the world. We marry to assist each other in this task.

—Tolstoy the Feminist

I feel great tenderness for her [his daughter Masha]. Her only. She makes up for the others, I might say.

—Tolstoy again

Note to the Reader

I was in Istanbul when the earthquake hit in 1999. At the time I lived in one of the most vibrant and diverse neighborhoods in the city, where the quality of houses varied as widely as the stories of the people who inhabited them. When I ran out of the building with everyone else at three in the morning amid shouts and screams, I saw something that stopped me in my tracks. Across the street was the local grocer—a grumpy old man who didn't sell alcohol and didn't speak to marginals—sitting next to a transvestite with a long, black wig and mascara running down her cheeks. I watched the man open up a pack of cigarettes, his hands shaking, his face as white as a ghost, and offer one to her. That was, and still is, the image of that night that has stayed most entrenched in my mind: a conservative grocer and a crying transvestite smoking side by side. In the face of disaster and death, our mundane differences evaporated and we were all One, even if for only a few hours.

But I have always believed that stories, too, have a similar effect on us. I am not saying that fiction has the magnitude of an earthquake, but when we are inside a good novel we leave our cozy, small apartments behind and, through fictional characters, find ourselves getting to know people we had never met before, and perhaps had even disliked as our Others.

Years later I would recall that night in a completely different context: After the birth of my first child I experienced a strong depression that separated me from the one passion in life that until then I had held above everything: writing fiction.

It was an emotional tremor for me. When I ran out of the building of the Self that I had carefully constructed all those years, there in the darkness, scared and shaken, I encountered a group of Thumbelinas— six tiny finger-women, each of whom looked like a different version of me—sitting side by side. I knew four of them already. The two others I was meeting for the first time. I understood that if it weren't for the extraordinary situation of my postpartum depression, I would have never seen them in a new light, and they would have kept living in my body and soul without ever listening to one another, like neighbors who share the same air but never a peaceful greeting.

Perhaps all women live with a mini harem inside and the discrepancy, tension and hard-achieved harmony among our conflicting selves is what really makes us ourselves.

It took me a while to get to know and love all of the six Thumbelinas.

This book is the story of how I faced my inner diversity and then learned to be One.

❧

I am a writer.

I am a nomad.

I am a cosmopolite.

I am a lover of Sufism.

I am a pacifist.

I am a vegetarian and I am a woman, more or less in that order.

That is how I would have defined myself until I reached the age of thirty-five.

Up to that moment, first and foremost I saw myself as a teller of tales. Once upon a time, people like me shared their stories around a campfire, under a sky so wide you could never be sure where it ended, if it ever did. In Paris, they scraped together the rent by writing for newspapers. In the palace of a despotic sultan each story earned them the right to live one more day. Be it the Anonymous Narrator, Balzac or the beautiful Shehrazat, I felt connected to those storytellers of old. The truth is, like many other novelists, I felt closer to dead writers than to contemporary ones, and perhaps related more easily to imaginary people than to those who were real—well, too real.

That was how I lived. That was how I planned to go on living. But then something totally unexpected, miraculous and bewildering happened to me: motherhood.

It changed everything, changed *me*.

I blinked at my new role, as baffled as a bat wakened by sunlight.

The day I learned I was pregnant the writer in me panicked, the woman in me became happily confused, the pacifist in me remained passive, the cosmopolite in me began to think of international baby names, the Sufi in me welcomed the news, the vegetarian in me worried about having to have to eat meat and the nomad in me just wanted to take to her heels and run as fast as she could. But that is what happens when you are pregnant. You can run away from everything and everyone but not from the changes in your body.

When the postpartum depression hit, it caught me completely unguarded. Stretching out in front of me like a dark tunnel that seemed to have no end, it scared me out of my wits. As I tried to cross through it, I fell down several times and my personality was shattered into pieces so small there was no way I could glue them back together again. Yet, at the same time, the experience helped me to look within and meet anew every member of the mini harem I had carried inside of me all those years. A depression can be a golden opportunity given to us by life to face head-on issues that matter greatly to our hearts, but which, out of haste or ignorance, have been swept under the carpet.

I am not sure what came first and what followed. Did I exit from my depression and then start writing this book? Or did I complete the book and in that way manage to crawl out of the tunnel? The truth is, I cannot tell. My memories of those days are vivid and intense, but they are far from being chronological.

I do know for certain, however, that this book was written with black milk and white ink—a cocktail of storytelling, motherhood, wanderlust and depression, distilled for several months at room temperature.

Every book is a journey, a map into the complexities of the human mind and soul. This one is no different. Every reader therefore is a traveler of a sort. Some tours introduce one to cultural heritage sites, while others focus on outdoor adventures and wildlife. In the pages that follow, I want to take you on two tours at the same time, one into the Valley of Babies, the other into the Forest of Books.

In the Valley of Babies, I will invite you to take a closer look at the many roles that make up our lives, starting with womanhood, motherhood and authorship. In the Forest of Books, I will discuss the lives and works of various women writers, past and present, East and West, to see how they have dealt with similar topics, successfully or unsuccessfully.

This book was written not only for women who may have shared, or will share, a similar depression but also for anyone—man or woman, single or married, parent or childless, writer or reader—who finds it difficult, at times, to balance the multiplicity of roles and responsibilities in their lives.

The Sufis believe that every human being is a mirror that reflects the universe at large. They say each of us is a walking microcosm. To be human, therefore, means to live with an orchestra of conflicting voices and mixed emotions. This could be a rewarding and enriching experience were we not inclined to praise some members of that inner orchestra at the expense of others. We suppress many aspects of our personalities in order to conform to the perfect image we try to live up to. In this way, there is rarely—if ever—a democracy inside of us, but instead a solid oligarchy where some voices reign over the rest.

Black Milk is an attempt to topple that oligarchy through peaceful means, to move forward into a full-fledged, healthy inner democracy. While it would be naïve to assume that a democratic regime is a bed of roses, it is still preferable to any kind of despotism. Only when we can harmonize and synchronize the voices within can we become better mothers, better fathers and yes, probably better writers.

But I am getting ahead of myself here and I shouldn't. I need to do a U-turn and go back in time, and look for the moment when everything started.

Black Milk

Lucky Dishwasher

There we were, my mother and I, caught in a bittersweet maze of feelings that only mothers and daughters are capable of getting caught in. But my heart was full of gratitude for the way she had responded to the sudden news and I thanked her for being so supportive.

"Oh, I am not being supportive at all, honey. I am just like a poor dishwasher who by chance finds a lottery ticket on the sidewalk and learns that he won the jackpot."

As accustomed to my mother's codes and ciphers as I am, I didn't get this one right away. "I'm afraid I don't understand."

"But it is so clear, sweetheart. You feared I would be upset when I heard you secretly got married in another country, and when you saw I wasn't upset in the slightest, you felt grateful. Is that right?"

I nodded. "Right."

"You see, only a mother who is certain that her daughter will get married someday would be disappointed upon learning that she has done it without notice. Frankly, I never had any expectations of you in that regard. It seemed like you would be the last person on earth to get hitched. So I didn't go and buy a lottery ticket every week and pin my hopes on it. Does that make sense?"

It was beginning to.

Happy to have my full attention, my mother continued enthusiastically. "So I accepted the situation as it was and went on with my life. Then one day out of the blue I found this ticket on the sidewalk and learned that I had won the lottery. That is how I felt when I heard the news of your nuptials, as astounded as a lucky dishwasher!"

I had recently gotten married in Berlin. It was no coincidence that we had chosen this city to tie the knot because our marriage, at least to us, seemed no less surprising than the unexpected reunification of Germany. Like East and West Berlin, we, too, had been together once, then separated, and were now getting back together. My husband and I also had—and still have—personalities as different as capitalism and communism. Eyup is a gentle and generous soul, an always-rational man bestowed with an amazing inner balance and the patience of the prophet Job, from whom he got his name. As for me, I would have to tick off pretty much everything opposite from his qualities, starting with "impatient," "impulsive," "irrational," "emotional" and "walking chaos."

We refrained from having a wedding as neither of us was fond of ceremonies. So we simply walked into the Turkish Embassy on Kbaum Avenue and announced our intention to get married. There was a homeless man sitting on a bench next to the entrance, his head full of lice and thoughts, his face turned up to the sky, happily basking under the sun. I thought he would make a perfect witness but when I tried to ask him if he would come inside with us, he spoke no English, I spoke no German, and the sign language we invented there and then was not creative enough to cover a subject this unusual. Instead we offered him a pack of Marlboro Lights, and in return he seemed to bless us with a toothless smile. He also gave us a shiny golden chocolate wrapper that he had carefully smoothed out. I accepted the gift with delight. It seemed like a good omen.

I didn't wear a wedding gown not only because of my distaste for such a ritual but also because I don't ever wear white. I have always had a hard time understanding how other people can. For years I could not even sit on a couch if it was too white, but I was gradually cured of this habit. My friends have several theories as to why I don't like white. They think I might have fallen into a cauldron of rice pudding when I was a baby (unlike Obelix falling into the Magic Potion, this gave me no supernatural powers) and ended up hating the color, but not the pudding. However, I have no such recollection, and their second theory about me being biased against doctors, dentists or lab technicians—people who wear white—isn't true either.

In any case, on that day in May, I adorned myself in my preferred color of choice: black. As for Eyup, he wore dark pants and a white shirt, to honor tradition to some extent. That is how we said "I do." Without fuss and on a whim. Although Eyup's parents and five sisters, and my mother and grandmother, would have loved it had we had a typical Turkish wedding with food, dance and music, when they found out that we had gotten married, they were kind enough to respect the way we chose to go about it.

Lucky dishwashers aside, my mother wasn't the only one who didn't expect me to get married. Apparently neither did my readers. As followers of my novels and essays, they had always been the first to understand what I felt. But this time they showed more shock than understanding. In letters, e-mails and postcards they expressed their surprise. Some even sent me clips of my earlier interviews where I had said, "Domestic bourgeois life? Forget it! It doesn't suit me," and, "I don't think raising kids is my thing, but I believe I could make a good stepmother someday. You know, someone you can easily take to a football game or to a prom dress rehearsal." Now, with a "gotcha" moment in their eyes, those smart readers with wry humor demanded to know what had changed.

There was only one answer I could give them: love.

I love my husband and always feel a strange calmness and happiness descend upon me when I am next to him. Yet there was a part of me that didn't know how to deal with such tranquillity and wouldn't or just couldn't settle down into wedded bliss. Perhaps it was because I couldn't settle down anywhere for too long. Having been born in Strasbourg, raised in Madrid, and resided in Ankara, Istanbul, Amman, Cologne, Boston, Michigan and Arizona, I had been living out of a suitcase all my life—certain that I could stay anywhere and everywhere on this planet as long as I didn't have to put down roots. As the only child of a single mother, I had accepted one truth about human nature early on that I saw others trying to resist in vain: that loneliness was an inseparable part of being human.

I liked loneliness. I cherished it. I knew people who would go nuts if they were alone for too many hours. It was the opposite with me. I would go nuts if I had to be in the company of other people all the time. I would miss my privacy.

My vocation as a novelist thrives upon solitude. In almost all areas of art one has to work with other people during the creative process. Even the most egotistical of film directors has to be good at harmonizing his energy with that of others, learning to function as a team. So, too, fashion designers, actors, dancers, playwrights, singers and musicians.

But not fiction writers. For weeks, months and sometimes years on end, we retreat into the novels we write; we stay inside that imaginary cocoon surrounded by imaginary characters, writing destinies, thinking we are God. As we develop plots, add sudden twists, create and destroy characters, we can easily end up presuming we are the center of the world. Self-absorption and an inflated ego are the two most harmful side effects of our profession. That is why we make poor lovers and even poorer wives and husbands. Writers are primarily asocial creatures—though we can easily forget that with a bit of fame and success. The novel is the loneliest form of art, as Walter Benjamin once said.

During the period after my wedding I was teaching in Arizona and every few weeks I would hop on a plane for a twenty-six-hour flight (with connections) to be with my husband and friends back in the crazy, chaotic, colorful rhythm of Istanbul, and then I would return to Arizona to retreat into my desert solitude.

The first thing you feel when you walk out of Tucson International Airport is the heat wave, rising from the depths of the earth, licking your face with invisible flames. The first thing you feel when you walk out of Ataturk International Airport in Istanbul is the wave of noise, a loud jumble of cars honking, motorcycles rumbling, jackhammers drilling and people talking, yelling and whistling, all at the same time.

Heat wave, noise wave. Back and forth. This went on for almost two years. Then one day, I learned I was pregnant.

I hadn't known I wanted to become a mother and it took me by surprise. But I wanted to have this baby. It was as if another part of me—a domestic, nurturing, maternal side—was now rebelling against the part that had dominated all those years. The insurgent forces of motherhood infiltrated the tiny little villages south of my personality with amazing speed and agility, but the vested powers sitting in the capital were still holding strong.

Yet, I didn't want to lose the wandering, independent, carefree spirit that I was. Inside my head there were six voices speaking all at once. Hence I entered this pregnancy with mixed feelings, as if I were being dragged toward the unknown by an undercurrent that was stronger than my heart. It didn't help that I was put on trial during the final stages of my pregnancy due to the sentences a few of my Armenian fictional characters uttered in my novel *The Bastard of Istanbul*. By coincidence the trial was set for the day after my delivery. Although I was acquitted at the first hearing, and the experience had no bearing on my subsequent depression, those tense days added to the challenges of the entire year.

I gave birth in September 2006, the most beautiful month of the year in Istanbul. Happy and blessed as I felt, I was also perplexed and unprepared. We rented a charming, quiet house on the islands where I could nurse and write. That was the plan. But it turned out I could do neither. My milk wasn't sufficient, and each time I attempted to go back into the world of fiction and start a new novel, I found myself staring at a blank page with growing unease. That had never happened to me before. I had never run out of stories. I had never experienced writer's block or anything that came close to it. For the first time in my adult life, as hard as I tried, words wouldn't speak to me.

Suddenly I was seized by the fear that something had irreversibly changed in me and I would never be the same again. A wave of panic surged through me. I started to think that now that I had become a mother and housewife, I would not be able to write fiction anymore. Like an old dusty carpet, my old Self was pulled out from under my feet.

Books had been my best friend since the day I learned how to read and write. Books had saved me. I had been an introverted child to the point of communicating with colored crayons and apologizing to objects when I bumped into them. Stories had given me a sense of continuity, center and coherence—the three Cs that I otherwise sorely lacked. I breathed letters, drank words and lived stories, confident that I could twist and twirl language in a passionate tango.

All this time my writing had filled the one suitcase I took with me wherever I went. Fiction was the invisible glue that held my different facets together, and when it was no longer with me, all my pieces fell apart. Without it, the world seemed like a melancholic place, infinitely sad. Colors that had looked bright and cheerful were now dull. Nothing was enough anymore. Nothing seemed familiar. I, who had traveled across continents, easily finding home in so many places, could not find the strength or will to go out into the street. My skin got so thin everything started to hurt me. The sun was too hot, the wind too harsh and the night too dark. I was full of anxiety and apprehension. Before I knew it, I had plunged into a severe postpartum depression.

After weeks of watching me cry, my maternal grandmother—a gentle but mighty woman with abundant superstitions—held my hand and whispered, in a voice as soft as velvet, "My dear child, you've got to pull yourself together. Don't you know that with every tear a new mother sheds, her milk turns sour?"

I didn't know that.

I found myself thinking about this image. What would happen if my milk curdled? Would it darken, acquiring a thick and murky texture? The thought of this not only alarmed me but also made me feel guilty. The more I tried not to cry the more I felt like doing so. How come every other woman I knew adapted to motherhood so easily, but

I couldn't? I wanted to breast-feed my child as long and best as I could. The image of spoiling milk nagged at me during the day, and attacked me in my dreams.

Then one morning, after months of depression, seclusion and unsuccessful treatment, I woke up with an urge to write again and sat at my desk. It was quiet, except for a few fishing boats in the distance and the baby sleeping in her cradle. There was a scent of jasmine in the air and the sky over the Bosphorus was a blue so pale that it had almost no color. Suddenly I had this most soothing realization that everything was okay and had always been so. As Rumi said, the night contained the day. We could start our lives over, anytime and anywhere.

It was okay that I had panicked and could not stop crying. It was okay that I had feared I couldn't manage writing and motherhood at the same time. Had my milk not been as white as snow, that, too, would be okay. If I started to write about the experience, I could turn my blackened milk into ink, and as writing had always had a magical healing effect on my soul, I could perhaps inch my way out of this depression.

That same day, I put the baby in her pram and walked out of the house into the bustling street. At first cautiously, then more daringly, I started talking to other women about their postpartum experiences. I was surprised to hear how many of them had gone through a similar emotional turbulence. Why didn't we know more about this? I had always been told that all women jump for joy as soon as they hold their babies in their arms. No one said that while jumping some of us hit our heads on the ceiling, making us temporarily dizzy.

As I kept writing *Black Milk* I had myriad moving conversations with women of all ages and professions. Slowly and steadily, it dawned on me that I wasn't alone. That helped a lot. It was ironic for someone who had always taken pride in her ability to be alone to seek solace in numbers, but I chose not to dwell on that. The simple fact is that postpartum depression is far more common than we, as a society, would want to believe.

Interestingly, women knew about this in the old days. Our great-grandmothers were aware of all kinds of postpartum instability and therefore better prepared. They passed on their knowledge to their daughters and granddaughters. But today we are so disconnected from the past that we have no real access to this wisdom. We are modern women. When we are weary and bruised inside we hide the signs with the latest makeup techniques. We think we can give birth one day and go on with our lives the next. Some of us do, of course. The trouble is, others simply cannot.

In Turkey, elderly women believe that during the forty days following the birth of a baby, a new mother should be kept in the company of her loved ones. If she were to be left alone, even for a moment, she might become susceptible to the attacks of the djinni—falling prey to a deluge of worries, anxieties and fears. That is why traditional families still decorate the bed of a new mother with scarlet ribbons and scatter sanctified poppy seeds around the room to ward off any supernatural powers looming in the air.

I am not trying to argue here that we should be guided by a bundle of superstitions or expect health care to cover decorations of garlic strings and evil-eye beads in maternity wards. What I am saying is that women of premodern times—through their old wives' tales, traditions and beliefs—recognized an essential fact that we are not that good at acknowledging: Throughout her life, a woman goes through several major stages, and the transition from one to the next might not be easy. She might require additional help, support and guidance before she starts living fully in the present again. As a woman moves from one day to the next, struggling, problem solving, organizing and controlling, there are times when the machine of her body may falter. It is this simple and age-old wisdom that we have lost touch with in our determination to be successful, strong and always perfect.

Mrs. Weakness is not a popular woman among the members of our generation. Nobody knows where she is now, but there are rumors that she has been sent into exile to an island in the Pacific or a village on the outskirts of the Himalayas. We have all heard of her, but it is forbidden to say her name aloud. At our workplace, school or home, whenever we hear someone talk about her we flinch, fearing the consequences. While she is not exactly on the Interpol List of the Most Wanted, nobody wants to be associated with her.

None of this is to deny that motherhood is one of the greatest gifts in life. It molds the heart like clay, bringing one in tune with the rhythm of the universe. There is a reason why countless women say motherhood was the best thing that happened to them. I agree with that from the bottom of my soul.

Nevertheless, a woman does not become a mother the very minute she gives birth. It is a learning process, and for some it simply takes longer than for others. There are those, like myself, who find themselves shaken to the core by the entire experience. I am not claiming that the transition into motherhood is more difficult for creative people, as I have seen women from all walks of life undergo similar trouble, albeit in varying degrees. No woman is absolutely immune to postpartum blues. Perhaps the strongest and most confident among us are the ones who are, in fact, most vulnerable. Interestingly, this psychological roller coaster can happen just as easily with the second, the third or even the sixth pregnancy as with the first.

After all, pregnancies are like snowflakes. No two are exactly alike.

PART ONE

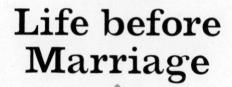

Life before Marriage

Signs

It is noontime in Istanbul. I am on the steamboat *Gypsy,* named after the way it dances in the blue waters, ferrying passengers between the islands and the mainland. Young lovers stealing kisses, high school students skipping class, office workers prolonging their lunch break, photographers lugging their cameras, salesmen backpacking their wares, tourists being tourists . . . Somehow people from all walks of life seem to have found themselves in this nutshell of a vessel that is swaying from side to side. I am squashed in a corner. With books on my lap, I am sitting between an overweight woman and a well-groomed, elderly gentleman. Having completed an interview for a literary magazine on one of the islands, I am on the return route. The city girl is going home. Alone.

Shortly after the boat leaves port, I realize I have forgotten my notebook at the place where I did the interview. Suddenly, I feel bad. Why do I always go around forgetting something or other? Umbrellas, cell phones, vitamins, mascaras, lipsticks, hair bands, gloves . . . I forget half-eaten sandwiches that I've put aside for a few minutes, and I forget, in public toilets, my silver rings after I've taken them off to wash my hands. Once I even forgot a glass bowl with two turtles in it, a birthday present from a dear friend. As I couldn't bring myself to confess to my friend that I had lost her present the very day she had given it to me, during the weeks that followed, every time she asked me about the turtles, I made up stories.

"Oh, they are doing great, gorging on my cyclamens, gaining weight."

Then I said: "You know, the other day one of the turtles sneaked out of the bowl without my noticing. I looked everywhere but couldn't find it. Then later, when I turned on the reading lamp, there it was. Sitting comfortably on the bulb! The shadow it cast on the wall looked like a monster."

I went on inventing the adventures of my two turtles until one day my friend looked me in the eye and asked me to please stop. Her voice suddenly dwindled into a whisper; she told me she had a confession to make.

"I need to get this off my chest," she said. "When I first bought the turtles I had serious doubts whether you would take good care of them. But you proved me wrong. You are doing such a great job that I think I owe you an apology."

I bit my lip and stood still, not breathing. That was it. After that I couldn't fabricate turtle stories and a few days later it was my turn to make a confession. I told my friend that she did not owe me an apology as it was I who had to apologize, not once but twice, for my carelessness and for my deception. I then explained to her that her turtles had never made it to my house.

"You know, I had a hunch," she said after a long, awkward silence. "When you told me the turtles were nibbling sunflower seeds out of your hands, I wondered if you were confusing them with caged canaries."

To my relief she broke into a laugh and I joined her. We made fun of my sloppiness. I didn't really mind. Other than the embarrassment of losing the gift, the incident induced no further self-criticism in my soul. What difference did it make if I was a good caretaker or not? After all, turtles weren't babies.

Suddenly the steamboat rocks, like a giant stretching out of sleep. All of us passengers live through a moment of panic. Lips move restlessly, hands reach for something to grab. Far ahead there is a Russian tanker creating massive waves. We watch the tanker uneasily, and yet as soon as the waves smooth out into ripples, we end our prayers, loosen our fists and sink back into lethargy.

But I have other concerns on my mind. Since realizing I no longer had my notebook, I have been thinking of nothing but writing. I guess I have a tendency to make life more difficult for myself. If I actually had paper, I might not have such a strong urge to take notes at this instant. But because I don't have paper, I *must* write. I furiously dig in my bag and empty everything onto my lap, but I can't find even a receipt to write on the back of.

I don't know why I am fretting. There is an idea buzzing in my head but just what it is I cannot tell until I put it in writing. Many people, including many writers, prefer to mull things over in detail before jotting them down, but I am the opposite. In order to understand the thoughts churning in my mind, I have to first see them in the form of letters. I know I have an idea now, but I need to put pen to paper to learn what it is. And for that I need paper.

I glance left and right. The woman next to me doesn't look like she could be of help. There appears to be a ton of knickknacks in her shopping bags, but I doubt there is a notebook among them. Now that I have paid attention to her, I realize how young she actually is. She seems to be around twenty-five. It is her extra weight that makes her appear, at first glance, ten to fifteen years older. She is wearing a balloon-sleeved, puffy-skirted azure dress—as if she has just walked out of a 1930s movie and got on a steamboat in Istanbul. Her hair, a wavy dark brown, is cut at shoulder length and newly combed. A pair of golden earrings dangles from her ears. Her toenails, visible through her open shoes, are painted a vivid red. Though the buttons of her dress look as though they are about to burst, she doesn't seem to mind. She has accepted the largeness of her breasts as a blessing and exhibits them as a favor to all mankind without discrimination. A woman who is proud of her womanhood and all the more womanly in her pride, she exudes a strong, bold and magnetic femininity.

As I do next to all women who glow with this kind of femininity,

I feel like an impostor, a poor imitation of my gender. To her, womanhood comes naturally, like a yawn or sneeze, just as effortless. To me, womanhood is something I need to observe and study, learn and imitate, and still can never fully comprehend.

If the woman next to me were a cat, she would be lying in a gorgeous basket beside a heater, her eyes narrowed to slits, or she would be curled up on the lap of her owner purring in delight, flicking her tail to a rhythm of her own. If I were a cat, I would be sitting anxiously by the windowsill all day long, watching the cars drive by and the pedestrians pass, and I would run from the house at the earliest opportunity into the wide world outside.

On the other side of the woman, there is a boy around eight years old, and next to him, a younger boy who strikingly resembles his brother. Both boys are wearing the same jeans and navy striped T-shirt. They have the same toys in their hands. Muscular, dark green, fully equipped plastic commandos, armed in one hand with a grenade whose pin is ready to be pulled, in the other with a Kalashnikov. Both boys are chewing wads of gum as big as walnuts, blowing one bubble after another. Every time a bubble pops, I flinch—as if they have shot at someone with those plastic commandos. Another enemy gets cleared off the steamboat.

Their toys may assault, but the boys are introverted. They don't even lift their heads to look at their mother. They are particularly careful not to come eye to eye with her. I suppose it is not easy for boys of their age to have a mother who is that attractive.

Convinced that neither the boys nor their mother can help me in my quest to find paper, I turn to the man on my left. He has metal-framed glasses, a serious expression, and though he must be forty at most, the top of his head is already balding. The man's body language screams, "I AM A SALESMAN." He is holding a leather bag, in which I'm certain there is paper somewhere. When I ask, he kindly offers me more than a few sheets, each sporting the letterhead SHOOTING STAR MARKETING LTD.

Thanking the man, I start to write, watching the ink dry as I move on. The letters pour forth as if of their own accord: THE MANIFESTO OF THE SINGLE GIRL.

I look at the paper in bewilderment. So this is what was on my mind.

The woman beside me edges closer, her head craned toward the paper on my lap. On Istanbul's steamboats you get used to people reading newspapers over your shoulder, but this woman is openly reading my notes. Though my first instinct is to try to cover what I've written, I soon accept the futility of looking for privacy in such a small, confined space and let her read.

1. Saying that loneliness is reserved for God the Almighty, and thus expecting everyone to pair up for life is one of the biggest illusions invented by Man. Just because we embarked on Noah's Ark in twos doesn't mean we have to complete the entire trip in pairs.

I'm writing and the woman is reading. At one point she leans so far onto my right shoulder that her hair touches my face. I inhale the scent of her shampoo, tangy and fruity. She seems to be having problems deciphering my notes, and, given my handwriting, I don't blame her. I make an effort to write more clearly.

2. How is it that in traditional societies, people who dedicated their lives to their faith and swore never to marry were revered by all, but in today's culture being a "spinster" is almost a disgrace, a pitied condition?

3. How is it that, even though marriage needs a woman and a man, and being unmarried is a condition that applies to both sexes equally, the term *spinster* has different—and more negative—connotations than *bachelor*?

My neighbor pulls out a pack of trail mix from her bag, shares half of it with her sons and turns her attention back to my writing, munching as she reads. Amid salty peanuts, roasted yellow chickpeas and pumpkin seeds, I write and she looks on, happily entertained.

4. Women who have been "left on the shelf" should have their dignity returned and be applauded for daring to live without a man to watch over them.

5. Those who use the expression "the female bird builds the nest" don't understand the bird. It is true that birds build nests, but with every new season they abandon the home they have made to erect a new one in a different place. There is no bird that stays in the same nest for the entirety of its life.

I notice the woman briefly shudder. The hair on her arms stands up as if the day were not pulsing with heat.

6. Change and changeability are life's alphabet. The vow to stay together "till death do us part" is a fantasy that runs against the essence of life. Besides, we don't die only once. It is worth remembering that human beings die many deaths before dying physically.

7. Therefore one can promise only to love at this very moment and nothing beyond that.

8. If I must resort to marriage as a metaphor, I can claim that literature is my husband and books are my children. The only way for me to get married is either to divorce literature or to take a second husband.

9. Since divorcing literature is out of the question and since there is no man among mankind who would agree to become "husband number two," in all likelihood, I will be single all my life.

10. Herewith this piece of paper is my manifesto.

I lean back and wait for the woman to finish reading. She is lagging behind, mouthing the words syllable by syllable like a schoolgirl who has just learned the alphabet. The gentle breeze that licks the deck carries the scent of the sea toward us and I taste salt on my tongue. After a few seconds the woman leans back and heaves a sigh, really loud.

I can't help but feel curious. What did she mean by that? Did she agree with me? Was it a sigh that meant, "You are so right, sister, but this is the way the world is and has always been"? Or did she rather want to say, "You write all this crap, honey, but real life works differently"? I have a feeling it is the latter.

Suddenly I am seized by an urge to needle her. This woman is my Other. She is the kind of woman who has gladly dedicated her life to her home, to her husband and to her sons. Since youth she focused her energy on finding an ideal husband and starting her own family, became a mother before saying farewell to her girlhood, gained weight for the cause, has aged before her time, has allowed her desires to turn into regrets and become sour inside. This woman, with her canned dreams, comfortable social status and bygone aspirations, is my antithesis. Or so I want to believe.

"For a woman, any woman, the right way to engender is through her uterus, not through her brain."* That is what some of the leading male novelists in my country believed. They claimed fiction writing as their terrain, an inherently manly task. The novel was a most rational construct, a cerebral work that required engineering and plotting, and since women were, by definition, emotional beings, they wouldn't make good novelists. These famous writers saw themselves as "Father Novelists" and their readers as sons in need of guidance. Their heritage makes me suspect that in order to exist and excel in the territory of literature, I, too, might have to make a choice between uterus and brain. If it ever comes to that, I have no doubt as to which one I will choose.

The steamboat is about to arrive at the shore. Unaware of my thoughts the woman next to me leaps to her feet. *Gather the bags, pack the chickpeas, ready the boys, bundle the Kalashnikovs, squeeze feet back into*

---

* Peyami Safa (1899–1961): a renowned Turkish writer who lived in Istanbul and was known for his novels, editorials and journalism.

shoes . . . In less than thirty seconds she is all packed. Pushing and shoving through the crowd with her boys by her side, she moves toward the exit, away from me.

Only then, only when the woman gets up, do I notice something I should have detected before. The woman isn't overweight. She isn't even plump. She is heavily pregnant, that's all. Her belly looks so huge, she could well be expecting twins or triplets.

For some reason unbeknownst to me, this insignificant detail turns my head. But there is no time to muse. The steamboat is at the dock. Everybody springs to their feet in a hurry, swarming chaotically toward the doors. In that commotion, I come eye-to-eye with the man beside me.

"Thank you for the paper. . . ." I say.

"You are most welcome," he says. "I am happy if I was able to help."

"Oh, you were," I say. "Just curious, what is Shooting Star Marketing?"

"We are a new company specializing in products for mothers and newborn babies," he says. "Electronic milk pumps, bottle warmers and things like that. . . ."

The man's smile blossoms into a grin. Or maybe it just looks that way to me. Suddenly it feels like somewhere in that bright blue sky where the sun has now begun to descend, the angels are pointing their milky-white fingers at me, making fun. There is an irony, when I come to think of it, in writing a single-girl manifesto on the letterhead of a company that sells products for new mothers.

Having noticed this irony, but not sure what to do with it, I stand there dumbstruck. A voice inside me says, "There are no coincidences in the universe, only signs. Can you see the signs?"

I brush the voice away and put my manifesto in my pocket, no longer completely convinced of its credibility. In this state I disembark the steamboat *Gypsy*.

Is this a sign I wasn't seeing? For no reason at all I had written the single-girl manifesto. In that same breath I had seen the woman beside me as my Other. She was "the housekeeper-mother-wife" I would never let myself become. Thinking I was not only different from but also far better than she, I swore to be Miss Spinster Writer. Meanwhile, I wasn't aware that above my manifesto glowed the name of a company that served new mothers. The universe was mocking my arrogance.

There must have been signs, not one but many, because months after writing this manifesto I fell head over heels in love. I even got married. As used to assuming that I would descend from Noah's Ark alone as I was, I awakened to the beauty of being part of a couple. Two years later I gave birth to my first child. During my pregnancy I often remembered how I had belittled the woman on the steamboat and I felt regret, piercing regret.

There must have been other signs, not one but many, because a few weeks after giving birth—when it became apparent that my milk was not going to be sufficient and had to be increased in quantity—we called a number that friends had given us and rented an electronic milk pump. When the machine was delivered to our house, I noticed a familiar logo on the package: SHOOTING STAR MARKETING.

Who knows, maybe it was the gentleman from the steamboat who dropped the milk pump at our house. . . . Who knows, maybe the no-longer-fat woman with her blue dress and sons, plastic commandos, roasted chickpeas and newborn twins or triplets was also there somewhere, hiding behind a bush, laughing at the change in my life, at this unexpected twist of fate.

In the Beginning There Was Tea . . .

A few weeks after the steamboat incident and long before the thought of getting married crosses my mind, I am having tea with a woman novelist. Little do I know that this encounter will motivate me to think harder about the choices we make between creating babies and creating books.

"I would like to meet you, Miss Shafak. Why don't you come over for tea?" she had said to me over the phone a few days earlier, and added with bright laughter: "The tea is only an excuse, of course. The real purpose is to talk. Come over and talk we shall." Eighty-one years old and still as passionate about writing as she was in her youth, Adalet Agaoglu is one of the foremost literary voices of her generation. I am excited to meet her.

Although she had given me meticulous directions to her home, on the evening of the meeting I spend some time looking for the address. As in many of Istanbul's neighborhoods, this one, too, has a maze of alleys that snake up and down, wind and intertwine into new streets under different names. Finally, when I find the apartment, I still have ten more minutes until the appointment, so I wander around a bit. Up at the corner there is a makeshift flower stand next to which two Gypsy women are sitting cross-legged in their dazzlingly-colored baggy trousers, jingling the gold bracelets on their wrists, puffing cigarettes. I admire them, not only for the perfect smoke rings they blow out but also for their total indifference to social limitations. They are the kind of women who can smoke cigarettes on the streets in a culture where public space and the right to smoke in the open belong to men.

Five minutes later, with a bouquet of yellow lilies in my hand and curiosity in my heart, I ring the bell. As I wait for the door to be opened, little do I know that this meeting will have far-reaching consequences in my life, triggering a series of reflections inside me about womanhood, motherhood and being a writer.

Ms. Agaoglu opens the door. Her skin is slightly pale, her smile cautious and her short hair the style of a woman who doesn't want to spend too much time with her hair.

"Here you are! Come on in," she says, her voice brimming with energy.

I follow her into the large sitting room. The place is spacious, immaculate and tastefully decorated. Every object seems to have fallen into its niche in seamless harmony. Though we are still deep in the heart of summer, it is a gusty day, with Istanbul's infamous northeast *poyraz* wind pounding on the windowpanes, penetrating the cracks in the doors. But her home is serene and smells of years of order and quiet.

I perch myself on the closest armchair. But no sooner do I lean back than I realize this happens to be the highest chair in the room and it might not be appropriate for me to sit here. I leap to my feet and try the sofa on the opposite side. It is so soft that I almost sink into it. Sensing I won't be comfortable there either, I slide over to the adjacent chair, which I instantly regret, because who would sit on a hard chair when there is a comfy sofa instead?

Meanwhile, hands folded on her lap, Ms. Agaoglu sits erect and composed, watching my every move from behind her glasses with an amusement she doesn't feel the need to hide. If it weren't for the look on her face I could have changed places again, but I hold my breath and manage to stay still.

"Finally we have met," she says. "Women writers are not great fans of each other, but I wanted to meet you in person."

Not knowing what to say to that, I smile awkwardly and try a less contentious beginning. "How very quiet it is here."

"Thank God it is," she says. "It is hard to admit this in a city as noisy as Istanbul, but I get disturbed by the slightest sound when I am writing fiction. It is crucial for me to have absolute peace and quiet while I work."

She pauses, measuring me with brightened interest, then continues, "But I understand you are not like that. I read your interview the other day. You seem to write on the move, enjoying disorder and displacement. I find that really . . ."

"Strange?" I offer.

She arches her thin eyebrows in dissent, searching for the exact word.

"Incomprehensible?" I make another attempt.

"Bizarre," she says finally. "I find it really bizarre."

I give a small nod. How can I explain to her that the order and quiet she so values give me the creeps? To live in the same house for decades, to know the face of every store owner and neighbor in the area, to be rooted in the same street, same quarter, same city, is an idea that I find harrowing. Steadiness and stability are Russian and Chinese to me. While I know they are great languages with rich histories, I don't speak them.

Silence is the worst. Whenever a thick cloud of silence descends, the yapping voices inside me become all the more audible, rising to the surface one by one. I like to believe I know all the women in this inner harem of mine but perhaps there are those I have never met. Together they make a choir that does not know how to tone down. I call them the Choir of Discordant Voices.

It is a *bizarre* choir, now that I think about it. Not only are they all off-key, none of them can read notes. In fact, there is no music at all in what they do. They all talk at the same time, each in a voice louder than the other, never listening to what is being said. They make me afraid of my own diversity, the fragmentation inside of me. That is why

I do not like the quiet. I even find it unpleasant, unsettling. When working at home or in a hotel room, I make sure to turn on the radio, the TV or the CD player, and sometimes all three at the same time. Used to writing in hectic airports, crowded cafés or boisterous restaurants, I am at my best when surrounded by a rich ruckus.

It suddenly occurs to me that this might be why I, unlike all my friends, never get upset with those drivers who roll down their windows and broadcast pop music over and beyond the seven hills of Istanbul. It's my belief that those *magandas*★ are just as scared of the quiet as I am. They, too, are afraid to be left alone with their inner voices.

Just like those showy types, I open my windows as I sit down to work on a novel. Surely my aim is not to invade the outside world with my personal music. I want the music of the outside world to invade my inner space. The cries of seagulls, the honking of cars, the siren of an ambulance, the quarrels of the couple living upstairs, the clamor of the children playing football across the street, the sounds of backgammon pieces coming from coffeehouses, the yelling of peddlers and the punk and postpunk music spinning on my CD player . . . Only in this hullabaloo is the revelry inside me briefly drowned out. Only then can I write in peace.

"Would you like to see the desk where I have written most of my books?" asks Ms. Agaoglu suddenly.

"Sure, I would love to."

It is an elegant mahogany desk topped with neatly organized manuscripts and books, decorated with carefully chosen memorabilia. A nice antique lamp radiates soft yellow light. She tells me she doesn't let anyone else clean her desk, as she wants to make sure every single object on it remains in the right place. I wonder for a moment whether that restriction applies to the entire room since there are also many items and photographs scattered all over the bookshelves, as well as

---

★ *Maganda*: Turkish slang for a man who is rude and crude; one who is stuck somewhere between Neanderthal and Man.

the coffee and end tables. A collector's passion for objects, each loaded with meaning and memory, is something that I have always found perplexing.

My relation with objects is based on serial disloyalty. I get them, I love them, I abandon them. Since childhood I have gotten used to packing and repacking boxes. When you move between neighborhoods, cities and continents, you can take with you only a certain amount of things. The rest of your possessions you learn to leave behind.

Born in France in 1903, Anaïs Nin was an author who left a big impact not only on world literature but also on the women's movement of the twentieth century. Though she was a prolific writer who produced novels, short stories and literary criticism, it was her diaries—most of which were published during her lifetime—that were most widely celebrated. Critics said most, if not all, the female characters in her fiction were her, a comment she heartily denied. One of the many intriguing things about her was how she, tired of dealing with the rules of the publishing world, decided to publish her own books. She bought a hand-fed printing press, learned how to run it and began to typeset. It was heavy labor, as she called it, especially for a woman who weighed no more than a hundred pounds. Later on when she talked about this experience, she said that printing her own books—setting each sentence into type—taught her, as a writer, how to be more succinct and less wordy.

Circumstances help us to learn how to be content with less.

Similarly, moving around has taught me how to survive with a minimal amount of furniture. What I buy in one city I abandon before leaving for the next. It is as if with every step I take and every gain I make, I lose something else somewhere. There is, however, one item in my hand baggage I have been able to take with me wherever I have gone. A satchel as old as the Dead Sea but as light as a feather, and not subject to customs anywhere in the world: the art of storytelling.

Even my most treasured books I could not keep together, piled as they are in cardboard boxes divided among the basements of relatives and friends. My Russian literature collection is in Ankara at my mother's house; all my books in Spanish, including *Don Quixote de la Mancha,* rest in the garage of a friend in a suburb of Istanbul; and *Arabian Nights,* all one thousand and one of them, still wait for me at Mount Holyoke College, where I was once a fellow.

In a strange way, such disorganization helps to bolster my memory. When you cannot keep your books with you, you have no choice but to memorize as many of the stories and passages as best as you can. That is how I have fragments of dialogue from Pasternak's *Doctor Zhivago* and poems from Rumi's *Mathnawi* carved in my mind. I cannot carry them with me, not books that thick or volumes that many, but I can always recite a few lines from Rumi off the top of my head. "Without Love's jewel inside of me, let the bazaar of my existence be destroyed stone by stone."

"Do you have a similar writing space you deem sacred?" Ms. Agaoglu asks.

"No, not really, but I have a laptop," I reply, knowing it sounds pathetic but saying it anyhow.

She gazes at me with eyes of wonder but then lets the subject drop. "Let's have tea now, shall we?"

I smile with relief. "Yes, please, thank you."

Back in the sitting room, as I wait for my host to return, a fact I have always known but never really faced plants itself in front of me: I have always clung, or maybe I wanted to cling, to bits and pieces of existence here and there, with no coherence, no center, no continuity in my life. There is a shorter way of saying this: I am a mess.

I see, in that precise moment, that however settled Ms. Agaoglu is, I am peripatetic to the same degree. However disciplined she is, I am disordered to the same extent. However hard I try to attach myself to an object, a home, an address or a relationship, the glue I use is never strong enough, and yet, odd though it is, such displacement has been both a curse and a blessing.

In a little while, Ms. Agaoglu reappears with a tray topped with porcelain teacups and plates. On my plate are pastries, the salty biscuits on the left, the sweet cookies on the right, all lined up in perfect symmetry and in equal number.

During the next half hour she tells me how it was for women writers in the past and, in her view, what has changed today. I listen, enjoying the conversation. There is no rush. No appointments to keep or tasks to accomplish. We speak of art and literature, of writers who have come and gone, and then of being a female writer in a patriarchal society.

Just then, out of the blue, Ms. Agaoglu catches me off guard by broaching a new topic. "I think at some point in their lives, women writers feel like they have to make a choice," she says. "At least that is what happened to me. I decided not to have children in order to dedicate myself to writing."

She tells me, in a voice calm but firm, that to be able to stand on her feet as a woman novelist and to write freely and copiously, she chose not to have any children of her own.

"I was lucky," she says, "because my husband backed me in this difficult decision. There is no way I could have done it without his support."

My stomach clenches. *Please don't ask me.* But she does.

"How about you? Is motherhood something you are considering?"

The manifesto I penned on the steamboat flashes in front of my eyes in gaudy capital letters. This might be the right time to recite some parts of it. But before I get a chance, the Choir of Discordant Voices begins to sing, as if an on button has been pressed.

"Shhh, be quiet," I whisper into my collar. "Shut up, girls, for God's sake."

"Did you say something?" Ms. Agaoglu asks.

"No, no . . . I mean, yes, but I was just murmuring to myself. . . . It's nothing really. . . ." I say, feeling the color rush to my face.

"And what were you murmuring to yourself?" Ms. Agaoglu asks, not letting me off the hook.

I swallow so hard that we both hear the gulp go down my throat.

I dare not say: "I was just reprimanding the four women inside me. You see, they hold opposing views on motherhood, as with all the important topics in my life."

I dare not say: "There is a mini harem deep down in my soul. A gang of females who constantly fight for nothing and bicker, looking for an opportunity to trip one another up. They are teeny-tiny creatures, each no taller than Thumbelina. Around four to five inches in height, ten to fourteen ounces in weight, that is how big they are. They make my life miserable and yet I don't know how to live without them. They can come out or stay put as they like. Each has declared a different corner of my soul her residence. I cannot mention them to anyone. If I did they would have me institutionalized for schizophrenia. But isn't the personality schizophrenic by definition?"

I dare not say: "Each member of the Choir of Discordant Voices claims to be the real me and therefore sees the others as rivals. So deep is their distaste of one another, if given a chance, they would scratch one another's eyes out. They are flesh-and-blood sisters but they function under Sultan Fatih's Code of Law.★ Should one of them ascend to the throne, I am afraid the first thing she would do would be to get rid of her siblings once and for all.

"Chronologically speaking, I don't know which finger-sized woman came first and who followed whom. Some of them sound wiser than others but that is less because of their ages than because of their temperaments. I guess I got used to hearing them quarrel inside my mind all the time."

I dare not say any of this. Instead I throw a question into the fray, taking the easy way out:

"Tell me, Ms. Agaoglu, if Shakespeare had a sister who was a very talented writer or if Fuzuli had a sister who happened to be a poet as gifted as he was, what would have happened to those women? Would

---

★ Fatih Code of Law: The Code of Sultan Fatih legalized fratricide in the fifteenth century in the Ottoman Empire, allowing rulers to kill their brothers so that they would not pose a threat to the throne.

they write books or would they raise children? I guess what I am wondering is, could they have done both?"

"That is a question I have tackled long ago. . . ." she says, her voice trailing off. "The answer I came up with was a clear no. But now, my dear, it is your turn to answer. Do you think a woman could manage motherhood and a career at the same time and equally well?"

A Talented Sister

In *A Room of One's Own,* Virginia Woolf makes the claim that it would have been impossible for a woman, any woman, to write the plays of Shakespeare during his age. To clarify her point she brings up an imaginary woman whom she introduces as Shakespeare's sister. She names her Judith.

Let's assume for a moment that this Judith was as passionate about theater as Shakespeare was, and just as gifted. What would have been her fate? Could she have dedicated her life to developing her talent like Shakespeare had done? Not even a chance, says Woolf.

The answer is no because a different set of rules holds for men than for women. Judith can be as talented as she likes, as fond of art and literature as she likes, but her path as a writer will be strewn with obstacles, small and large. She will have a hard time finding wiggle room in the "sociable-wife, meticulous-housewife, faithful-mother" box she is expected to fit into. More important, between her womanly tasks and motherly roles, she will not be able to find the time to write. Her whole day will pass with household chores, cooking, ironing, taking care of the children, shopping for groceries, tending to her familial responsibilities . . . and before she knows it, she will become a Sieve Woman, all the time in the world leaking through the holes in her life. In those rare moments when she finds herself alone, she will give in to exhaustion or frustration. How will she write? When will she write?

From the very beginning, the opportunities presented to Shakespeare will be barred from Judith. In this world where girls are discouraged from developing their individuality and are taught that their primary role in life is to be a good wife and mother, where women are vocal in the realm of oral culture but mostly invisible when it comes to written culture, women writers start the game down 7–0.

Let us now apply Virginia Woolf's critical question to the Middle East.

Fuzuli was one of the greatest voices of the Orient, a renowned sixteenth-century poet highly respected today by Arabs, Persians and Turks alike. Let's say Fuzuli had a talented younger sister—he very well may have had one—and her name was Firuze, meaning "turquoise," the color of her eyes.

This Firuze is a whiz kid, an explorer by nature, bent on learning, bubbling with ideas. Her hair is curly, her smile dimply and her mind is full of questions, each tailing the next one. Like images in opposite mirrors, her ideas multiply endlessly, extending into infinite space. Imagination flows out of her sentences like water through the arches of an aqueduct, always fresh, always free.

She loves stories, the more adventurous and dangerous the better. Day and night she spins stories about pirates carrying human skulls with rubies set into their eye sockets, magic carpets that fly over spice bazaars and crystal palaces, and two-headed green giants who speak a language alien to all ears but hers. She endlessly tells these tales to her mother, grandmother and aunts. When they can listen no more, she relates them to guests, servants and whoever else should come calling.

The elders in the family shake their heads in unison and say, "Girl, you have an imagination deeper than the oceans. How do you come up with all these stories? Do you sneak up to the peak of the Kaf Mountain in your sleep and eavesdrop on the talks of the fairies till morning breaks?"

Firuze wonders what kind of a place is this Kaf Mountain. How she would love to go there and see it with her own eyes. The world is full of wonders, and there are some corners of Earth that remind you of paradise; this she knows not through experience but through intuition. She has read the verses about paradise in the Qur'an where it says, "Those who are accepted into heaven will be adorned with golden bracelets and be given clothing made of the finest green silk." One of her favorite pastimes is to close her eyes and imagine herself donned in fine silks, jangling crafted bells on her ankles as she walks by streams of the coolest waters, picking juicy fruits from the trees, each bigger than an ostrich egg.

Dream is a rosy-cheeked lass, as charming as a water nymph, and just as playful. If you attempt to hold her in your arms, she will slip out of your grip, lithe and nimble, like a fish, like the mirage she is. Those who crave her touch only wear themselves out.

Reality is a crone with hair as gray as stormy skies, a toothless mouth and a chilling cackle. She is not ugly, not really, but there is something disturbing about her that makes it difficult to look her in the eye.

Dream is Firuze's bosom buddy, her best friend. While they play, laughing and joking as they skip about, Reality watches them from a distance with eyes narrowed to slits.

"Someday soon," says Reality, "that spoiled Dream will be out the door and I will languish in that throne of hers. Firuze can play with Dream for a while longer. But she'll be a woman soon and then she'll have to part ways with that adored playmate of hers."

One morning Firuze wakes up with a strange wetness between her legs and a red blotch smeared upon her nightgown. Her heart skips a beat. She fears she has cut herself on something. Sobbing, she runs to her mother. But no sooner has she said a few words than she receives a whopping slap.

"Be quiet," says her mother, the tenderness in her gaze not matching the sharpness in her tone.

"But what is going on, Mother?" asks Firuze in a horrified whisper.

"It happens to all women," replies her mother. "Just don't tell anyone about it, especially your brothers. Here, take these cloths and go clean yourself."

"It happens to all women," Firuze repeats incredulously.

"That is right, and it means you are not a girl anymore. From now on you have to watch how you behave. You cannot run around or skip rope. You cannot talk loudly or giggle. You are a woman now."

When? Why? How did she switch from girlhood to womanhood? She had always thought becoming a woman was like walking a long, winding road with trees on each side, learning your way step by step. Why had no one told her that it was, in fact, a trapdoor you stepped on and tumbled into without knowing it was there?

Firuze feels dirty and guilty, not due to something she has done, but due to what she *is*. Her grandmother tells her not to touch the Qur'an until her bleeding has stopped and she has thoroughly cleansed herself. It seems even God doesn't want her anymore.

Firuze feels hurt. The color goes from her face, the smile from her eyes. That carefree girl whose laughter echoed in the house like a dozen tinkling bells is now replaced by a woman whose body weighs down on her. Her head bent low, her face clouded by thoughts, Firuze is in a foreign land even as she sits by the brazier with Reality.

The elders of the family do not take their eyes off her, whispering among themselves about possible suitors. Matchmakers come and go, bearing *lokum* wrapped in silk handkerchiefs. As her parents haggle for her bridal price, it becomes ever more important that Firuze be modest. But no matter how strictly they supervise her, they can't stop her from running up to the second floor and pressing her nose into the latticed windows. She stays there until the holes leave marks on her face like chicken pox, inhaling the smell of the wild herbs carried by the wind from the valleys afar.

If only she could walk out of the house and find a caravan that would take her beyond the city of Karbala to the ends of the world. She wants to go to school like her brother Fuzuli, and study theology, *tafsir*★, astronomy and alchemy. If only she could walk along the streets proudly carrying books and brick-thick dictionaries under her arms. If only her parents would say, "Well done, Firuze. May you become a great poet like your brother, God willing!"

★ *Tafsir*: the art of commenting on the Qur'an.

Firuze has a secret she won't reveal to anyone: For years now she has been writing poems. In the beginning she used to scribble down whatever was weighing on her heart, without any expectations, as if talking to herself. Before long she realized that this, to her, was more than a pastime. It was a passion.

Her writing progresses like an illness that has infected and invaded her body and soul. More often than not, inspiration comes at dawn. She rises before the morning breaks, puts a shawl on her thin shoulders and starts to write. Those who hear the soft tinkering from her room think she has risen to pray. They don't know that in a way she has. Poetry to her is true prayer, rising from the depths of her soul, addressed to a force far higher and mightier. If there were no poetry, Firuze believes, God would be too lonely.

She reads the works of other poets, especially the Iranian Hafiz and the Turkish Nesimi. She also adores her brother's poems, one of which she came across today and instantly memorized:

All that is in the world is love
And knowledge is nothing but gossip

Though she loved the poem she couldn't help thinking that only a man who had been well educated and versed in grammar and language could make such a statement. For Firuze, and all who had been excluded from school, knowledge was surely much more than gossip.

It was burning thirst.

There is an aged concubine, a woman with skin darker than ebony, who has been taking care of Firuze since the day she was born. When she walks she glides across the room as silent as silk; when she talks, she does so in whispers. One morning while crocheting a lace bedspread together, Firuze turns to her nanny and says, "I want to go to the madrassa★ and be a famous poet."

★ A school that is often part of a mosque.

"Is that so?" The nanny chuckles, her large breasts jiggling.

"Why are you laughing?" says Firuze, sounding hurt.

"Allow me to tell you a story first," the nanny says, suddenly serious again.

And this is the story she tells: One day Nasreddin Hodja was working in a watermelon patch when he stopped for a break and sat under a walnut tree. Looking up, he murmured to himself, "God Almighty, I don't understand Your ways. Why on earth did You grow huge watermelons on the thinnest stems and put those tiny little walnuts on those thick branches? Wouldn't it have been better the other way around?"

Just as he finished speaking a strong wind blew and a walnut fell down from the tree, falling square on his head.

"Ouch!" Nasreddin Hodja yelled in pain. As he massaged his bruised head, he understood his mistake. "God forgive me and my silly tongue," he said. "Now I understand why You didn't place watermelons on a tree. If Thou had replaced watermelons for walnuts, I wouldn't be alive now. Keep everything in its place, please. You know better!"

Firuze listens, hardly breathing. "What's that got to do with me?"

"Crazy girl, don't you see?" the nanny asks. "Who has ever heard of a female poet? There is a reason why God made everything as it is and we'd better respect that reason, lest we want watermelons raining on our heads."

That afternoon Firuze walks into the backyard. She walks past the well straight to the hen coop in the corner. Opening the small wooden gate, she enters, inhaling the pungent smell of earth, dust and dirt. Neither the rooster nor the chickens pay attention to her. The hen coop is her room. This place, with its sharp odor and noisy residents, is her only breathing space.

Under the feeding bowls, inside a velvet box, she keeps her poems. Cleaning off the dust, she grabs the box and goes to see her brother.

"Hey, little sister, what are you doing?" Fuzuli says, surprised to see her standing by the door.

She hands her poems to him, the smile on her face as tight as an oud string. "Read them, will you?"

He does. Time slows down and moves to a different rhythm, like a sleepwalker. After what seems like an eternity, Fuzuli lifts his head, a new flicker in his eyes that wasn't there before.

"Where did you find these poems?" he asks.

Firuze's eyes flicker away from his face. She dares not say the truth. Besides, she wants to know whether her poems are any good. Does she really have talent?

"One of the neighbors came calling the other day. The poems belong to her son," she says. "She implored you to take a look at them, and tell her, in all honesty, if her son has any talent."

A shadow crosses Fuzuli's face as if he were suspicious but when he speaks his voice is calm and assuring. "Tell that neighbor her son should come and see me. This young man has a great talent," he says, stroking his long, brown beard.

Firuze is alight with joy. She plans to tell her brother the truth when the right moment comes along. If she can convince her brother, he can convince the whole family. They will understand how much words mean to her. Believing in poetry is believing in love. Believing in poetry is believing in God. How can anybody say no to that?

But the moment she waits for never comes. Only weeks after their conversation, Firuze is married off to a clerk eighteen years her senior.

With drums and tambourines they sing on her henna night. The women first dance and laugh with joy, then their faces crumble, awash with salty tears. On wedding days at the celebrations of women, and only then and there, happiness and sorrow become two different names for the same thing.

Yesterday she was a child/swimming in a sea of letters/she bled poetry
A stain grew on her nightgown/dark and mysterious
In a heartbeat/in a blink/she became a woman
Her name a forbidden fruit. . . .

Due to her husband's connections, it is decided that the couple shall settle down in Istanbul. Firuze is swept away from her home, her family and her childhood. As she leaves her house, she does not pay a last visit to the hen coop. She doesn't care. Not anymore. Hidden in a hole under the feeding bowls, her poems go to waste. Her big secret turns to dust and the dust is swept away.

Months later in Istanbul, Firuze sits in a *konak* by the Bosphorus watching the dark indigo waters. She gags but manages not to throw up this time, being seven weeks into her pregnancy. She hopes it will be a son to carry her husband's name across generations and to the ends of the Earth. Sometimes she utters poems but she doesn't write them down anymore. The words she breathes disperse in the wind like shards of a broken dream she once had but can no longer remember.

Who knows how many women like Firuze lived throughout Middle Eastern history? Women who could have become poets or writers, but weren't allowed. . . . Women who hid their masterpieces in hen coops or dowry chests, where they rotted away. Many years later, while telling stories to their granddaughters, one of them might say,

"Once upon a time I used to write poems. Did you know that?"

"What is that, Grandma?"

"Poetry? It is a magical place beyond the Kaf Mountain."

"Can I go there, too? Can I?"

"Yes, my dear, you may go but you cannot stay there. A short visit is all you are allowed."

And she would say this in a whisper, as if that, too, were a fairy tale.

Perhaps the question that needs to be asked is not: Why were there not more female poets or writers in the past? The real question is: How was it possible for a handful of women to make it in the literary world despite all the odds?

When it comes to giving an equal chance to women like Firuze, the world has not advanced so very much. Still today, as Virginia Woolf argued, "when one reads . . . of a woman possessed by devils, of a wise woman selling herbs, or even of a very remarkable man who had a mother, then I think we are on the track of a lost novelist, a suppressed poet, of some mute and inglorious Jane Austen, some Emily Brontë who dashed her brains out on the moor or mopped and mowed about the highways crazed with the torture that her gift had put her to."

Still today there remains a rule in place: Male writers are thought of as "writers" first and then "men." As for female writers, they are first "female" and only then "writers."

One More Cup of Tea

"Are you all right?" Ms. Agaoglu asks. "You look like you're miles away."

"Oh, do I?" I smile guiltily.

Glancing meaningfully across the table, she offers me another cup of tea and says, "Being a mother and a writer are not opponents, perhaps, not necessarily. But they are not best buddies either."

My mind acts like a computer gone awry. Names and pictures bounce around on the screen, disconnected and displaced. I think of women writers who are also mothers: Nadine Gordimer, Margaret Atwood, Annie Proulx, Anita Desai, Jhumpa Lahiri, Naomi Shihab Nye, Anne Lamott, Mary Gordon, Anne Rice, the legendary Cristina di Belgioioso. . . . A large number of female writers have one or two children. But there are also those, like Ursula K. Le Guin, who are mothers of three or more.

Yet at the same time, there are also many poets and writers who did not have children, for their own good reasons. Emily Dickinson, Virginia Woolf, Emily Brontë, Dorothy Parker, Lillian Hellman, Ayn Rand, Gertrude Stein, Patricia Highsmith, Jeanette Winterson, Amy Tan, Sandra Cisneros, Elizabeth Gilbert . . .

Then there are female writers who chose to both give birth and adopt. Of these, the most remarkable is a woman who was not only a prolific writer but also an advocate of racial and sexual equality, a woman with a great heart, winner of the Nobel Prize for Literature, Pearl S. Buck.

Noticing that the adoption system in America discriminated against Asian and black children in favor of white, in the early 1950s Buck decided to fight the system and help the disempowered. After a long struggle she founded the Welcome House—the first international, interracial center for adoption—and changed the lives of countless children. While doing all of this, she never gave up literature, or slowed down her writing. Quite to the contrary, her motherhood and activism seem to have propelled her career as a writer.

Last, there are also women writers who *might* have wanted to have children, but their husbands didn't, and therefore neither did they. Many believe that that was the case with the renowned British writer Iris Murdoch. There have been claims that her husband, John Bayley, never wanted to have kids and she went along with his wishes. A biography published after Murdoch's death outlined this lesser-known side of their relationship, causing quite a stir.

I try to find a formula, a golden formula, that could apply to most, if not all, women writers, but obviously there is none.

J. K. Rowling started writing the Harry Potter series after her son was born and dedicated the subsequent books to her newborn daughter. She says motherhood gives her inspiration. One assumes that a mother who writes about magic must be telling supernatural stories when she tucks her children into bed, but J. K. Rowling says she doesn't believe in witchcraft, only in religion. I don't know how smoothly her household runs, but Rowling seems to have a real knack for fusing motherhood and writing.

Then there is Toni Morrison, who had two small sons that she was raising by herself when she first began to write. For many years she could not work in the daylight hours, her rendezvous with pen and paper taking place before dawn, when the boys would wake up. As difficult as life was for her then, she says she drew inspiration from each hardship.

Sometimes the biggest award a woman writer hopes to receive is neither the Man Booker Prize nor the Orange Prize but a good-hearted, hardworking nanny. It is a dream shared by many, to hear those five magic words: "And the Nanny goes to . . ." No wonder some of the grants Sylvia Plath won were written up as "nanny grants"—money with which she could hire a professional caretaker so as to find the time and energy to write.

But then there is the other side of the coin. In her thought-provoking "Notes to a Young(er) Writer," Sandra Cisneros tackles head-on the question of class, and women writers and poets having "a maid of their own." "I wonder if Emily Dickinson's Irish housekeeper wrote poetry or if she ever had the secret desire to study and be anything besides a housekeeper," Cisneros writes. "Maybe Emily Dickinson's Irish housekeeper had to sacrifice her life so that Emily could live hers locked upstairs in the corner bedroom writing her 1,775 poems."★ As much as the literary world avoids talking about such *mundane* things, money and social class are still privileges that empower some more than others.

One should also pay attention to the children, not only to the mothers. Susan Sontag's son, David Rieff, followed in his mother's footsteps in becoming a writer and an editor. In fact, he was his mother's editor for a while. Kiran Desai speaks of the close writing relationship she has with her mother, Anita Desai. Likewise, Guy Johnson, the son of one of the most beloved voices of American poetry, Maya Angelou, also chose to become a poet.

"If these children had for some reason hated their mother's world, surely they would not have followed the same path," I think to myself. "I suppose female writers don't make such shabby mothers after all."

But even as I say this I know that there are also examples to the contrary, cases that are much more difficult to talk about. There are women writers who had great talent but perhaps were not great mothers. We do not know a lot about them. Relationships that seem enviable from the outside might tell a different truth behind closed doors. Beyond pretty photographs and bright façades there are bruised hearts that we seldom hear about.

One well-known example is Muriel Spark.

Spark is, no doubt, one of the most influential female authors of the past century. She wrote more than twenty novels and dozens of other

---

★ Geoffrey Sanborn, "Keeping Her Distance: Cisneros, Dickinson, and the Politics of Private Enjoyment," *PMLA*, 2001.

works, including children's books, plays and storybooks. When she passed on from this world at the age of eighty-eight, friends, relatives, publishers, editors, critics, readers and journalists attended her funeral. There was only one person who didn't: her son, Robin.

One wonders what must have transpired for a son, an only son, upon learning that his mother has passed away, to decline to go to her funeral. How much hurt, how much suffering, does that take? And how could a mother, knowing she is going to die soon, spend her final days making sure her son is left out of her will? What sorrow, what pain, could have led her to make that decision?

Born in Edinburgh, Spark left her homeland shortly after getting married and moved to Rhodesia (Zimbabwe), where her husband had been offered a teaching position. In 1938 the couple had a son. I don't know if they were any unhappier than the families around them, but sometime later Muriel Spark decided to return to Britain. Alone. When she walked away from her six-year-old son, did she sense that it would be the hardest moment of her life, or did she believe, in all sincerity, that she would soon come back? In any case she never did. Robin was raised by his father and paternal grandmother.

As the years went by, the distance between mother and son widened. But it was not until the day Robin, now a grown-up man, announced his wish to become Jewish that whatever ties remained completely snapped. Spark, who had become a devout Catholic, reacted bitterly to her son's attempts to prove that his grandmother (and, therefore, mother) was, in fact, Jewish. She claimed that her son was seeking to create sensationalism and scandal just to get back at her. After that her relationship with her son was so strained that when a journalist asked her if she ever saw him, she answered: "As long as he stays away from me he can do as he pleases."

And that is how they remained . . . apart.

Outside on the street, behind the half-drawn curtains, the wind speeds up, rustling the leaves of the acacia trees through the slanted evening light. Simultaneously, time speeds up. It now flows so fast that I feel a surge of panic as though I'm late for something, but what exactly, I don't know. How old am I? Thirty-five. Numbers start to go up like the spinning digits on a gas pump. Thirty-six, thirty-seven, thirty-eight, thirty-nine . . . How many more years can I postpone the decision to have children? The clock on the wall, the clock inside my head, the clock in my heart, the clock in my uterus, they are all ticking at once. Suddenly I undergo a strange emotion—as if all these clocks were set to go off at the same time: now.

It is precisely then that the mini women inside me begin to bang against the walls of my chest. They all want to get out. They all want an urgent meeting.

Doing my best to look confident and collected, I jump to my feet. "I am sorry, may I use the restroom?"

"Sure, it is up there to the left," says Ms. Agaoglu, scrutinizing my face with those dark brown eyes of hers.

But I have no time or wish to explain. I dash to the bathroom, lock the door behind me and turn on the faucet to scalding water so that Ms. Agaoglu doesn't hear me talking to myself.

"Okay, you can come out now," I whisper.

Dead silence. On the counter in front of me there is an aromatic candle that smells of green apples. I watch its flame bob with the draft of my movements.

"Hello? Come out already!" I know I am yelling but I cannot help it.

That is when a liquid voice drenched with lethargy responds, "Oh, stop shouting like you have a stomachache, will you?"

I wonder which one of them she is, but prefer not to ask.

"Why aren't you coming out? I thought you wanted to have an urgent meeting. Because of you, I've locked myself in the toilet in a house where I am only a guest."

"We had wanted to meet, but then we realized it was dinnertime. Everyone went home to grab a bite, so we can't come outside just now."

"Oh, great!"

"Don't be cranky. I'll tell you what, why don't you get yourself down here, dear?"

Unlike Alice in Wonderland, I do not need to drink some magic potion and shrink to thumb size in order to travel to another realm, because it is not my body but my consciousness that is doing the traveling. I can take on any shape I want and still have no shape at all. Knowing this, I take a deep breath, grab a candle and start descending the mossy stairs to the dungeons of my soul.

It is time to have a serious talk with my four finger-sized women.

The Harem Within

It is dark and foggy down here. With its labyrinthine alleys and secret passages, my soul is a perfect setting for a gothic novel or a vampire movie. As I look left and right, I realize that I am completely disoriented. So many times I have walked these cul-de-sacs and dimly lit side streets, and yet I still get lost.

Far ahead there is a crossroads from which four separate paths spill. Blinking repeatedly, I lift the candle up to eye level and peer into the thick, uninviting fog. Which way should I go? I try to think of a giant, round machine, something between a compass and a wheel of fortune. This is a mental exercise I visualize when I am indecisive, although I am not sure if it really helps. In my mind's eye, I spin the wheel as fast as I can until it slows down and comes to a stop at the letter *W*. I quickly determine that this means West, and dutifully head in that direction.

There, in a city as neatly organized as Brussels, in a chic and modern flat furnished minimalist style, lives Little Miss Practical. She is the side of me who has great common sense and even greater pragmatism. I press her doorbell and, upon being screened by a camera, hear a buzzer that lets me inside. She is sitting at her desk, looking sprightly and sporty. On the plate in front of her is a sandwich of goat cheese and smoked turkey on wheat bread. Beside the plate is a thimbleful of Diet Coke. She has been watching her weight for as long as I can remember.

She is four and a half inches tall and weighs barely thirteen ounces. She wears casual, comfortable clothing: a breezy beige shirt, red bone-framed glasses and a pair of brown linen pants with lots of pockets to keep everything at hand. On her feet are leather sandals; her dark blond hair is cut short so that it doesn't need extra styling. Washing (shampoo and conditioner all in one) is good enough. Drying her hair would be one step too many.

"Yolla, Big Self," she says cheerfully. "What happened to you? You look awful."

"Yeah, thanks," I grumble.

"What's up, yo?" she asks. For some reason beyond my comprehension, she loves speaking in rapid-fire sentences peppered with slang, sounding like a street kid by way of Tucson.

"Oh, Little Miss Practical, you've got to help me," I say.

"*Nema problema!* Help is on the way."

"Did you hear the question Ms. Agaoglu asked me? I don't know how to answer. Is it possible to be a good mother and good writer at the same time? Do I want to have kids? If not, why not? If so, when, why, how?"

"Hey, be easy, Sis," she says as she pats her mouth dry with a napkin. "Don't sweat the small stuff. One can be a writer and a mama, why not? All you need to do is to trust me."

"Really?"

"Yup. Here's what we'll do. We'll split your time into two chunks: writing time and nursing time." She pauses with an impish smile, measuring my reaction. "That means you'll have to start wearing a watch."

"You know I never wear a watch," I say. "Watches, the color white and wasabi . . . The three *W*s I'd rather stay away from."

"Well, there's a *W* word you might welcome," she says mysteriously. "Because it happens to be the answer to your problem."

"What is it?"

"Winnowing!"

Seeing me draw a blank, she laughs. "Separating the grain from the chaff," she remarks. "That's exactly what you need to do."

Again I look vacantly: Again she smiles with confidence as if she has the pulse of the world under her finger.

"Think of it this way, Sis. The human brain is like a set of kitchen drawers. The cutlery is placed in one drawer. The napkins in another. And so on. Use the same model. When you are nursing, open the 'motherhood' section. When you are writing, pop open the 'novelist' one. Simple. Close one drawer, use the other. No confusion. No contradictions. No fretting. All thanks to winnowing."

"Wow, that's splendid, but there is a small detail you left out: While I'm writing, who will take care of the baby?"

"As if that's a problem," she says with a snort. "Hello. The age of globalization is here. Snap your fingers. You can find a nanny. Filipino, Moldavian, Bulgarian . . . You can even choose her nationality."

Little Miss Practical thrusts her hand into one of her pockets and produces a paper. "Look, I've made a list of all the information you'll need. Phone numbers of the nanny agencies, babysitters, nursery schools, pediatricians. You should also get an assistant to answer your e-mails. It'll make life easier. And if you get a secretary and a tape recorder, you can stop writing altogether, ya' mean?"

With a heavy heart I ask, "What do you mean?"

"I mean, instead of *writing* your novels, you can *speak* them. The recorder will tape your voice. Later, your secretary can type up the whole text. Isn't it practical? That way you can finish a novel without having to leave the kid."

"Just curious," I say as calmly as I can manage. "How exactly am I going to afford a nanny, an assistant and a secretary?"

"Oh, you're being so negative," she says. "Here I'm offering practical solutions for material problems and you see only the downside."

"But money is a *material* problem," I object, my voice cracking. For a brief moment neither of us says a word, mutually frowning and sulking.

"Besides, even if I had the money," I say, "I still couldn't do what you suggest. It goes against my sense of equality and freedom. I can't have all those people working for me, as if I were a raja or something."

"Now you're talking nonsense," snaps Little Miss Practical. "Don't you know that every successful female writer is a raja?"

"How can you say that?"

"How can you deny that?" she asks back. "Remember that wolf woman you adore so much."

Just when I am about to ask what wolf woman she is talking about, it dawns on me that she is referring to Virginia Woolf.

"Do you think that lady of yours had only a *room of her own*? No way. She also had a cook of her own, a maid of her own and a gardener of her own, not to mention a butler of her own! Her diaries are full of complaints about her many servants."

Laden with curiosity I ask, "Since when do you read about the lives of novelists?"

Little Miss Practical's readings are based solely on two key criteria: efficiency and functionality. *How to Win Friends and Hearts, The Key to Unwavering Success, Ten Steps to Power, The Art of Knowing People, Awaken the Millionaire Inside, The Secret to Good Life* . . . She gobbles up self-help books like popcorn, but never reads novels. Fiction, in her eyes, has no function.

"If it's *useful,* I'll read it," she says defensively.

"And what is the *use* of the wolf woman?"

She turns a disparaging dark gaze on me. "That lady of yours used to write orders to her servants on scraps of paper. What chores needed to be done, what dishes needed to be prepared, which dresses needed washing . . . She would write them down. Can you imagine? They lived under the same roof but instead of talking to them, she *wrote* to them. . . ."

"Well, we don't know her side of the story," I say meekly.

"Everything was *her* side of the story. She was the writer, Sis!"

I don't feel like quarreling. With a ruler in her hand, a calculator in her pocket and plans in her head, Little Miss Practical is used to measuring, calculating and planning everything. I take the list she has prepared for me and leave in a hurry, still feeling uneasy.

I spin the wheel again. It stops at letter *E*. This time, I walk east.

There, in a city as spiritual as Mount Athos, beyond a wooden door, sits Dame Dervish—her head bowed in contemplation, her fingers moving the amber prayer beads. On the tray in front of her there is a bowl of lentil soup and a slice of bread. Her thimble is full of water. She always makes do with little. On her head is a loosely tied turban that comes together in the front with a large stone. Patches of hair show from beneath the turban. She wears a jade dress that reaches the floor, a dark green vest and khaki slippers.

Seeing she is in the midst of a prayer, I sneak in and listen.

"God, Pure Love and Beauty, may we be of those who chant Your name and find restoration in You. Don't let us spend our time on Earth with eyes veiled, ears deafened and hearts sealed to love."

I smile at these words and I am still smiling when I hear her next words.

"Please open Elif's third eye to Love and broaden her capacity to grasp the Truth. Connections are the essence of Your universe; please don't deprive her of Your loving connection."

"Amen to that," I say.

She flinches as she surfaces from her thoughts. When she sees me standing there she breaks into a smile, lifting her hand to her left breast in greeting.

"I need your help," I say. "Have you heard the question Ms. Agao-glu asked me? I don't know how to answer it."

"I heard it indeed and I don't know why you panic so. God says He sometimes puts us through a 'beautiful test.' That is what He calls the many quandaries we face in this life. *A beautiful test*. There is no need to rush for 'the answer' because all answers are relative. What is right for one person may be wrong for another. Instead of asking general questions about motherhood and writing, ask God to give you what is good for you."

"But how am I supposed to know what is good for me?"

She ignores my question. "Whether you have children, write books, sell pastries on the street or sign million-dollar business con-tracts, what matters is to be happy and fulfilled inside. Are you?"

"I don't know," I say.

Dame Dervish takes a deep breath. "Then let me ask you another question. Are these novels of yours really yours? Are you the creator of them?"

"Of course they are mine. I create them page by page."

"Rumi wrote more than eighty thousand splendid verses and yet he never called himself a creator. Nor did he see himself as a poet. He said he was only an instrument, a channel for God's creativity."

"I am not Rumi," I say, a bit more harshly than I intended.

Our eyes meet for a second and I look away, uneasy. I don't want to confer the authorship of my books to another, even if it be God.

"Let me tell you a story," Dame Dervish says. "One night, a group of moths gathered on a shelf watching a burning candle. Puzzled by the nature of the light, they sent one of their members to go and check on it. The scouting moth circled the candle several times and came back with a description: The light was bright. Then a second moth went to examine it. He, too, came back with an observation: The light was hot. Finally a third moth volunteered to go. When he approached the candle he didn't stop like his friends had done, but flew straight into the flame. He was consumed there and then, and only he understood the nature of the light."

"You want me to kill myself?" I ask, alarmed.

"No, my dear. I want you to kill your ego."

"Same thing, isn't it?"

Dame Dervish sighs and tries again. "I want you to stop thinking. Stop examining, stop analyzing and start living the experience. Only then will you know how being a mother and being a writer can be balanced."

"Yes, but what if . . ."

"No more what-ifs are needed," she says. "Did the moth say 'what if'?"

"Okay, I am not Rumi, I am not a moth. I am a human being with a mind and four mini women residing inside me. Surely my way of dealing with things is more complicated."

"Uh-huh," says Dame Dervish, chewing her bread.

It is the kind of "uh-huh" that can mean only, "You aren't ready yet. Like a fruit that needs more time to ripen, you are still hard on the inside. Go and cook a little, then we'll talk again."

Shuffling my feet, I take my leave and walk toward the south.

There, in a city as crowded as Tokyo, behind a thrice-bolted door, is the relentless workaholic Miss Ambitious Chekhovian. Four and a half inches in height, ten and a half ounces in weight, she is the skinniest of all the finger-women. She is always eating away at herself, so naturally she doesn't gain any weight.

"Time is not money, time is everything," she is fond of saying.

In order not to lose time, instead of cooking supper and setting a table she munches on crackers and chips and takes a lot of vitamins as supplements. Even now, there is a pack of biscuits, tiny cubes of cheese and a minuscule box of orange-carrot juice in front of her. There is also a vitamin C tablet and a gingko biloba pill beside her plate. This is her dinner.

Of all the statements made by men and women since time immemorial, there is one by Chekhov that she has taken up as her life's motto: "He who desires nothing, hopes for nothing, and is afraid of nothing, cannot be an artist." That is why she is a good Chekhovian. She desires, hopes and fears, all abundantly and all at the same time.

Today, Miss Ambitious Chekhovian is wearing an indigo skirt that reaches just below her knees, two strands of pearls around her neck and a matching jacket with an ivory silk blouse inside. She has a tiny bit of foundation on her snow-white skin and is wearing dark red lipstick. Her chestnut hair is held back in a bun so tight that not a single strand of hair manages to get loose.

Every inch of her is groomed, clipped and buffed, as always. Her porcelain teeth gleam in their straight rows like expensive pearls. She is determined, resolute and hardworking—excessively so.

"Miss Ambitious Chekhovian, will you please help me," I say. "You heard what Ms. Agaoglu asked. What is *your* answer?"

"How can you even ask?" She frowns at me with her thinly plucked eyebrows. "Obviously, I am against you having a baby. With all that we have to do ahead of us, it is hardly time for children!"

I look at her with puppy eyes.

"But I was next to Dame Dervish a minute ago and she said that there is no point in running amok in life."

"Forget that crazy finger-woman. What does she know? What does she understand of worldly desires?" she says offhandedly. "She has lost her mind somewhere inside those prayer beads of hers."

She pops a biscuit into her mouth, then a vitamin pill, and takes a sip of juice to wash it all down. "Listen, dear, let me summarize again my philosophy of life: Did we ask to be brought into this world? Nope. No one asked our opinion on the matter. We just fell into our mothers' wombs, went through arduous births and *voilà*, here we are. Since we came along in such an accidental manner, is there anything more sublime than our desire to leave something worthy and lasting behind when we depart the world?"

I find myself nodding heartily, though the more she speaks, the more lost I am becoming.

"Unfortunately too many lives are crushed in a monotonous routine. Such a pity! One must actually aim to be special. We have to become immortal while we are still alive. You have to write better novels and develop your skill. 'You need to work continually day and night, to read ceaselessly, to study, to exercise your will. . . . Each hour is precious.'"

"Was that Chekhov again?" I ask suspiciously.

"It was Anton Pavlovich Chekhov," she says with a frown, and to hammer home the point, she repeats his name in Russian. "Антон Павлович Чехов."

"Right." I sigh.

"Look, I made a calculation: If you write a new novel every year for the next ten years, give a lecture every month, attend all the major literary festivals in Europe and tour the world, then in eight years and two months you'll have reached new heights in your career."

"Oh, give me a break, will you?" I say, exasperated. "Do you think literature is a horse race? Do you think I am a machine?"

"What is wrong with that?" she says nonchalantly. "Better to be a machine than a vegetable! Instead of living like a sprig of parsley, passionless and lifeless, better to live with the dash and zest of a working machine."

"And what about motherhood?"

"Motherhood . . . motherhood . . ." she says, glowering, as if the word has left a bad taste in her mouth. "Better leave motherhood to women who are born to be mothers. We both know you are not like that. Motherhood would upset all of my future plans. Promise me. Say you won't do it!"

I look into the horizon, longing to be somewhere else. In the ensuing silence Miss Ambitious Chekhovian slowly gets up, walks to her bag and fishes out a piece of paper.

"What is this?" I ask when she holds it out to me.

"It is an address," says Miss Ambitious Chekhovian. "The address of an excellent gynecologist. Guess what! I already got you an appointment. The doctor is expecting you at six-thirty on Tuesday."

"But, why?"

Miss Ambitious Chekhovian's eyes light up as her voice gets an eerie softness: "Because we want to solve this problem once and for all. This operation will do away with all of the existential questions that have been messing with your mind. I've decided to have you sterilized."

"What am I, a stray cat!?" I say, flushing scarlet with rage.

Dissatisfied, she shrugs and turns around. "It is up to you."

I know I should mind my temper but I can't. Still grumbling, I leave her to her veterinary campaign and head up north.

There, behind an ornamented iron door, in a city as bustling with ideas as New York, lives Miss Highbrowed Cynic. Her windows are covered with burgundy velvet curtains and flimsy cobwebs, her walls with posters of Che Guevara and Marlon Brando.

She wears slovenly hippie dresses that reach the floor and mirror-threaded Indian vests. She wraps bright foulards around her neck and wears bangle bracelets of every color up to her elbows. When she feels like it, she goes to get a tattoo or another piercing. Depending on the day, she either leaves her shoulder-length hair loose or puts it up in a haphazard bun. She does raja yoga and advanced Reiki. All the acupuncture she's received has yet to help her quit smoking. If she isn't smoking a cigarette or a cigarillo, she chews tobacco.

Her handbags are cluttered sacks, where she fits in several books, notebooks and all sorts of knickknacks. She usually doesn't wear makeup, not because she is against it but because when she puts a mascara or lipstick in her handbag, she can never find it again.

Miss Highbrowed Cynic is following an alternative diet nowadays. She has a plate of organic spinach, organic zucchini and some kind of mixed vegetables with saffron in front of her. She is a staunch vegetarian on the verge of turning vegan. It has been years since she last ate meat. Or chicken. Or fish. She claims that when we consume an animal, we also consume their fear of death. Apparently that is the reason we get sick. Instead, we are meant to eat peaceful leafy greens, such as spinach, lettuce, kale, arugula . . .

"Hello, Miss Highbrowed Cynic," I say.

"Peace, Sister," she says, waving her hand nonchalantly.

"I need to pick your brain on an important matter," I say.

"Well, you came to the right place. I am *brains*."

"Okay, what is your opinion about motherhood?"

"What is the use of asking rhetorical questions when it is a well-known fact that everyone hears only what they want to hear," she says. "Wittgenstein wrote about the limits of language for a reason. You ought to read the *Tractatus*."

"I don't have time to read the *Tractatus*," I say. "Ms. Agaoglu is still in the living room waiting for an answer. You've got to help me now."

"Well, then, I urge you to think about the word *envy*."

"Come again?"

"Envy is not a simple emotion, mind you, but a deep philosophical dilemma. It is so important, in fact, that it shapes world history. Jean-Paul Sartre said all sorts of racism and xenophobia stem from envy."

"I am afraid I don't get a word of what you are saying. Could you please speak more plainly?"

"All right, let me put it in simple terms: The grass is always greener on the other side."

"Which means?"

"It means if you have a baby, you will always be envious of women who don't have children and focus fully on their careers. If you choose to focus on your career, however, you will always envy women who have kids. Whichever path you choose, your mind will be obsessed with the option you have discarded."

"Is there no way out of this dilemma?" I ask.

She shakes her head desolately. "Envy lies at the root of our existential angst. Look at the history of mankind, all the wars and destruction. Do you know what they said when World War I broke out? The war that will end all wars! Of course that is not what happened. The wars didn't end because there is no equality and no justice. Instead we have an imbalance of power and income, ethnic and religious clashes. . . . All of this is bound to generate new conflicts."

I take a long, deep breath. "You are making me depressed."

"You *ought* to be depressed," she says, wagging a finger in my face. "To live means to be saddled with melancholy. It is no coincidence that Paul Klee painted the Angel of History so lonely and hopeless. Remember the look on the face of *Angelus Novus*. I highly recommend that you read Walter Benjamin on . . ."

"You are making me soooo depressed," I interject.

She stares at me as if seeing me for the first time. "Oh, I see. In the age of Internet and multimedia, no one has the time or patience for in-depth knowledge anymore. All right, I will cut to the chase."

"Please."

"My point is, whichever woman you will grow into, you will wish to be the Other. According to the great French philosopher Emmanuel Levinas, the essence of ethics is the point where you come face-to-face with the Other. Of course, from a phenomenological stance, we could speak of the 'other' inside the 'I.'"

"Ugh, hm!" I say.

"Read Heidegger to see how a human being, any human being, cannot be taken into account unless seen as an existent among the things surrounding him, the key to all existence being Dasein, which is being-in-the-world." She widens her dark green eyes at me. "Therefore, my answer to your banal question is as follows: It doesn't really matter."

"What do you mean?" I say, trying to keep frustration from my voice.

"Whether you don't have children or you have half a dozen of them, it is all the same," she says with customary assurance. "In the end, it all boils down to the envy of the Other, and to deep existential dissatisfaction. Humans do not know how to be satisfied. Like Cioran said, we are all sentenced to fall inside ourselves and be miserable."

A freezing wind blows in through an open window. The candle in my hand flickers sadly and I shiver. Miss Highbrowed Cynic's voice, stiff with relish and conviction, scratches my ears. I begin to walk away from her.

"Hey, where are you going? Come back, I haven't finished yet."

"You'll never be finished," I say. "Bye now."

It is getting late and talking to Miss Highbrowed Cynic has demoralized me so profoundly I cannot stand to hear another word on this subject. I clamber up the stairs of the Land of Me, two at a time, panting heavily, and fall back into Ms. Agaoglu's bathroom. I make a move to wash my face but the running water is too hot and adjusting the temperature requires an energy I am not sure I have now. So I turn off the faucet and, doing my best to look calm and composed, return to the living room.

Everything is the way I left it. The paintings on the walls, the books on the shelves, the porcelain teacups on the table, the cookies on the plates, the ticking of the clock, are the same and the house preserves the same solemn silence. Ms. Agaoglu is tranquilly waiting in her seat.

The question she asked me a while ago still hangs in the air between us. But I don't have an answer. Not yet.

"Umm . . . thank you so much for your hospitality," I say. "But I should really get going."

"Well, it was nice talking to you," she says. "Woman to woman, writer to writer."

When I step out into the street I catch sight of the two Gypsy women sitting in the same spot. Judging by the flushed looks on their faces, they are excitedly talking about something, but upon noticing me, they go quiet.

"Hey, you," one of them says. "Why do you look so down in the dumps?"

"Probably because I am down there," I say.

The woman laughs. "Come, give me your palm and I'll tell you the way out."

"Forget about telling my fortune," I say. "What I need is a cigarette. Let's have a smoke together instead."

It is as if I've suggested robbing a bank. They get serious and become suspicious all of a sudden, eyeing me distrustfully. I ignore their gaze, sit down on the sidewalk and take out a pack of cigarettes from my bag.

That's when a smile etches along the lips of the Gypsy who offered to read my fortune only moments ago. She slides over to me. A few seconds later the other one joins us.

As darkness falls, only paces from Ms. Agaoglu's living room, the Gypsy flower sellers and I are seated cross-legged on a sidewalk, puffing away. Above us a wispy cloud of smoke lingers lazily. For a moment, the world feels sweet and peaceful, as if there were nothing to worry about, no questions gnawing at my mind.

Moon Woman

In 1862, Leo Tolstoy married a woman sixteen years his junior: Sophia Andreevna Bers. Although the marriage was to become known as one of the unhappiest in literary history, there may have been much love and passion between them—at least in the early years. There was a time when they laughed together, he like a wild horse galloping at full speed, she like a mare cantering across the paddock, timid but excited. Thirteen children came of this union (nineteen, according to some). Five of them died during childhood. Sophia raised the remaining eight (or fourteen). She spent a large portion of her life as a young woman either pregnant or breast-feeding.

She was like the moon in its phases, glowing against the starry skies. Her body changed every minute of the day, every week, and every month, filling out, rounding up to fullness, and then slimming down only to fill out again. Sophia was a moon woman.

While Tolstoy was in his room, writing by the light of an oil lamp, Sonya—the Russian diminutive for Sophia—distracted the children lest they disturb their father. Her diaries bear witness to her dedication. When Tolstoy asked Sophia not to nag him for not writing, she was so surprised she wrote down in her diary, "But how can I nag? What right do I have?" Night after night, year after year, she worked hard to make the process of writing easier for him. And in the hours that were not consumed by her kids, she acted as her husband's secretary. Not only did she keep the notes for *War and Peace,* she rewrote the entire manuscript seven times over. Once when she suffered a miscarriage and fell gravely ill, she was worried that because of her illness he would not be able to write. She inspired, indulged and assisted him—a fact that is hard to remember when one sees the depth of the hatred that cropped up between them later in life.

Then he wrote the marvelous *Anna Karenina*—the novel that begins with one of the most quoted lines in world literature: "Happy families are all alike; every unhappy family is unhappy in its own way." One question literary historians and biographers are fond of bringing up is to what extent Tolstoy's real life influenced the subject matter of the novel. How many of Tolstoy's own fears, with regard to his wife and his marriage, found their way into *Anna Karenina*? Perhaps the famous writer, then forty-four, steered his story into the stormy waters of adultery as a warning to Sophia, who was then only twenty-eight. Perhaps by writing about the disastrous consequences that a high-society lady could suffer through infidelity, he was simply cautioning his wife.

As if a married woman's debauchery isn't sinful enough, when lovers live not in the high mountains in isolation but in the heart of the civilized world, it is a sin far worse. The first time Alexey Alexandrovitch has a serious talk with his wife, he makes this very clear: "I want to warn you that through thoughtlessness and lack of caution you may cause yourself to be talked about in society." Things get out of hand not when a woman has feelings for a man other than her husband but when the knowledge of this becomes public.

It is also probable that through his novel, Tolstoy wasn't only sending his wife a message but was also teaching his daughters of varying ages a lesson in morality. Strangely enough, the novel ended up having more impact on him than on his wife or daughters. He went through a moral torment, the first of many, which would end up paving the way for a very different sort of existential crisis—one that would strike at the very essence of his marriage.

No matter how we interpret the events that followed, this much is true: Sophia never saw Anna as a role model, positive or negative. The fictional character who wore dark lilac, who wished to be like a happy heroine in an English novel, who worked on a children's book and who smoked opium—although similar in some ways to Sophia—was clearly not her. Despite the concerns her husband harbored, *she* never abandoned him or loved another man. On the contrary, she remained attached—perhaps too attached—to her husband and to her family, until it drove her over the edge. Every year a new baby came, and with every child Sophia turned a bit more irritable and their marriage took another blow.

A day would not pass without an argument erupting within the house, the husband's and wife's energies drained by petty squabbles no bigger than a speck of dust. In this way, the Tolstoys waded through the thick fog of marriage for several more years. Sexuality was still a way of reconnecting, but when that, too, was gone—more for him than for her—and the fog began to dissolve, Tolstoy couldn't bear to see what it had been hiding all that time.

When Tolstoy peered into the soul of his wife, he saw youth, desire and ambition, and was displeased with what he found. When Sophia peered into the soul of her husband, she saw self-centeredness mixed with the seeds of altruism, and never sensed how much this would affect their lives in the future. He stared at her and wondered how she, as comfortable and well brought up as she was, could still have worldly aspirations. She stared at him and wondered how he, as pampered and respected as he was, could love anything, be it his writing or God, more than he loved her.

Like Dr. Frankenstein, who struggled to rid himself of the creature he had designed and crafted, Tolstoy made an unhappy, argumentative wife out of the young girl he had married years earlier.

For a while he tried to put up with her, but his patience rapidly ran out. In a letter written to his daughter Alexandra Lvovna, he complained of Sophia's "perpetual spying, eavesdropping, incessant complaining, ordering him about, as her fancy takes her. . . ." In the same breath, he said he wanted freedom from her. He suddenly, abrasively and irreversibly distanced himself from his wife and from everything that was associated with her.

Then one day, he simply took off.

That afternoon, for the first time in a long while, he felt freedom by his side, not as an abstract concept or an idea to defend, but as a presence, so close, solid and tangible. He walked. He skipped and jumped. At the top of his voice, he sang songs that no one had heard before. The peasants working in the nearby fields solemnly watched the most respected novelist in Russia doing one crazy thing after another, and they spoke about it to no one. As if in return for their silent support, that same evening, Tolstoy decided to give away his possessions to the poor. The man who came from an aristocratic background, who had been sheltered all his life, was now determined to shed all the privileges of his station.

When Sophia, the matriarch, heard about this, she went berserk. Only a fool would squander his wealth like that, she was certain—only a fool with no wife or children to care for. Before long, and much to her chagrin, Tolstoy publicly declared that he had wiped his hands clean of the material world. He gave away all of his money, all of his land. Abandoning the banquets he was so fond of, he swore off eating meat, hunting and drinking, and put himself to work like a village craftsman.

Sophia watched his transformation in absolute horror. The nobleman she married, the writer she adored and the husband for whom she bore children was gone, replaced by a badly dressed, flea-ridden peasant. It was an insult that drove straight into her heart.

She called Tolstoy's new habits "the Dark Ones," as if speaking of a fatal illness, like a plague that had tainted their household. Her lips chapped from biting them, her mouth contorted in unhappiness and her face that of a woman older than her age, she suffered one nervous breakdown after another. One day her son Lev asked Sophia if she was happy. It took her a while to answer a question as simple and challenging as this. Finally she said yes, she was happy. Her son asked, "So why do you look like a martyress?"

The love between husband and wife, as strong as it might once have been, could not accommodate the woman and man they had grown into, generating mutual rage and resentment, like a wound bleeding inwardly.

Finally, in the fall of 1910, a few months after secretly taking his wife out of his will, and giving the publishing rights of his novels to his editor, Tolstoy fell sick with pneumonia. Fading in and out of consciousness, the way he had faded in and out of his wife's life for decades, he died in a train station where he had fled to after yet another argument at home. It is symbolic that the writer, who had started his literary walk by claiming that true happiness lies within family life, ended his life by walking away from his family, away from her.

For a long time Sophia was seen as solely a mother and wife. Her great contribution to Tolstoy's literary legacy was either ignored or belittled. It is only recently that we are beginning to see her in a different light—as a diarist, intellectual and businesswoman—and can appreciate her as a talented, selfless woman with many abilities and unrealized dreams.

PART TWO

Winds of Change

What the Fishermen Know

Two months later, I am walking by the seaside at six o'clock in the morning on a Sunday. I am an early riser, not because I don't like sleep—which I don't, really—but because waking up after the sun comes out leaves me feeling slightly irritated, as if the whole world has been whooping it up, and I am catching only the end of the party.

So here I am, up and out for a walk. The only other life forms awake at this hour are the seagulls, the street cats and Istanbul's amateur fishermen. Music on my iPod (Amy Winehouse), popcorn in my pockets (suffice it to say, I believe that in a better world, popcorn would make it onto the breakfast menu), I walk briskly, mulling over the life of Sophia Tolstoy.

There is a crystalline quality to the air, and the sky hangs indigo above me, furrowed by rose-flushed clouds that move toward the hills far ahead. Istanbul looks rejuvenated and clean, like a young bride fresh out of the *hamam*. One can almost imagine that this is not the same city that drives its inhabitants crazy day after day. Now it looks picturesque and alluring, a city dipped in honey. I suspect Istanbul is at its prettiest when we Istanbulites aren't around—yet another reason to wake up early.

Along the coastline toward Bebek there are twenty to thirty fishermen—from teenage boys to grandfathers with canes—strung along in a perfect line, facing the sea. Like prayer beads on a thread, they stand side by side with their plastic buckets and jars of wriggling worms, their eyes fixed somewhere on the horizon and their fingers clutched around fishing rods. They do not talk or joke around. They simply, patiently wait for the fish to come and take the bait.

Later in the hour, the sun is rising, but I notice it has company. The moon is still there—a day or two shy of fullness. My eyes are riveted on the sky. Doesn't the moon know it is in the wrong place at the wrong time? As I watch its faint aura, I think about Sophia again.

"If Sophia had been a novelist, would Leo Tolstoy have assisted her in the same way she assisted him?" I wonder. "Would he have made copies of his wife's manuscripts over and over again? Would he have taken the children out for a walk, and met their every need, so that his wife could have more hours of peace and quiet to concentrate on her writing?"

Laden with these questions, I walk toward the park in the midst of the neighborhood. The playground, which is packed with mothers, children and babies during the day, is empty now. I sit on a bench, watching a few pigeons waddle around, poking at the crumbs of bread stuck in the crevices.

Suddenly, a scream pierces the air, pulling me out of my reverie. I rise to my feet, my heart pounding. "Who's there?"

In lieu of an answer comes another scream, shrill and loud, followed by a bang, like something being dropped, or someone being slapped. The sounds are coming from behind the mulberry bush a few feet ahead. More curious than cautious, I tread in that direction.

"Heeelp!"

I know this female voice from somewhere, but where, I cannot tell.

"Oh, shut up! HELP ME INSTEAD!"

This time it is a different person shouting. Are there two ladies being robbed?

"Is there no one to save me from this shrew?" the first voice yells.

Or are there two ladies robbing each other?

"Huh, it's *you* who is harassing me," the other snaps. "I'm sick and tired of you standing in my way. Why don't you take a vacation? Go to Disneyland."

"Why should *I* leave? You should go. I've had enough of you confusing Elif with your harebrained ideas!"

Hearing my name, I freeze and strain my ears.

"It's because *you* want to influence Elif. But I will never let that happen. Over my dead body, you hear me?"

That is enough eavesdropping. I part the bushes and there, standing on a tree trunk, their hands clutched around each other's throats, I see the unmistakable profiles of two finger-women.

"Hey, yo, Big Self. Wassup?" says one of them, forcing a smile.

The second woman takes her hands off her adversary, and makes a sign of peace. "Good to see you, Sister."

I frown from one to the other. "Little Miss Practical! Miss Highbrowed Cynic! What are you doing here?"

These two have been on a collision course for as long as I've known them. At first glance, they both seem to embrace reason and rationality. But that is as far as their similarities go. While Little Miss Practical wants to overcome every challenge in a pragmatic way, Miss Highbrowed Cynic isn't interested in easy solutions. The former wants to solve things as quickly as possible while the latter opts for a detailed, complicated, philosophical approach. Where one prefers to be clear and concise, the other favors ambiguity and abstraction. One likes answers, the other prefers questions.

Without a further word, I pick them up by the napes of their necks and place one on each of my shoulders. In this fashion, I walk back toward the Bosphorus. It doesn't take long before another line of amateur fishermen appears before us.

"Look at those fishermen," says Little Miss Practical, craning her head from where she sits on my left shoulder. "They're wack. How many fish do they think they'll catch like that? They stand there for hours, and go back home with a couple of sad rockfish in their buckets. In the time they spend here, they could work and earn real cheddar. They could buy a huge salmon!"

"What do you know?" Miss Highbrowed Cynic says, with a snort, from my right shoulder. "What can any pragmatist know about philosophy, art and literature, and the things that make life worth living?"

"What have fishermen got to do with that?" asks Little Miss Practical.

"Fishing's got to do with that," comes the answer. "It is the perfect way to contemplate the endless mysteries of the universe."

I nod in agreement, but the truth is, I don't understand the fishermen either. How does it feel, and what kind of state of mind does it require, not to rush, not to push? What level of humility does it take to be satisfied with what you have, and be happy to go home with two flimsy fish in a plastic bucket at the end of a long day?

Of all the prophets, it is Job who, on some level, I cannot empathize with—Job who, according to the Qur'an, is the symbol of patience, humbleness and peaceful surrender. I have never understood how he doesn't get angry, not even upset, in the face of the ordeals God puts him through, and remains ever thankful, ever accepting.

Unaware of my thoughts, Miss Highbrowed Cynic continues her dissertation. "Many books have fishermen as their central characters."

"What books?" asks Little Miss Practical. There is nothing about awakening the fisherman within in her enormous self-help collection.

"*Scire tuum nihil est, nisi te scire hoc sciat alter!*"

"What the hell was that?"

Miss Highbrowed Cynic raises her voice over the incipient hum of the city. "I said: Your knowledge is nothing when no one else knows that you know."

"Poser!" hisses Little Miss Practical.

"My point *is,* how can you follow Melville's adventures of Ishmael and Captain Ahab, and not contemplate our tiny little place in this universe? What about Hemingway's epic battle of wills between the old fisherman and the giant fish he longs to catch? And take Ursula K. Le Guin's *A Fisherman of the Inland Sea*—you will be thinking twice as hard as you ever have about the roles of good and evil. You see how fishing is intertwined with philosophy?"

"All right, all right, I get the point. While you're at it, you might want to tell the philosophers over there something about efficiency," says Little Miss Practical. "There must be, what, thirty of them. Why don't they, say, rent a fishing boat together? Then, when they go out to sea and cast their nets, their output would increase tenfold."

Miss Highbrowed Cynic heaves a sigh. "Fishing has depth. It has wisdom. You will never understand if your only concern is productivity. Why am I wasting my breath? No philosophy or art will ever come from the shallow waters you swim in."

"You're all big talk! You always talk about *depth*," grumbles Little Miss Practical. "What are you, a scuba diver?"

"Ladies, ladies, please," I interject. I know I need to handle this as delicately as I can. "Let's not argue on this beautiful morning."

"What is wrong with arguing?" objects Miss Highbrowed Cynic. "The German philosopher Ernst Bloch used the concept *noch nicht*— not yet what things could be. Instead of trying to be complete, we should embrace the idea of being without a beginning and an end, a state of continuous regeneration. That is why questions should not be answered. They should be deepened with more questions."

"That is the craziest thing I've heard in a long while!" comes a grumpy voice from around the corner.

We turn our heads and see Miss Ambitious Chekhovian ahead of us, standing amid the feet of the fishermen. I am scared out of my wits that someone will accidentally step on her, but she doesn't seem the least bit concerned.

"Deepen dilemmas with more questions? What next? Do you know how much time this stupid Sunday morning walk has already cost our career? Elif, you should be writing right now. Not wasting your time like this!"

I shoot a glance left and right. The fishermen are busy staring at the water. I wonder if there is anyone other than me who can see Miss Ambitious Chekhovian.

I drop my voice to a menacing whisper. "What are you doing?"

"Well, I was hoping you might have had time to reconsider what we were talking about several weeks ago," she says nonchalantly. "You know, the hysterectomy."

"You are nuts," I say, and the two finger-women on my shoulders show their support by clapping their hands.

"All right, if you want to become a *moon woman,* I'm not going to stop you," Miss Ambitious Chekhovian says. "Go and get pregnant, gain all the pounds, and worry about breast-feeding, then raising the child, sending him to school, sending him to college, and before you know it, you will forget all about literature and writing."

I want to protest but she doesn't give me a chance.

"Don't you dare tell me that the literary world is not a competition, and you don't have to rush or push, because that is gibberish. Even if you're not racing against other writers, you are racing against yourself, and your own mortality."

I open my mouth again, and again she interrupts me.

"And don't you forget that the writer was Leo Tolstoy, not the moon woman Sophia."

"What does that mean?" I ask.

"It means what it means. Remember the woman on the steamboat. The woman who was twenty-five years old but looked forty. The woman who collected pounds and resentments like free cakes. Do you want to become her?"

"You talk as if she were the only one who is unhappy in this world," says Miss Highbrowed Cynic, "whereas all humanity is in a similar position. Melancholy is central to being human."

We ignore her.

"Yo. Women can be both good mothers and good career women. And they can be happy. . . . It's simple. The key is time management." This from Little Miss Practical.

Miss Ambitious Chekhovian snorts. "Of course, there are women like that, and I call them circus jugglers. Send the kid off to school in the morning, cook the husband a perfect omelet, two eggs and a table-spoon of butter, dress in a hurry, make it to work, rush home in the evening, set the table, feed the kid, then pass out on the couch while watching TV. . . . Yes, those women do exist. But they never write novels."

"You are the Queen of Hyperbole," I chide.

Her dark eyes smoldering with agitation, Miss Ambitious Chekhovian gives me a faint smile. "The point is, my dear, jugglers can manage only the moment. That's it. They can do motherhood and do their jobs. That much is true. But just how far can they rise in their careers? That is another question."

"Literature and writing is more than a career," I say.

"Exactly," she says. "It is a lifestyle. It is a lifetime passion. An artist needs to be ambitious and passionate. You don't work nine to five. You breathe your art twenty-four hours a day, seven days a week. That's why you should consider a hysterectomy."

Half an hour later, we are back in the park, sitting on another bench—the four of us, feeling drab, almost drowsy. That is what happens when more than two finger-women get together. This much quarreling tires us all, draining our energies, yet these Thumbelinas do not know how not to quarrel.

"Hello, everyone! May I join you?" It is Dame Dervish, suddenly mushrooming on the bench, like a Sufi version of Houdini.

She wears a plain smoky-gray dress and a long cloak of the same color, fastened with a pearl brooch. The hem of her dress is fluttering softly in the breeze. She wears a necklace sporting the name Hu,★ written in Ottoman script.

"Welcome, dear Sufi," I say. "Come and join us."

"Thank you," she says. "I feel welcomed, but I wish you could as well. Look at yourself, always evaluating, always in haste. Sometimes you try to do five things at once and then fall flat from exhaustion. Do one thing at a time. What is the hurry? Give yourself over to the moment. Time does not exist beyond that. The Seven Sleepers in the

---

★ In Sufism, Hu is a name of Allah, and is used in conjunction with Allah (Allah Hu, which means "God, the Real"). The word denotes a "dimensional beyond" without quantity and quality. It symbolizes Oneness, where everything is interconnected.

Qur'an slept for three hundred years in a cave, but when they woke up they felt like only a few hours had passed."

"Do you want me to sleep?" I frown.

"I want you to stop competing with time."

I try to give myself over to the moment, and realize I don't have a clue what that really means.

"Dame Dervish . . ."

"Hmm?"

"Do you think . . . I mean, if I ever were to do this, not that I want to, of course, just a question, if I were to someday . . . I mean, hypothetically . . ." I take a deep breath and try again. "Do you think I could make a good mother?"

Her dark green eyes widen, creasing around the edges. "If you fulfill three conditions you will make a wonderful mother."

"What three conditions?"

"First of all, God needs to want it, so a new chapter must be written in your storybook," she says. "Second, you need to want it, of course, deep in your heart, and your partner's, too."

"Well, what is the third condition?"

"The third condition has to do with the fishermen," she says. "You have to learn what they know."

"Not the fishermen again!" Little Miss Practical says with a snort, raising her hands, palms up.

I look around in bewilderment. What could these fishermen possibly know about becoming a mother? What could they know that I don't know?

"Dear Elif," says Dame Dervish, as if writing me a letter.

"Yes?"

"Have you ever seen a fisherman run at the sea? You can't have—because he, who you call fisherman, doesn't chase fish. He waits for the fish to come to him."

"Which means . . . ?"

Dame Dervish regards me for a beat before she answers. "It means: Stop running after the waves. Let the sea come to you."

Just then a young mother pushing a stroller passes in front of us and jolts me back to my senses. Despite myself I look at the baby—her pink fingers, powder-soft hair, dimpled cheeks—and I find myself smiling.

"Come on, let's go. What are we waiting for?" asks Miss Ambitious Chekhovian, pulling at my arm. "Time is money."

"Let's go and read novels," says Miss Highbrowed Cynic.

"The shortest route," orders Little Miss Practical. "Let's catch a cab."

Suddenly, I don't want to hear or see any of them. At least for a while. "Go ahead," I say gently, but firmly. "I'm staying."

Thankfully, after a few protests, the four finger-women leave. Arguing among themselves as to which road to take, they walk away on their little feet, their voices trailing off into the air.

I notice a fat, tawny cat nearby, following them with his fixed eyes. Can the cat see them? The thought first excites, and then frightens, me. What if the cat confuses them with mice or birds and tries to gobble them up? But to my relief, even if the feline could see my finger-women, he shuts his eyes and resumes his nap, realizing, perhaps, that they would give him indigestion.

Taking a deep, deep breath, I watch the little women exit the park. What am I going to do with them? They make everything harder for me, and yet I love them.

For one long moment, I, too, want to be a fisherman.

Of Poets and Babies

She was the girl who wanted to be God so that she could create the entire universe from scratch. Such was her desire to live with real intimacy; she couldn't fit into her body or her past. In her youth she was a teacher for a while, though it didn't take her long to decide that being part of the workforce was not for her. She was made to write. Determined to earn her living from her writing, never satisfied with what was placed in front of her, she pushed and shoved. Waiting patiently for tomorrow to come didn't suit her well. She wouldn't make a good fisherman.

To her close friends she was Syl, to her family, Sivvie. To the rest of the world she was Sylvia Plath.

Her marriage to Ted Hughes has been the subject of numerous heated discussions among scholars, feminists and nonfeminists alike. Many have taken either her side of the story or his but the truth must lie somewhere in between, in a hue other than black or white. The essays and books written about her—even after all these years—tend to be as emotionally charged as she was. Perhaps somehow all her biographers end up falling in love with her.

Hers was a rocky marriage that caused much pain. Yet, like many other relationships that ended up similarly, it had started out as an uncontrollable magnetic pull. They were two poets in love: Sylvia Plath and Ted Hughes. Shared metaphors, conflicting subjectivities, powerful personalities. Can two poets be in love without competing with each other in the long run? It is not impossible, of course, but it is hard. They were young, headstrong and free. They had things to say to each other and a world to change together. Thus, they fell in love, fought endlessly, made love with passion and urgency, did and said things they bitterly regretted later, forgave each other and themselves, all through words. Words were their particular pride.

There is a poem she wrote titled "I Want, I Want." The central figure is a God-like baby who is yet to be born. Immense, bald and open-mouthed, this is not a cute, angelic baby but a powerful natural force that wishes to come into this world and demands to be given love and attention, and gets them. It is a baby that wants *to be*. The poet uses a volcano as the symbol of feminine fertility—the ability to breed, broaden and bear life within. But a volcano is also a dangerous and destructive force. Even when it is asleep you cannot be fully sure that it will not erupt at any moment. It cannot be tamed. It cannot be predicted.

Throughout her life, Sylvia Plath underwent various anxieties with regard to womanhood and motherhood. First, she feared she was sterile and could never have babies. Then she lost many nights' sleep fretting over the pains of giving birth. How excruciating was it? Would she survive? And once she had babies, she worried about the outside world and its cruelties.

But she was equally convinced that being a mother would add great things to her life and to her writing. After having a baby, she was going to be a different woman—one whom she would depict in her poems as a superhuman being, a magical mortal who was transformed with the mere touch of a baby's pink thumb. In her diary she wrote, "I must first conquer my writing and experience, and then will deserve to conquer childbirth." Another time she said, "I will write until I begin to speak my deep self, and then have children, and speak still deeper." Maybe she was right, after all. She would write her greatest work, *Ariel,* after becoming a mother.

Before long she gave birth to a daughter, and sixteen months later to a son. Staying at home to raise her babies was a critical choice, but one that she made. From then on, she would take care of her house and her family, and write her poems and stories. Sometimes the two occupations would overlap, and she would find herself scribbling pages and pages in her diaries about changing diapers and baking chocolate cookies.

As she immersed herself in household chores, she would watch from the sidelines the goings-on in the literary world. She took note of the new works being published and the emerging writers being feted, especially the female ones. She was no stranger to envy. Just like she was no stranger to anger, angst and self-destruction. And that perhaps is one of the things that makes her so real and her presence so palpable so long after her death. Plath openly and brazenly wrote about the myriad dark energies in life that we all recognize but often pretend not to.

In the repetitive rhythm of daily habits, she felt both elated by and frustrated with her motherly duties. Her husband, in the meantime, continued frequenting literary events they used to attend together. He carried on with his life as it had been, writing his poetry, making new contacts, fortifying his fame. Perhaps fatherhood was not as great a rupture in a man's life as motherhood was in a woman's. Or perhaps, she suspected, it was just their own unique situation.

Inasmuch as babies were powerful metaphors in her poems, poems were babies to Sylvia Plath. When she spoke about her works that were not yet complete, she called them "unborn babies." She even described how her poems smiled at her, how "their little foreheads bulged with concentration," and how they changed every day, moving their tiny fingers and toes. She was the mother to not only two children but a thousand poems. And there were times when they were all hungry and crying at once, craving her attention and compassion, and no matter how hard she tried, she couldn't keep them all happy.

Her split with her husband was a major turning point in her life. After the emotional breakdown, she decided to put herself back together in a more indomitable way, to reinvent herself, to become a brand-new woman. She was ambitious. She was talented. She was alone. Often she started the day at four in the morning—the one or two hours that she had to herself before the children woke up were the most precious time of the day. The poems she wrote during those months are perhaps her brightest—such as "Medusa," "Daddy" or "Lady Lazarus," where she shocked her readers by saying, "Dying / Is an art, like everything else. / I do it exceptionally well." At the kitchen table, in the bathroom or in bed under the covers, she wrote wherever and whenever she could, scribbling furiously in her extra-careful hand, at an incredible speed—as if she were racing against God, against the men she loved and loved no more, against her numerous shortcomings, each of which she despised.

There is a poem she called "For a Fatherless Son." It is about a father who has left his home, his wife and his children. There is more sorrow in this poem than resentment, more surrender than fight. One can sense that something changed in her. For it was not quite rage or rebellion she experienced but a feeling of perpetual sadness. She spoke of the emptiness that was left in her children's lives after their father's departure, an *absence that grew beside them like a tree* that they would have to learn to live with.

That was the stage in her life when she desired to be many things at the same time, and excel equally in each. A mother, a housewife, a writer, a poet . . . She wanted everything to happen immediately and flawlessly. Perhaps she was also in love with her creations. She stubbornly retained the belief that she could be an ideal mother and an excellent poet: the perfect Poet-Mother. It was not an easy combination, especially in the climate of the 1950s, when everyone thought a woman had to make an either-or choice. She refused to choose.

Nevertheless, her effort to become "superwoman" wore Sylvia Plath down. Before long she noticed that she was pushing herself too hard. When she made it to one place, she discovered she had skipped over another; when she fixed one thing, something else was falling apart. Slowly but surely, she realized she could not be perfect. That is why her poem "The Munich Mannequins" begins like this:

"Perfection is terrible, / It cannot have children."

With the money she got from literary prizes or grants she would pay for a nanny. While writing her first and only novel, *The Bell Jar,* in an attempt to establish a deeper connection with her past and soul, she deliberately prodded the places of fear in herself—fear of sanity, of being like thousands of others; and fear of insanity, of being so fundamentally different there was no hope of mingling with society. She wrote in detail about mental breakdown, electroconvulsive therapy and the suffocating monotony of modern life: "To the person in the bell jar, blank and stopped as a dead baby, the world is the bad dream." When the book was published in January 1963, readers were divided and Plath herself was deeply distressed by the tone of the reviews it received.

As she ran out of steam, unable to meet the extremely high demands she had placed on herself, Plath decided that she would rather die than live in the way it had been prescribed for her by others. The creative person with unbridled passion that she was, she wanted everything or nothing at all. . . . She had tried suicide before, an overdose of sleeping pills at the age of twenty. Yet at the time she had wanted both to die at her own hands and to be rescued. This time she wanted only the former.

It was a cold morning, February 11, 1963, one that reeked of tedium and induced a sense of isolation. After checking on her two children in their beds, and leaving milk and bread on their bedside table, she closed their door and sealed the cracks. She went into the kitchen, turned on the oven's gas and took a dozen sleeping pills, swallowing them one by one. Then she stuck her head in the oven, and as the gas licked at her face, she fell into eternal sleep. She was only thirty years old.

To this day, Plath's legendary heritage is unsurpassed. In Turkey, I have met numerous female college students who admire her work so much they organize special reading nights on campuses for her. In America, there is a colorful, intriguing blog called "Playgroup with Sylvia Plath." In Germany, I once talked to a Filipino woman who had named her daughter Ariel after her. In France, at an international women's organization, I met a chic businesswoman who asked us all to "toast to Sylvia."

No other literary suicide has been talked and written about so much. No other woman writer, after her death, turned into such an icon beyond place and time.

The Midnight Coup d'État

One night toward the end of the summer, I hear voices in my sleep. A door opens and closes somewhere in the house, footsteps on the stairs, whispers in the dark. Thinking I'm having a nightmare, I toss and turn in bed. Then someone pokes me on the shoulder, shouting, "Hey, wake up!"

I try to ignore the voice, hoping the moment will pass, as all moments tend to do, but there follows a second command, this time louder.

"Get up! Wake up already!"

I open my eyes and find Miss Ambitious Chekhovian literally right in front of my nose. She has climbed up my shoulder and crawled her way to my face, where she now stands on my chin, legs and arms akimbo. She is looking at me with a kind of triumph I find more puzzling than disturbing in my present state. Her makeup is perfect, her bun of hair is tight, as always. Even at this hour she looks prim and proper. It takes me an extra second to notice she is wearing a military uniform with a badge of rank on her shoulders. Before I get a chance to ask her why on earth she has dressed up like that, she speaks in a tone I can barely recognize.

"There is a matter of great importance. You better get up!"

"Well, can't it wait till morning?" I grumble. "I was sleeping, in case you hadn't noticed."

"No, it cannot possibly wait," she says. "The best time for a military takeover is the wee hours of the night, when everyone is asleep and resistance is slim."

I sit up in bed and stare at her, stunned, like an animal caught in the headlights. "What did you say?"

To my dazed expression she responds with a glacial look. In all these years we have known each other, I have never seen her like this before.

"As of this moment we have declared a coup d'état," she says. "The regime in this house has changed."

What on earth is she talking about? My hair standing on end, anxiety bubbling up in my throat, I try to make sense of the situation.

"In two minutes we expect you in the living room. Don't be late, the committee won't like that," says Miss Ambitious Chekhovian, and leaves.

Still groggy from sleep, I put on a shawl, wash my face and go downstairs. A surprising scene awaits me when I step into the living room. The members of the Choir of Discordant Voices are there, all of them frowning. The tension in the room is so thick, I can almost touch it. In the corner the CD player is blasting the kind of songs I have never heard under this roof. They sound disquietingly aggressive, like anthems of a country that has waged war on all its neighbors and all the neighbors of its neighbors.

I see Miss Highbrowed Cynic first. She is sitting inside the fruit bowl on the table, dangling her legs as she puffs away on her cigarette. I don't usually allow the finger-women to smoke indoors, but something tells me this is not the right moment to remind her. There is an unusual flicker in her gaze, an odd furtiveness, which I can't quite put my finger on. She is wearing a military-style jacket over her hippie dress, a wacky combination that makes me dizzy.

Behind her, leaning against a tissue box, is Little Miss Practical, wearing a parka, black, bulky boots and commando-style trousers with a matching green hooded top. Her arms crossed over her chest, her brows furrowed, she sighs loudly. For some reason unbeknownst to me, she is staring at the wall, clearly avoiding any eye contact.

Next to the potted petunia under the window, her knees drawn up to her chest, sits Dame Dervish. A clump of her reddish hair has escaped from her turban, and is casting a shadow on her face. Upon closer inspection, I notice she is chained to the radiator with handcuffs.

"What is going on here?" I ask, a trace of panic creeping into my voice.

"Tonight, while you were sleeping, we had an emergency meeting," says Miss Ambitious Chekhovian. "We reached the conclusion that it was high time for a shift in the regime. From this moment onward, I have changed my name to Milady Ambitious Chekhovian and I have taken charge of the Choir of Discordant Voices."

Suddenly Miss Highbrowed Cynic coughs.

"I beg your pardon, *we* have taken charge," says Milady Ambitious Chekhovian. "That means, Miss Highbrowed Cynic and I. Together, we have performed a coup d'état."

This has got to be a joke, but all the finger-women look so serious and intense that it's better not to laugh.

"As the chairwoman of the executive committee," Miss Highbrowed Cynic joins in, "I am pleased to announce that we will soon introduce a new constitution that, for the next thirty-five years, will make it impossible to overthrow us. After that, our children will start to reign."

"Hey, that is a far cry from democracy," I object.

But Miss Highbrowed Cynic pretends not to hear. She is extremely agitated tonight and tries to conceal it, which makes her anxiousness even more pronounced, causing her to look as if she were high on amphetamines. "I am proud to announce," she says, "that as the new government our first act has been to consolidate peace and order in the house."

"I don't see any change," I say under my breath.

"Now that peace and order have been consolidated," continues Milady Ambitious Chekhovian, "our second act will be to send you away from this city."

"What . . . Why . . . Where am I going?" I ask, dumbfounded.

"To America," roars Milady Ambitious Chekhovian, enjoying her newfound power. "We are going to the New World, all of us."

"Okay, girls, that's enough," I say. "I am not going anywhere until you explain to me—in clear and proper terms—why you want me to go to America."

They go quiet for a moment, as if they were not expecting this reaction. Do they really believe they are army generals and cannot be questioned?

"This is not about America, it is about you. It could well have been anyplace, like Australia or Japan," says Milady Ambitious Chekhovian. "What matters is that you need to leave Istanbul at once."

Miss Highbrowed Cynic smacks her lips approvingly. "We are going to America because it just so happens that we applied for a fellowship in your name. Congratulations! You have won. Now get packed!"

I feel a lurch in my stomach, only now realizing how serious they are.

"We have decided that you should take this trip in order to grow as a writer," Miss Highbrowed Cynic adds. "It will be inspiring for you to get away for a while. We are doing this for your own good."

"For my own good," I repeat.

If she heard the scorn in my voice, Milady Ambitious Chekhovian doesn't seem to be bothered by it. "I will be honest with you," she says. "We have been planning this coup d'état for a while. But it was you— with your recent irrational behavior—who accelerated the process."

"What *irrational behavior* are you referring to?" I ask as calmly as I can manage.

"Lately, your state of mind has not been well," says Milady Ambitious Chekhovian, her voice shaky with emotion. "All these years, we have slaved away so that you could excel as a novelist. We never took off, we never fooled around. People might think novels pop off an assembly line, but they don't. Behind every book, there is toil. There is sweat and pain."

"All right," I say. "Why do you bring this up now?"

Milady Ambitious Chekhovian raises her chin and straightens her shoulders, like the military hero she has become. "Did we do all this for nothing? How dare you throw away the years of sweat in one fell swoop?"

"Wait a minute, I am not throwing away anything," I object. "Where are you getting all of this?"

"From your behavior, of course. I have been watching you for some time. Don't think I haven't noticed!"

"Noticed what?" I bellow. I am not calm anymore, and don't try to be.

"I can very well see that you're considering having a baby."

"Oh my God, is that what this is about?" I ask.

"Yes, sir," she says. "You are wondering: 'Could I become a mother? What kind of mother would I make? I'm getting older. My biological clock is ticking.' All these harmful thoughts are bouncing around your head! I don't see this going anywhere good. Do you think I didn't notice the way you were looking at that baby the other day?"

"How did I look?" I ask suspiciously.

"With sparkling eyes . . ."

"What is wrong with that, is it—" I try to defend myself, but Milady Ambitious Chekhovian cuts me off immediately.

"There can be only two reasons why a woman looks with sparkling eyes at another woman's baby: (a) she wants to be a baby again; (b) she wants to become a mother. In your case, I am afraid it's the latter."

Miss Highbrowed Cynic joins in. "Obviously, if you stay around here, you will be led astray."

"Led astray from what?" I ask, incredulous.

"From your literary trajectory, of course!" Miss Highbrowed Cynic and Milady Ambitious Chekhovian exclaim in unison. "From being a writer and an intellectual . . . Your path is to write and read."

I am more amazed by their show of solidarity than by the things they are spouting. When *did* these two become such chums?

I turn to Miss Highbrowed Cynic, managing a smile. "I thought you weren't against motherhood. You said it made no difference. You said, one way or another, we are always miserable."

"Exactly," she says, nodding. "I have *now* decided that it is better to be a miserable writer than a miserable writer, housewife, spouse and mother."

My head starts to spin. What about Little Miss Practical, I wonder. She's been unusually silent. Noticing my inquisitive gaze, she guiltily plays with the zipper of her parka.

"What is your take on this?" I ask. "I thought you were on the side of liberal democracy and free market economy."

"True, a junta isn't my cup of tea," she admits. "But I'm down for it, under the extenuating circumstances."

"What extenuating circumstances?"

"Well, at first I wasn't thrilled with the coup. But *then* I saw the benefits. Life in America is far more stable and orderly. My needs will be better met. How pragmatic is that!"

"That is called opportunism, not pragmatism," I say.

"There is no need to get upset," says Miss Highbrowed Cynic. "If we take the time to read Habermas's theory of communicative action, we will see that we all can coexist. Since system rationality and action rationality are not the same thing, as autonomous finger-women agents we can relate to one another through communicative reasoning and develop mutual understandings."

"Yo, I don't know what she is talking about but I couldn't agree more," says Little Miss Practical.

I can't believe what I'm hearing. I always thought the members of the Choir of Discordant Voices were, well, discordant, but apparently the military takeover has brought them together.

It is then that I look at Dame Dervish, who is still sitting on the floor with a brooding expression and concern-filled eyes. She is the only one not wearing a military outfit.

"What about her?" I whisper.

This question makes my tormentors uneasy. After an awkward

pause, Milady Ambitious Chekhovian offers an answer. "Unfortunately, Dame Dervish did not approve of our midnight coup d'état. Despite our best efforts, we could not change her mind. She told us she would not fight us or stand in our way, but she would not, under any circumstances, support us."

"And why is she handcuffed?" I ask.

"Well, it's her fault, really. She tried to stage a peaceful protest, parking herself like a turbaned Gandhi under our feet, and left us with no other option than to arrest her."

"She is a political prisoner now," adds Miss Highbrowed Cynic.

I cannot believe my ears. My finger-women have gone wild, and I don't know how to control them—if I ever did, that is. I want to talk to Dame Dervish privately, but I'll have to wait for an appropriate moment.

A mantle of silence canopies the room: the militarists among us pacing the floor, the handcuffed pacifist sitting on the floor and me staring at the floor. Finally, Little Miss Practical approaches me with an envelope.

"What's this?" I ask.

"Your plane ticket. You're leaving tomorrow. It might be a good idea to start packing. I made a list of the things you need to take with you."

"So soon? But where am I going, what fellowship did I win? I don't know anything!"

The answer comes from Milady Ambitious Chekhovian. "Ninety minutes from Boston, there is a beautiful college called Mount Holyoke. That is where you are going. It is an all-girls campus!"

Miss Highbrowed Cynic joins in with pride: "You won a fellowship given to a limited number of women artists, writers and academics from around the world. It is a lively intellectual hub, you'll see."

After that, I cannot go back to sleep. My instinct is to take off to the end of the world as soon as it is morning, but how far could I run from those voices within? My courage melting like hot wax, I sit there, tense and wary, watching the sun rise. In that husky light, everything around me seems to quickly evaporate—the night, the names, the places. . . .

In that instant I know, in my bones and soul, that the summer has come to an end. Not gradually and imperceptibly, but in a single moment, in a quantum jump.

Perhaps all summers are like that. They go on and on, uneventful and lazy, and just when you have gotten used to the sluggish rhythm, they end abruptly, leaving you totally unprepared for the cold autumn.

All I know is a new season is under way.

PART THREE

Brain Versus Body

Where the Fairies Hang Out

An hour later, when the three women in uniform leave the room to pack their suitcases, I go to rescue their detainee. Feeling like some hero in a war movie, *Saving Private Dame Dervish,* I sneak toward the captive, careful not to make any noise. With the help of a pair of tweezers, I unlock her handcuffs. She rubs her wrists, giving me a tired smile.

"Thank you, dear," she murmurs.

Finished with Operation Freedom, we steal out of the house. I'm walking and she, having crawled into my bag, pokes her head out once in a while to have a look around. The minute we make it to the street, I begin to complain.

"I cannot believe they are doing this to me. Have they lost their minds? This time they've crossed the line."

Dame Dervish listens with raised eyebrows, saying nothing.

"And now they want me to go to the States. Just like that, out of the blue," I continue. "You know what? Maybe you and I should take up arms, organize an underground resistance and topple them. They'd be so freaked out."

"I am a pacifist. I don't take up arms," says Dame Dervish. "'Whenever you are confronted with an opponent, conquer him with love.' That's what Gandhi teaches."

"With all due respect, let's not forget that Mr. Gandhi had not met Milady Ambitious Chekhovian," I say.

"'Nevertheless, an elephant cannot swallow a hedgehog.'"

"Was that Gandhi again?"

"That was a slogan from the Prague Spring," says Dame Dervish. "In 1968. If you can say that against the Soviet tanks, you can say it against any finger-woman you want."

She never ceases to surprise me, this Sufi of mine.

"Look around you, Elif. What do you see?" asks Dame Dervish.

Pedestrians hurrying up and down the street, commuters standing still in public buses that are full to the brim, peddlers selling replica designer bags, street children cleaning the windshields of the luxurious cars that stop at red lights, billboards advertising fast money and glitzy lifestyles, a city of endless contradictions . . . That is what I see when I look around in Istanbul.

"All right, now look at yourself," says Dame Dervish. "What do you see?"

A woman who is split inside, half East, half West. A woman who loves the world of imagination more than the real world; who, year after year, has been worn down by useless paradoxes, wrong relationships, mistaken loves; who is still not over the hurt of growing up without a father; who breaks hearts and has her heart broken; who cares too much about what other people think; who is afraid that God may not really care for her and who can be happy or complete only when writing a novel. In short, "a personality under construction" is what I see when I look at myself. But my tongue won't cooperate in making this confession.

At my uneasy silence, Dame Dervish says, "You have to accept the universe as an open book that is waiting for its reader. One must read each day page by page."

Her voice sounds so calm and soothing, I feel embarrassed about my outburst a minute ago. "Then, tell me, how am I supposed to read this very day?"

"There is a voyage knocking at your door," says Dame Dervish, as if she were holding an invisible cup in her hand and telling my fortune from the configuration of the coffee grounds at the bottom. "If you don't leave Istanbul, these three finger-women will not let you be. From morning till night, they will pick at you."

"Tell me about it," I say, exhaling loudly.

"I think one of these days you should sign a peace treaty with all of us," says Dame Dervish. "The reason why the finger-women are quarreling so much among themselves is because you are quarreling with us. You think some of us are more worthy than others. While in truth, we are all reflections of you. All of us make up a whole."

"You want me to make no distinction between you and Milady Ambitious Chekhovian? But you two are completely different!"

"We don't have to be identical. She and I share the same essence. If only you could understand this. Until you realize that every voice inside you is part of the same circle, you will feel fragmented. Unite us all in One."

"You are talking about my embracing them, but those rascals instigated a coup d'état while I was asleep, for God's sake. It is only a pacifist who trusts a despot. It's never the other way around!"

Dame Dervish gives me a nod, her smile as warm as a caress. "May be."

I look at her, awaiting an explanation. That is when she tells me this story.

"Once upon a time, there was a dervish who spoke little. One day his horse ran away. When they heard the news, all the neighbors came to see him. 'That is terrible,' they remarked. The dervish said, 'May be.'

"The next day, they found the horse with a gorgeous stallion next to it. Everyone congratulated the dervish and said this was wonderful news. Again, he said only, 'May be.'

"A week later, while trying to ride the stallion, the dervish's son fell off and broke his leg. The neighbors came to say how sorry they were. 'How awful,' they exclaimed in unison. The dervish replied, 'May be.'

"The next day, some state officials came to the village to draft young men to the war zone. All the boys had to go, except the dervish's son, who lay in bed with a broken leg."

"You see what I mean?" asks Dame Dervish.

"I guess so," I answer.

"I want you to see the fellowship in Massachusetts not as something imposed on you but as an opportunity. Turkey or the United States, it isn't important, really. What matters is the journey within. You won't be traveling to America, you will be traveling within yourself. Think of it that way."

There is a confident serenity about her, which I like. She might well be right. I have to learn to live peacefully, fully, every day with the voices inside me. I'm tired of constantly being at war with them.

With a sudden urge and zest, I flag down a passing taxi. "Come on, then, let's go," I say as I open the door to the cab.

"Where to?"

"To the train station," I announce, beaming.

"Did you decide to go to America by train?" Dame Dervish asks as she chuckles to herself.

I shake my head. "I just want to go and smell the trains. . . ."

I just want to spend some time at the station—inhale its strange, pungent aroma, the odor of people rushing in all directions, the heavy tang of the destitute with their dreams of affluence, the refreshing hint of new destinations. Whenever I feel the need to contemplate a mystery or observe the world, whenever the nomad in me wakes up, I go there.

Airports are too sterile, clean and controlled when compared with train stations, where the heart of the underprivileged still pulsates.

Haydarpasha Station is an old, majestic building with too many memories. And like many old, majestic buildings, it, too, has its own djinn and fairies. They perch on the high windows and watch the passengers below. They watch couples split, lovers meet, families unite, friends break up. . . . They gaze at the thousand and one predicaments of the sons of Adam and daughters of Eve, and still find us puzzling.

If you ever go there and walk right into the middle of the station, if you then stand still amid the hullabaloo with eyes firmly closed, listen, you can hear them whispering, the djinn and fairies of the station . . . uttering strange words like poetry, in a language long forgotten. . . .

Perhaps, like the Greek poet Konstantinos Kavafis, they, too, are saying,

New lands you will not find, you will not find other seas.
The city will follow you . . .
You will roam the same streets.

Women Who Change Their Names

I was eighteen years old when I decided to change my name. By and large, I was happy with my first name, Elif, which is a fairly common girl's name in Turkey, meaning tall and lithe, like the first letter of the Ottoman alphabet, aleph. The word is encountered in Arabic, Persian, Hebrew and Turkish, although to my knowledge, it is only in the latter that it is used as a female name. That same year, I had read Borges's "The Aleph" and I was familiar with his description of the word as a virtually untraceable point in space that contained all points. Not bad, I thought. Striding along with all the vanity of my youth, I did enjoy being likened to a letter, though I would have much preferred the entire alphabet.

It was a different story, however, with my surname. It upset me that as women, we were expected to take first the family names of our fathers, then our husbands. Having grown up without seeing my father, I couldn't understand, for the life of me, why I should carry his name. Since I was also determined to never get married and take my husband's name, I concluded that the rule of surnames simply didn't apply to me.

I had been pondering this paradox for a while when a prestigious literary magazine in Turkey selected for publication a short story I had written. The editor, an intellectual in his midforties, gave me a call to congratulate and welcome me into the literary fold, which he said was "no different from a jungle with wild egos." As he was about to hang up, he told me to let them know if there were any last-minute changes I would like to make before the magazine went to press.

"Yes," I said urgently. "My last name. I am changing it."

"Are you getting married? Congratulations!"

"No. Not like that," I interjected. "I have decided to rename myself."

He chuckled, the way people tend to do when they don't know what to say. Then he said, very slowly and loudly, as if talking to a child with a hearing impairment, "O-kay, and how do you want us to write your name?"

"I don't know yet," I confessed. "It's a lifetime decision. I'll have to think about it."

There was an awkward silence at the end of the line, but then the editor gave another laugh. "Well, of course, go ahead and do it. What's the harm? You are a woman, there's no reason for you to take this too seriously. Even if you choose the most poetic surname for yourself, you'll end up with your husband's anyhow."

"Give me a day," I said. "I will find the surname I will have forever, whether I get married someday or not."

Every name is a magic formula. The letters dance together, each with their own spin and charm, each an unknown as much as the other, and together they concoct the mystery that a name holds. Like sorcerers in the dark, adding letter upon letter, ingredient after ingredient, the language unit by which we are known puts a spell on us. There are names that help us soar high in the sky; there are names that weigh on our shoulders and slyly pull us down.

Men live without ever feeling the need to change their family names. Their credentials are given to them at birth. Settled and stable. They inherit their surnames from their fathers and grandfathers, and pass it on to their children and grandchildren.

As for women, whether they know it or not, they are name nomads. Their surnames are here today, gone tomorrow. Throughout their lives, women fill out official forms in different ways, apply for new passports and design several signatures. They have one last name when they are young girls, and another upon marriage. They go back to their maiden names if they get divorced—though sometimes they retain their ex-husbands' family names for practical purposes, which doesn't necessarily make things easier—and adopt an altogether different one if they get remarried.

Men have one constant signature. Once they find the one that suits them, they can keep it till death without changing a single curve. As for women, they have at least one "old signature" and one "new signature," and sometimes they confuse them. Signature of the bachelorette, signature of the married woman, signature of the divorcée.

Women writers have also undergone a series of name-change operations. The late-nineteenth-century Ottoman novelist Fatma Aliye wrote her novels and novellas mostly in secret, as she did not want to upset her husband and family with her "independent ways." One day she stopped using her name and published her next work under the pseudonym "A Woman."

For that's what she was. A woman. Any woman. All women. Getting rid of her name was like casting off the heavy mooring that tied her to the mainland. Once she ceased to be Lady Fatma Aliye and became only "a woman," she was free to sail anywhere.

In the 1950s a romance novel called *Young Girls* appeared in Turkey, by a certain Vincent Ewing. The book quickly became a national best seller, finding good coverage in the media. Strangely, no one knew the writer. No journalist had managed to get any interviews from him. Only three things were known about the author: He was American, he was Christian, he was male. Turkish people read the book with that information in mind.

Years went by. One day it was announced that the author of *Young Girls* was, in fact, a young Muslim Turkish woman. Nihal Yeğinobalı was her name.

When asked why she had chosen to hide her identity, her answer was intriguing:

"I was a young girl myself when I wrote *Young Girls*. There was a considerable degree of eroticism in the novel that was considered inappropriate for a young woman such as myself. So I picked a male pseudonym. In those days there was more interest in translated novels. This is why we decided that the writer of my novel should be American. My publisher pretended it was translated from English."

Publishing a book under a specific male name, like "Vincent Ewing," or a generic appellation, like "A Woman," furnishes us with an armor to shield ourselves. We need the protection even more when we write about sexuality, femininity and the body. I don't know of any male writer who agonizes about upsetting his mother (or grandmother or great-aunts or neighbors or any distant relatives) should he write a novel that touches on eroticism and graphic sex. If there are, they must be few in number. Yet, worrying about the permission to tell the story—be it personal or familial—is particular to women writers all around the world. This is the unspoken pressure Margaret Atwood writes about in her riveting essay regarding her great-aunts. "The pressure is most strongly felt, by women, from within the family, and more so when the family is a strong unit," she says. From Turkey to Canada, from industrial to postindustrial society, women who take up writing traverse several invisible boundaries in marriage, family, class and society. Each crossing can be one more reason to modify a name and obscure its gender.

It is not for naught that another well-known writer, perhaps the greatest novelist of the Victorian period, chose a male pseudonym— determined, smart, persevering Mary Ann Evans, otherwise known as George Eliot. Britain in the 1800s did have its share of female writers— only, most of them wrote about romance, love and heartache: topics deemed suitable for womankind. As for George Eliot, she openly disliked all such books. She wanted to write on an equal footing with male novelists. She wanted to write "like a man," not "like a woman."

George Eliot's distaste for "women's literature" was so intense and unabashed that in 1856 she penned an article called "Silly Novels by Lady Novelists." She divided fiction written by women into four categories in accordance with their degree of silliness, and named them as the frothy, the prosy, the pious and the pedantic. I enjoy reading this extremely interesting piece not only to get a glimpse into the Western literary tradition but also to see how cruelly a woman writer can bad-mouth her own sex.

But Eliot was no stranger to standing out among other women. In a letter to Herbert Spencer, the biologist and philosopher, she boldly challenged conventional society and set herself apart from the members of her own sex: "I suppose no woman ever before wrote such a letter as this—but I am not ashamed of it, for I am conscious that in the light of reason and true refinement I am worthy of your respect and tenderness, whatever gross men or vulgar-minded women might think of me."

Similarly, the Brontë sisters, too, felt the need to remold their names. Selecting pseudonyms that retained their initials, Charlotte adopted Currer Bell while Anne took on the name Acton Bell and Emily became Ellis Bell. It was easier to evade prejudices against women when one had an androgynous name. The sisters played this mischievous game as long as they could, their only challenge being how to deceive the village postman when packages arrived. The dilemma was solved by making sure all correspondents sent their letters to a certain "Currer Bell in care of Miss Brontë."

Another female writer who chose a pseudonymous cross-dressing was the legendary George Sand, though one sometimes gets the impression that she might simply have wanted to get rid of the baggage of her long name: Amantine-Aurore-Lucile Dupin, Baroness Dudevant.

George Sand married Baron M. Casimir Dudevant in 1822. They had two children together. But before long the couple split apart. Sand welcomed her unattached state as liberation from social bonds. Being divorced, single and wealthy gave her the chance to be much more daring than other women, and take steps that they could not dream of.

Sand had also started wearing male clothing—a topic that the gossipers jumped upon with joy. As an aristocratic woman it was her civic duty to dress to the nines, paying great attention to her attire, speech and manners, but she did just the opposite by choosing comfortable and serviceable male outfits. Her fondness for pipe smoking was an even bigger scandal. In an era in which women were expected to be agreeable, sociable ladies and nothing more, she walked around in men's clothes with a pipe in her mouth and radical ideas in her head. Like a tall tree that attracts lightning, she drew attention and anger. In the end, her aristocratic title was taken away from her. But nobody could confiscate the name she had given herself. She was, and is today, George Sand.

As Ivan Turgenyev once said, she was "a kind hearted woman, and a brave man!"

Jane Austen fell in love once. She was someone who criticized women marrying for wealth, status or a sense of security, firmly believing that one could marry only for love. Yet, though she loved and was loved in return, due to class differences, the marriage was not allowed to happen. His name was Tom Lefroy—a young man who had nothing to his name but would one day become the chief justice of Ireland. In a letter dated January 1796 and addressed to her sister Cassandra, Austen confessed that Tom was the love of her life. But she quickly added, "When you receive this, it will be over. My tears flow at the melancholy idea." Heartbroken, she retreated to her corner, to her writing.

"I think I may boast myself to be, with all possible vanity, the most unlearned and ill informed female who ever dared to be an authoress," she said. It was not true, of course, and she knew it. Austen was very knowledgeable on a wide range of subjects, having been admirably educated by her father—a clergyman—brothers, aunt and then through her own uninterrupted reading. She had a sharp tongue and a penchant for playfulness and sarcasm.

Years later, she was offered marriage again, this time by a respected man of great means. Though she was fond of her "solitary elegance," as she once called her singleness, she accepted the offer. Finally she was going to become a wife, start a family and manage her own home. With these thoughts and hopes, she went to bed early. When she woke up the next morning, the first thing she did was to send a note of apology to her suitor. She had decided not to marry.

I often wonder what happened that night. What surreal place did

Jane Austen visit in her dreams that made her change her mind? Did she have nightmares? Did she imagine herself scrubbing the staircase of a hundred-floor paper house with a bucket full of ink, watching every stair crumble as she cleaned and cleaned? What was it that made her decide against walking down the aisle?

Of all the American women writers of earlier generations, there is one that holds a special place in my heart: Carson McCullers. Perhaps it is because I came upon her work at a time when I was discovering the world and myself. Her words had a shattering effect on me. It was my last year of high school when I read *The Heart Is a Lonely Hunter,* drawn more to the title of the book than the name of the author. The year before I was very popular at school, if only for a few weeks, having newly arrived in Ankara from Madrid, where I had spent my teenage years. The kids in my new class had been thrilled to learn that I could speak Spanish and had even been to a bullfight. But the introvert in me had not taken long to show up and the sympathetic curiosity in the eyes of my classmates had been gradually replaced first by an absolute indifference, then a judgmental distance. Girls thought I was unsociable, boys thought I was bizarre, teachers thought I was aloof, and I trusted no one but books. That is when I met Carson McCullers.

I was a Turkish girl who had never been to America and yet the stories of lonely people in the American South moved me deeply. But there was more to it than that. Twenty pages into the book, I was dying to know the person who could write like this.

She was born Lula Carson Smith. By shortening her name to Carson she was not only trying to be noticeable but also standing on an ambiguous ground where it was hard for her readers to guess her gender. She was someone who did not easily blend with her peers and could be, at times, quite unfriendly. Instead of dressing up in stockings and shoes with high heels and slender skirts, as was the fashion in the 1930s, she preferred to walk around in high socks and tennis shoes, happy to startle her classmates. Despite her indifference to the established codes of beauty, I find it interesting that when she met the love of her life, Reeves McCullers, the first thing that struck her were his looks. "There was the shock, the shock of pure beauty, when I first saw him." Though their relationship was beset with doubts and difficulties—they divorced at one point and then remarried—they remained inseparable for nearly twenty years—until the day he died.

So it is that world literary history is full of women who have changed their minds, their destinies and, yes, their names.

The next morning I gave the editor a call.

"Hi, Elif. . . . It is nice to hear from you," he said briskly, but then paused. "Or did you change your name already? Shall I call you by a different name?"

"Actually, that's the reason why I called," I said. "I found my name. And I want you to use this new one when you print my story."

"O-kay," he said, once again, very slowly and loudly. By now I had figured out that was how he spoke when he couldn't see where the conversation was heading. "How does it feel to shed your old name?"

"That part is easy," I said. "The difficult part is to find a new one."

"Hm . . . umm," he said in sympathy.

"I have been researching the lives of writers, perusing words in dictionaries, reading literary anecdotes, looking for an unusual name. I mean, not as unusual as David Bowie's child Zowie; or Frank Zappa, of course, who named one of his children Moon Unit. But perhaps it is a bit easier when you are trying to name a newborn baby with endless potentials and unknowns than to name your old, familiar, limited self."

"David Bowie has a child named Zowie Bowie?" he asked.

"Yup," I said.

"All right, go on, please."

"Well, I once had a boyfriend who wanted everyone to call him 'A Glass Half Full' because he said that was his philosophy in life. He even wrote the name on his exam papers, getting funny reactions from the professors. But then he graduated and went into the military. When he came back, he didn't want anything to do with A Glass Half Full. He had gone back to his old name, Kaya—the Rock."

"O-kay," the editor said.

"Anyhow, I decided I didn't have to go that far. Actually, I didn't have to go anywhere. Better to look at what I have with me here and now," I said. "Instead of carrying my father's surname, I decided to adopt my mother's first name as my last name."

"I'm not sure I am following," he said.

"Dawn," I explained. "Shafak is my mother's first name. I will make it my surname from this day on."

A month later when the magazine was published, I saw my new name for the first time in print. It didn't feel strange. It didn't feel wrong. It felt just right, as if in a world of endless shadows and echoes, my name and I had finally found each other.

The Fugitive Passenger

On the first day of September 2002, the Turkish Airlines flight from Istanbul to New York takes off with me on it. The plane is jam-packed with undergraduate and graduate students, businessmen and businesswomen, trained professionals, journalists, academics, tourists and a newlywed couple on honeymoon. . . . Besides Turks and Americans, there are Indians, Russians, Bulgarians, Arabs and Japanese who have come from connecting flights. This will be my first visit to America. I think about Anaïs Nin arriving in the United States in 1914 with her brother's violin case in one hand and a yet-to-be-filled diary in the other. I am smiling at the curious little girl in my mind's eye when I notice something and stop.

A young, lanky man two rows in front of me is grinning sheepishly at me. He thinks I was smiling at him. There is no way I can explain it was for Anaïs Nin. In order to cause no more misunderstandings, I slide down in my seat and hide my face behind a book: *In Favor of the Sensitive Man and Other Essays.*

Shortly after the food service, I walk down the corridor to go to the toilet. Out of the corner of my eye, I check to see what the other passengers are reading, craning my head left and right to decipher the titles of the books they are holding. I notice some Westerners reading books on Turkey or Istanbul (including a novel of mine), which intrigues me, because most tourists read about a foreign country *before* they go to see it, but very few continue reading *after* they have seen it.

There are two vacant restrooms. As soon as I open the door of the first one and step inside, I freeze on the spot. There, next to the liquid-soap dispenser beside the sink, stands a finger-woman. I'm just about to say "excuse me" and leave when she calls out.

"No, please, stay. . . . I want to talk to you."

I look at the stranger quizzically. She kind of resembles the others in the Choir of Discordant Voices. She is no taller than them, but probably weighs more. She has a kind, round, freckled face, a pointy chin, hair the color of Turkish coffee and eyes so blue they suck you in. She's wearing no makeup except for eyeliner and perhaps some mascara on her long lashes, it's hard to tell. She seems to be in her early or mid-thirties, and I am sure I've never seen her before.

"Who are you?"

"Don't you recognize me?" she says again, sounding slightly offended.

I scan her from head to toe. She is wearing an aquamarine dress that reaches her knees, red shoes without heels, a belt of the same color, beige nylon stockings. Her wavy hair is held back in a ponytail by a modest hair band. The chubbiness of her cheeks is due to her extra pounds, but she seems to be at peace with her body. She doesn't have the tense air that the calorie-counting Little Miss Practical radiates.

"I'm one of your inner voices," she says finally.

"Really? I've never seen you before. Did you just arrive?"

"Actually, I've been with you since you were a little girl playing with dollhouses," she says.

Confused and clueless, I ask her name.

"They call me Mama Rice Pudding."

I break into a laugh, but when I see her scowl I swallow my chuckles and put on a serious face.

"I see you find my name amusing," she says coldly.

"I am sorry, I didn't mean to hurt your feelings."

At my guilty pause she smiles. "What strikes me is that you don't find the names of the others amusing at all," she says. "You don't laugh at Milady Ambitious Chekhovian or Miss Highbrowed Cynic, do you?"

She's right. I have nothing to say.

"My name is what it is because I happen to be a motherly, loving person," she continues, flipping her hands upward to make a point.

"Really?" I say, under my breath.

"Yes, I relish hanging bamboo wind chimes on the porch, growing begonias in cute little pots, pickling vegetables in the summer, making pink grapefruit marmalade. . . . You know, keeping the home fires burning. I know how to get ink stains off carpets, what to do when you spill olive oil on your best skirt, how to clean a rusted teapot and other important tricks. I bake pastries and desserts. Just this month one of my recipes has been featured in a cooking video, and they named it Mama's Heavenly Rice Pudding."

For almost a minute I don't say anything. I am sure there must be a mistake and I consider how to kindly break the news to her. There is no way a finger-woman like her can be one of my inner voices. I lack the skill to crack eggs for an omelet or the patience to boil water for tea. I hate house chores and other domestic duties, and avoid them as much and as best as I can. My friends don't need to know about this, but I could live in a room without cleaning it for days and weeks, and if the going gets rough, I'd prefer to redecorate the room than to have to clean it. And if the entire house gets too dirty, I'd rather move into a new one than have to vacuum, scrub and polish it thoroughly. My take on this is that of a hotel client, easygoing and laid-back: I like to sleep in my bed knowing that I'll not have to wash and iron the sheets the next day.

Mama Rice Pudding purses her lips and pouts as if she can read my thoughts. "You never let me speak, not once! You stored me away in the depot of your personality, and then forgot all about me. All these years, I've been waiting for you to accept and love me as I am."

That is when a bigger wave of guilt begins tugging at the edges of my mind. I feel like an old-fashioned conservative parent who has renounced his son for being gay and pretends he doesn't even exist. Is that what I have done to the maternal side of me?

"How about the other finger-women?" I ask. "Do they know about you?"

"Of course they do," replies Mama Rice Pudding. "But they prefer not to tell you about me and the other chick."

"What do you mean by 'the other chick'?"

But she ignores my question. "Like many young women I, too, want to get married, wear a wedding dress, have a diamond ring, raise children and cruise the sales aisles of supermarkets. But you pushed away all my desires and looked down on them with such force that I couldn't even mention them. I was silenced, suppressed and denied."

I think of Anaïs Nin again—a vigorous woman who once said, "Ordinary life does not interest me"; who believed that a critical writer such as herself could never make a housewife. She had an unruly side, a mostly disordered lifestyle and more than one lover by her side. "Life shrinks or expands in proportion to one's courage," she would say.

"What are you thinking about?" Mama Rice Pudding asks.

"Anaïs Nin . . ." I murmur, not expecting her to recognize the name.

But she does. "Those edgy avant-garde writers!" she says, spitting the words out. "You know what your problem is? You read too much, that's your problem."

"Wait a minute, what kind of criticism is that?"

But she raves on about the terrible effects of books on my soul, getting more and more carried away. "You convinced yourself that you couldn't be a *normal* woman. Why do you frown upon the ordinary?"

Seeing that this conversation is taking on political overtones, I try to navigate my way through it as delicately as I can. "Hmm . . . Miss Highbrowed Cynic always says whatever calamity has befallen humanity is because of ordinary people. She quotes the bright Jewish woman philosopher Hannah Arendt, who has shown us that fascism has thrived and grown due not to the *bad* people with wicked aims but, in fact, to the *ordinary* people with good intentions."

"Oh my God," she says, rolling her eyes. "Do you see what you are doing to yourself? Here I am talking about marriage and motherhood and muffins, and you respond by alluding to Hitler and the Nazis."

Baffled, I gape at her without so much as a blink.

"Forget about all the other finger-women," she continues. "They've been eating away at you for years. Don't belittle the beauty of the ordinary, of seeking simple pleasures. You and I can have so much fun together."

"Really? Like what?"

She beams. "We can go to the farmers' market every weekend, buy organic zucchini. We can wait in front of stores at dawn with thermoses in our hands, and dash inside the second the doors open and start grabbing sale items before anyone else. We can decorate our home from top to bottom with scented candles and flowers of matching colors. Trust me, you'll love it. Have you ever set a beautiful dinner table? Do you know how gratifying it is when your family and friends commend your culinary skills?"

Before I find the chance to give her an obvious answer, we hear a sudden noise at the door. I open it slightly and peek out.

To my surprise, there is a line in front of the restroom. And at the very front stands Milady Ambitious Chekhovian in her dark green general's uniform. Tapping her military boots and fidgeting nervously, she appears to be in mighty need of going to the toilet.

A shadow of panic crosses Mama Rice Pudding's face. "Oh, no! Not that monster!"

"What do you want me to do?" I ask.

"Please don't tell them I am here. They'll tear me to shreds, those witches!"

She is right. Milady Ambitious Chekhovian with her doggedness, Miss Highbrowed Cynic with her pessimism, Little Miss Practical with her intolerance of anything that takes longer than ten minutes to prepare, would tear Mama Rice Pudding apart. I need to protect her from her sisters.

"Don't worry, you are safe with me. I won't whisper a word."

Smiling warmly she reaches for my hand and gives it a gentle squeeze. Her fingers are not manicured and well groomed like Little Miss Practical's; they aren't decked with rings like Milady Ambitious

Chekhovian's or chewed up like Miss Highbrowed Cynic's. They are rough from hard work, pink and plump. I am bewildered by the affection I feel for her. If she is my motherly side, isn't it weird that I feel the need to mother her?

"Wait a minute, how are you going to get into America?" I ask. "Do you have a visa?"

"I don't need a visa," she says. "They don't even search finger-women like me at airports."

I can see why. It'd be hard to find a terrorist streak in her.

"I'm not worried about the external world," she says. "You just keep that coven of finger-women away from me and I'll be just fine."

"Okay."

"Please promise me that you will not let them ever crush me again."

As I ponder how to skirt this demand and how to get her out of this restroom without the other Thumbelinas seeing her, the plane experiences turbulence. The pilot announces that everyone must return to their seats and fasten their seat belts.

A few seconds later, I open the door. The line has dispersed and I can see that Milady Ambitious Chekhovian is already in her seat.

"The coast is clear now," I say to Mama Rice Pudding. "You can go out."

"I will," she says with a new edge to her voice. "But you haven't given me your promise yet."

It is one of those moments when I know I should be totally honest and tell the truth, but for the sake of courtesy or out of pure cowardice, I simply can't. Instead, I tell her what she wants to hear, even though I know deep down inside that I can't keep that promise.

"I swear I will not let the other finger-women silence you."

A huge smile lights up her face. "Thanks. I know I can trust you."

"By the way, who is this other chick you were talking about?" I hear myself asking.

"You will meet her when the time is ripe."

"But why is she hiding?"

"She is not hiding. None of us is. It's *you* who doesn't acknowledge our presence. For years, you've given all your attention to Little Miss Practical, Miss Highbrowed Cynic, Milady Ambitious Chekhovian and Dame Dervish."

"I understand," I say, although I am not sure I do.

"Okay, we need to go now."

"Well, it was really nice to meet you."

"Likewise," she says, blushing. "I guess I will see you around."

Still smiling, she slips out the door. I stay in the restroom a few more seconds, slightly shaking—not knowing whether it's due to the turbulence or to the confusion in my mind.

It dawns upon me that I don't know myself very well. Throughout my adult life, I've favored certain voices inside me at the expense of others. How many inner voices are there that I have yet to meet?

I go back to my seat.

Until the plane touches down in New York, this is all I think about.

A Festive Banquet

Simone de Beauvoir, even more than fifty years after her death, remains a diva in the history of the feminist movement. At her funeral in 1956, thousands of mourners heard an unforgettable phrase: "Women, you owe her everything"—a phrase that says a lot about her charisma and legendary heritage. You may not agree with everything she said, you may not even like her personality, but you cannot turn a blind eye to her work or intellectual legacy.

"One is not born a woman, but becomes one," she stated famously. For centuries girls were taught that their most important roles in life were sexuality, childbearing and motherhood. Armed with the small task of ensuring the continuation of the human race, young women were rarely, if ever, encouraged to pursue their studies and make more of their talents. In the France of the 1940s, motherhood was almost a religious duty, unquestionable and sacrosanct. Simone de Beauvoir knew what she was talking about, being raised by a staunch Catholic mother.

Waging a passionate war against bourgeois norms, she questioned the institutions of marriage and motherhood at great length. She said many women longed to rediscover themselves in their children—a "psychological need" she clearly did not share. She and Sartre were a committed but free couple—independent, self-reliant and sufficient for each other. Bourgeois marital life was full of lies, deceptions and unrealistic pledges of fidelity. Determined not to repeat the mistakes of their parents, they had made a pact: They would tell each other everything. They were both open to the idea of "experiencing contingent love affairs." Besides, she believed that maternity was incompatible with the life she had chosen as a writer and intellectual. She needed time, concentration and freedom to pursue her ideals.

In *The Second Sex,* de Beauvoir reiterates Hegel's famous dictum that the birth of children often goes hand in hand with the death of parents. Yet, despite her strong feelings on marriage and motherhood, de Beauvoir's writings bear traces of another truth underneath: that if Sartre had wanted to have children, in her desire to please him she could have become a mother. She adored him. To her the sun of a new society rose from the depths of his eyes. He was the only man she respected more than she desired—the man whose time, work and ideas she had had to share with hundreds of other people, some of whom were women far more beautiful and ambitious than she was. And yet she knew how special she was in his eyes. Since the day their paths intersected in 1929 when they were both students at the *École Normale Supérieure*, he had been many things to her—a comrade, a lover, a father, a son, a brother, a tutor, a best friend and an impossible dream.

One should not be fooled by the terms of endearment she uses in her letters to him: "my little man," or "my dear little being." He was a giant to her—a man she addressed with the formal *vous* all the time. If he had wanted to start a family, she would have probably gone ahead, even though she clearly thought that motherhood was not meant for the likes of her. Though she was hurt by Sartre's infidelities, she continued to defend the pact they had made. Simone de Beauvoir was a woman of impeccable analyses and unexpected conflicts.

If the broader society was not ready to address motherhood in a critical light, the intellectual circles—by definition progressive and open-minded—were just as unprepared, not to mention disproportionately male. There was a widespread silence in the world of books when it came to issues such as premenstrual syndrome, postpartum depression or menopause. Likewise, hardly anyone wrote about the Bermuda triangle of "ideal wife–diligent housekeeper–selfless mother" whereby so many women's creative talents disappeared into the vortex.

In a milieu such as this de Beauvoir faced deeply rooted prejudices and clichés. She wrote and spoke fervently on how women were being "forced to choose" between the brain and the body.

She was equally critical of those women who had willingly internalized gender inequalities, seeing themselves as inferior to their male counterparts. "Even the lowliest of men sees himself a demi-God when faced with a woman," she remarked. Her mind was corrosive, her pen was sharp and her personality was highly contentious. Once she said she found it quite normal that many people among the middle class hated her. "If it were any other way, I would begin to doubt myself."

It wasn't only Western feminists who questioned the romanticized sacredness of motherhood. In the East, too, there were heated debates. The Japanese feminist movement opened up the term *bosei*—the natural motherly instinct—for discussion. They put forth the claim that maternal roles were more cultural than natural and biological.

Female writers in Japan brought new blood to these debates, questioning gender stereotypes through their fiction. In 1983 Yuko Tsushima published *Child of Fortune,* which features a remarkable female protagonist—a headstrong, nonconformist divorcée—torn between the realities of her heart and the ideal of womanhood taught by society. Although she doesn't necessarily consider herself a feminist writer, Tsushima has critically explored themes of gender and sexuality in her works. Perhaps she is spiritually connected with another Japanese author of the past century, Toshiko Tamura—one of the country's earliest, most outspoken female writers—whose royalties, after her sudden death in 1945, were used to establish a literary prize for women writers. In a story titled "A Woman Writer," Tamura describes a scene where an angry husband, himself a writer, reprimands his wife, who is struggling to write a passage. The husband believes women are not good writers. They are indecisive and insecure, wasting a hundred pages to write only ten. His words reiterate the belief that men write for more serious and sublime reasons, and are therefore earnest writers, whereas for women writing is merely a hobby.

There is a similarly influential woman writer in Turkish literature whose unique voice continues to echo today, long after her passing. In the antagonistic environment of the 1970s, when the country was divided between leftists and rightists, Sevgi Soysal questioned, in clever, flowing prose, patriarchal precedents on all sides.

She was the writer of women dangling on the threshold—between sanity and insanity, society and the individual, setting the table and walking away, endless self-sacrifice and impromptu selfishness. . . . She created female characters who straddled the divide between living for others and following their hearts. One of her unforgettable fictional characters is Tante Rosa:

> Tante Rosa left a letter behind. She left three children, one of them still on the bottle, a recipe for roasted goose and apple pie, and instructions on how to clean the table cloth for the maid whom she had also taught the art of arranging shelves. She left a little garden with marigolds, a house with a wooden staircase, high ceilings, and a grandfather clock; a husband who went to church every Sunday morning, and crawled into her bed every Sunday afternoon; neighbors who had big, bright hats, snot-nosed children, their own husbands and roasted goose. . . . She left her left breast behind, the breast that covered her heart. And walked away.

Soysal's female characters are, for all intents and purposes, the exact opposite of the "ideal women" of Turkish society. Hers are women who make mistakes, stumble on their path and hurt their knees, and yet, each time, somehow manage to pull themselves together.

In another novel, she writes about a woman named Oya, who is deeply fragmented in her desires and obligations.

> "I'll go to the sea. Any sea shore at all." The beautiful scenery along the shore road that begins in Alanya and curves its way up to the Aegean Sea flashes before her eyes. Blue. Wide. Sea. Rocks. Forest. And what of her husband? What of her house? What of her children?

And her other responsibilities? At the moment there is no blue, no freedom, no forest. There is only more duties creeping ever closer.

∽

In my mind I organize a banquet in heaven. A long table with a snow-white tablecloth, elegant cutlery and silver candleholders. A huge glittering crystal chandelier hangs over the center of the table. There is roasted goose, rice with saffron and mouthwatering desserts on vast plates. Simone de Beauvoir sits in a high chair at one end of the table. Though she gives the impression of sulking, she is actually happy. On her right is Toshiko Tamura with her elegant eyeglasses, eating fried rice with chopsticks, putting thought into each grain. On her left is Sevgi Soysal, who doesn't have much of an appetite, but she, too, is in a good mood. Humming a slow tune, she takes a sip from her wineglass.

A French woman, a Japanese woman and a Turkish woman—three determined writers, three autonomous individuals, who lived worlds apart but spoke the same language—could they be dining together in heaven now? I'd like to think so.

In Search of the Mother Goddess

On the second day of September, I descend from a bus that has PETER PAN written in gaudy, capital letters on both sides. The name suits my mood. I, too, feel like "a boy who wouldn't grow up," and this place with its unfamiliar landscape and fickle weather could very well be Neverland. I drag a big, blue suitcase on wheels, and carry a cat box—except there is no cat inside, but four finger-women. Though they had raised no complaints during the eleven-hour flight from Istanbul, in the one-and-a-half-hour bus ride from Boston they have been constantly whining or puking.

As soon as I step down onto the sidewalk, the silence on the campus is like a slap on the face. My ears are so used to the constant chaos and crazy rhythm of Istanbul that I fear I may go deaf here. I see people, but nobody is shouting, yelling or whistling. Even the squirrels seem to tiptoe so as not to make noise. I find the stillness unsettling.

But the campus is lovely. It is vast and green as far as the eye can see. There are tall, thick trees everywhere, speaking in gnarled mystery. There are dozens of other languages being spoken here—the college being home to more than two thousand students from almost seventy countries. One out of every three students is a foreigner like me.

This impressive, cosmopolitan college is the outcome of one woman's vision. In 1837, an idealistic teacher named Mary Lyon began to advocate for the right of female students to be given the same level of education as male students. At a time when women did not yet have the right to vote, her views were quite radical. But Mary Lyon persevered, and after much struggle and several setbacks, she managed to collect the necessary funds to found the college. Since then, thousands have graduated from Mount Holyoke, and perhaps with each new graduate, Mary Lyon's spirit has been rejoicing.

Mount Holyoke and neighboring Smith College were nerve centers of the 1960s and 1970s American feminist movement. When I set foot here, the tradition is still visibly alive. In addition to feminists, postfeminists and half-and-half feminists (those who appreciate feminism but do not necessarily like feminists), there are also plenty of Wiccans in search of spiritual union with Mother Goddess, and quite a number of bisexual and lesbian activists.

All this—squirrels and lesbians—I write about in a column for a widely circulated Turkish newspaper known for its conservative readership. Understandably, the feedback to my columns is mixed. Overall, my readers in Turkey seem to be more surprised by the fact that nobody catches the squirrels and cooks them (not that we have a national squirrel dish; I don't know where they get this idea from) than by the sight of lesbian couples walking hand in hand. I take this as a progressive sign.

There is one poster that grabs my attention from day one—that of a female worker wearing blue overalls, a red and white bandana on her head and a shirt with one sleeve rolled up to reveal a tensed and muscled bicep like that of Popeye the Sailor Man. She adorns the walls around campus. "You can succeed, you can stand tall and be strong in this male-driven world" is the slogan everywhere.

On my second day, I discover the building that will become my favorite place during my entire stay: the gigantic, gaudy, gothic library. It's love at first sight. From handwritten books to modern literature, political philosophy to botanical science, I roam the aisles touching the books, smelling them.

But no one appreciates the library more than Miss Highbrowed Cynic. The second she spots the building, which resembles Rapunzel's castle from a distance, she jumps with joy and yells so loudly, she damages her vocal cords.

Fall goes by and the trees shed their first leaves, painting the entire campus in amber, red and brown. In the mornings, Little Miss Practical and I go jogging. One day on the way back we stop by the library.

We find Miss Highbrowed Cynic sitting on a shelf, hunched over an open book. Using a sharpened pencil as a pole, she vaults from one stack of books to the next. She also has a string ladder to climb to higher shelves. Every time she moves, the peace-sign earrings on her lobes and the bangles on her arms jingle. The black T-shirt she is wearing over her jeans has this message written across: "ANTI-WAR / ANTI-RACISM / ANTI-HATE."

"Hi, Sister," she says to me, and slightly frowns at Little Miss Practical. Since we have come to America the conflicts among the finger-women have surfaced again, their temporary coalition dissolving fast.

"What are you reading?" I ask.

"The Sense and Non-Sense of Revolt," she says.

Little Miss Practical casts a confused glance over my shoulder. "Another fisherman's story?"

"A book by the French critic Julia Kristeva, who happens to be one of the leading thinkers of our times," says Miss Highbrowed Cynic.

"Smart cookie, huh?" asks Little Miss Practical.

"She sees the Oedipus complex as a key to understanding women," continues Miss Highbrowed Cynic, her tone not so much annoyed as haughty. "A young girl adores her mother, copying everything she does. But then she finds out that she does not have a penis, and feels flawed and incomplete, like a eunuch. To compensate for this deficiency, she attaches herself to her father. The mother who was loved and admired until then is now pushed aside, seen as a competitor. There are girls who from this stage onward develop a hatred for their mothers."

Little Miss Practical and I listen, without a word, without a breath.

"Women writers are affected by the Oedipus complex more than you may think. Did you know, for instance, why Sevgi Soysal became a novelist? She began to write at age eight because she was jealous of her father's affection for her mother. She saw her mother as a rival, and through her writing and imagination she wanted to win her father's favor."

"Oh, really?" I say.

"Oh, yes, she writes about this in her memoirs," Miss Highbrowed Cynic says, with her know-it-all attitude. "Every child wants to rejoin her mother's body. This is an impossible wish, of course. That 'oneness' is long gone, severed forever, but the child cannot help longing for it. The 'symbolic order' represented by the father awaits the individual who cannot rejoin his mother's body."

"Come again?" says Little Miss Practical.

Miss Highbrowed Cynic volleys on. "In order to survive in this order, we suppress our imagination, temper our desires and learn to be 'normalized.' No matter how hard we try, however, our imagination can never be stifled. In the most inopportune places and at the oddest times, it surfaces. The mother's semiotic rises up against the father's symbolic order."

"Such confusing things!" says Little Miss Practical. "What's the point of making life so complicated? These French thinkers are not practical in the least. No wonder French movies are so depressing."

Miss Highbrowed Cynic stares at the other finger-woman with an air of condescension but says nothing. Instead she turns to me. "Kristeva talks about three ways for a child to create her identity. First, to identify with the father and the symbolic. Second, to identify with the mother and the semiotic. Third, to find a shaky balance in between."

I pretend to follow what she is saying, but Miss Highbrowed Cynic doesn't fall for it: "Don't you get it? If you pursue the third option, you could use the father's symbolic order and the mother's semiotic in your work."

"Hmm . . . Is there a writer who has ever done that?" I ask.

"Yes, Sis. Take a closer look at Virginia Woolf's *The Waves*. She was writing precisely in that precarious balance."

I don't object. It might or might not be true. Writing fiction is a tidal river with strong currents. While flowing with it, one doesn't think, "Let me now add a splash of symbolic order and a dash of the mother's semiotic." You don't chew on such things when developing a novel. You are too busy falling in love with your characters.

That is what Miss Highbrowed Cynic doesn't understand. Novelists write without thinking. It is afterward, when literary critics and scholars weigh writers' every sentence that theories are applied. And then when people read those theories, they get the impression that novelists were purposefully creating their stories in such a way—which is not true.

"There's something I don't get," Little Miss Practical says.

"Why am I not surprised?" scoffs Miss Highbrowed Cynic.

"You're so into the theory of motherhood. All this *semiotic, symbolic, bucolic* . . . But when it comes to the practicalities, I am sure you'd fall flat on your face."

"My knowledge would guide me," says Miss Highbrowed Cynic.

"Whoa, come on, Sister, you couldn't even change a diaper. I may not know anything about your theories, but I can get the hang of motherhood faster than Speedy Gonzalez runs."

The shape of her eyebrows indicates that Miss Highbrowed Cynic doesn't appreciate the remark. I leave them quarreling, and walk out of the library.

I wander around the campus. Being rid of the finger-women—if only for a short while—lightens my heart and my mood. Like a walking sponge, I soak up every detail I see, every sound I hear, every smell I sniff, and store it all away inside me. That is what happens when you are a foreigner; you collect details as if they were seashells on a shore.

In the cafeteria, I get in line and end up standing in front of a lesbian couple. One of the women is short and has spiky, carroty hair. The other is quite tall and heavily pregnant. We move forward, pushing our trays along inch by inch. Just when we reach the dessert display, the short woman chirps up.

"Ah, would you mind if we take that, since there is only one left?"

There on top of a glass shelf, where the woman is pointing, is one lone piece of raspberry cake. I move back.

"Of course, go ahead."

"Thank you, thank you! Shirley has been craving raspberries since this morning," says the woman, giving me a wink.

"Oh," I say. "You're expecting a baby, how wonderful."

"Yes," says Shirley as she pats her belly. "Six feet one, chess and amateur tennis champion, professional artist, IQ over 160, interested in Buddhism and Far Eastern philosophy—"

"Excuse me?"

"The father," she says. "We picked him out of thousands at the sperm bank. . . . He's going to be a very special baby."

There is something in all this meticulous advance planning that freaks me out. Perhaps it is not surprising that women would look for athletic, charismatic, wealthy and influential sperm donors. But as someone who has grown up without a father, I am thinking, what does that ultimately mean to a child who will never know his or her biological father? Besides, the things we lack in life—such as blue eyes, a muscular body or conversational eloquence—might help us to develop other qualities that are dormant inside. Many talents are born in the shadows, out of necessity. The search for perfect babies misses the surprising role of oddities, coincidences and absences in our personal development.

In the evening I return to my room. The place I am staying in is about 130 square feet. It has the tiniest kitchen counter and a shower so small you can wash only half of yourself at a time.

Before me, there was an Indian painter residing here—the walls still smell of her paints. And before her, a Zimbabwean sociologist. The room has seen dozens of women from all over the world. The Indian artist left behind paint stains and an intricately designed rolling pin. The Zimbabwean scholar left a scary mask on the wall, which casts a long and thin ebony shadow.

What will I leave to next year's fellow? "Before me, there was a

Turkish author staying here," she will say. I can't find anything but words to hand down to her. Perhaps I can leave one of my favorite Turkish words, which also exists in English: *kismet*.

I lie down on my bed. The solitude that I so enjoyed only this afternoon now darkens my mood. What am I doing here so far away from Istanbul, from my loved ones, from the place where my novels are set, from my friends, my mother and my mother tongue? Am I throwing myself into unknown waters just to see if I can swim?

What if I can't?

I recall my mother telling me I was too good at being alone. "It is as if you don't need anyone," she had said. "But you should. Too much independence is not good. You should be dependent, even if a tiny little bit."

This, coming from someone who had refused to remarry at the expense of being "a woman without a male protector" in the eyes of the society, had surprised me. But now I find myself thinking of her advice in another light.

Women of my age have husbands, children and picnic baskets. They don't hop on Peter Pan buses and go roaming Neverland. You should do that in your early twenties, when you are fresh out of school and your "life" hasn't started yet. But you don't do it in your midthirties. There should have been some order and stability in my life by now. Women my age have scrambled eggs in the mornings with their families and social rituals they like repeating. I'm still being dragged around by the winds, like a kite whose string has snapped.

The members of the Choir of Discordant Voices seem pleased to be here, doing their own thing. Miss Highbrowed Cynic doesn't look like she's ever going to leave the library. When she has a spare moment she attends either a workshop or a conference. Little Miss Practical keeps taking computer classes—PowerPoint, Excel, Linux. The last time I saw Dame Dervish she was meditating in this place where nature is so beautiful. As for Milady Ambitious Chekhovian, she is always on the Internet writing, applying for this and that, finding things to do.

Everyone is in their own world. But where is Mama Rice Pudding?

I haven't seen her since the airplane. Maybe she didn't come to America. Maybe she couldn't get through passport control after all. Or maybe she got lost somewhere in New York. . . . Suddenly my heart aches. Can a person miss a side of her whom she doesn't even know? I do.

As I fall asleep, I think of Mama Rice Pudding. I wish I knew her better.

Normal on the Outside

Courtney Love once said: "I like to behave in an extremely normal, wholesome manner for the most part in my daily life—even if mentally I am consumed with sick visions of violence, terror, sex and death." Everything is normal, as long as we appear so on the outside. But what is normal? And who exactly is a normal woman? Which womanly attributes are natural? Which others are cultural? Are girls genetically predetermined to be maternal, nurturing and emotional, or do their families and societies mold them that way? Or else, are the natural and the cultural qualities so intricately interwoven that there is no telling which characteristics shape whom anymore?

Adjectives come in pairs. For every *beautiful,* somewhere there is an *ugly.* Perhaps, in preparation for the Great Flood, adjectives, like animals, boarded Noah's Ark in twos. That's why we always think in terms of dualism. If there is an established definition of what constitutes "ideal womanhood," it is thanks to a similarly entrenched definition of "ideal manhood." Both definitions, and the expectations that ensue from them, can be equally harrowing for real women and real men.

I grew up seeing two different types of womanhood. On the one hand was my mother—a well-educated, modern, Westernized, secular Turkish woman. Always rational. Always to the point. On the other hand was my maternal grandmother, who also took care of me and was less educated, more spiritual and definitely less rational. This was a woman who read coffee grounds to see the future and melted lead into mysterious shapes to fend off the evil eye. Many people came to see her, people with severe acne on their faces or warts on their hands. My grandmother would utter some words in Arabic, take a red apple and stab it with as many rose thorns as the number of warts she wanted to remove. Then she would draw a circle around each thorn with dark ink.

Some of the most vivid memories of my childhood are about red apples, rose thorns and dark circles. The truth is, of all the people who visited my grandmother for their skin conditions, I didn't see anyone walking away unhappy or unhealed. I asked her how she did this. Was it the power of praying? In response she said, "Yes, praying is effective, but also beware of the power of circles." From her I learned, among other things, one crucial lesson: If you want to destroy something, be it a blemish, acne or the human soul, all you need to do is to surround it with walls.

It will dry up.

There are many similarly "irrational" lessons from my life that I greatly cherish today. To a strictly logical person they might seem pure nonsense, even crazy. Society and culture teach us what exactly is normal and acceptable. My grandmother's cures were "commonplace" for many people in a middle-class neighborhood in Ankara in the early 1970s, although to someone in Vienna they might have looked pretty bizarre. But individuals also differ in their perceptions of normal and abnormal. My mother never believed in the superstitions my grandmother held dear. "Coffee is for drinking, not for reading," Mom said. As for me, I deeply suspected that there were sprinkles of magic in life and love, and that someone who looked like a handsome prince at first glance could easily turn into an ugly frog.

As every writer of fiction knows, when we are developing a story we do not need to be constrained by the limits of logic. Just the opposite, we can dive headfirst into that bottomless lake of irrationality. We can write about superstitions, magic and fairies. There is room for all in literature. This despite the fact that in our daily lives we conform to a different set of rules, moving in a solid and rational world.

For many centuries all around the globe, girls and women have been expected to conform to one set of attributes, while men and boys measure up to another. If and when the traits of an individual included elements from both sets, life became much more complicated. Even today, a woman who is thought to be "manly" can face a bulwark of reactions, as can a man who is deemed "womanly." The more conventional the society is, the less likely the two sets intersect—at least outwardly. But the exclusivist approach to gender relations is by no means specific to traditional societies. Though constantly changing, it is fundamentally universal. From ancient myths to modern graphic novels, from folklore to advertisements, this dualistic way of thinking has infiltrated many areas of our lives.

Man	Woman
Masculine	Feminine
Bold	Modest
Dominant	Passive
Culture	Nature
Day	Night
Rational	Emotional
Brain	Body
Intelligible	Sensitive
Vertical	Horizontal
Moving	Settled
Polygamous	Monogamous (or multiple partners)
Doer	Talker
Objective	Subjective
Logos	Pathos

Oddly enough, women, too, are used to thinking of themselves in these terms. The relationships we build with one another, the talks we have among ourselves and the way we raise our own daughters are overshadowed by the dichotomy of gender patterns.

How much of my womanhood is biological, how much of it is socially learned? Of the will to become a mother, which part is innate, which part is imposed? Is it sheer coincidence that I have started contemplating motherhood in my midthirties? Is it because my biological clock is ticking? Or is it because the social chronometer, which continuously compels us women to measure ourselves against one another, is speeding ahead?

When everything is so culturally loaded, how am I going to know what is really natural and what is environmental?

Sitting on the Edge

Zelda Sayre Fitzgerald was born on July 24, 1900, in Alabama. She was a fearless, bouncy kid who received much love from her mother, perhaps at the risk of being fairly spoiled. As for her distant father, who was a formidable judge, she got far less affection and attention from him. Her childhood vacillated between these two emotional extremes. A vivid illustration of her personality lies in a small predicament she caused when she was just a child.

One morning the local police received a call that a child was walking across a rooftop. When the officers reached the address, they found little Zelda sitting on the roof waiting for them. After a lot of hassle, they managed to get her down. The truth behind the story was discovered a bit later. It was Zelda who had called the police. First she had made the phone call, then climbed onto the roof, crept right to the edge and sat down and waited to be rescued. This, more or less, remained the modus vivendi in her life. Even as a grown-up woman, she continued to go to the edge and then calmly watch the panic she had caused.

The essays and books written about Zelda Fitzgerald almost always revolve around three points:

1. She was the wife and greatest love of F. Scott Fitzgerald.
2. She was a gifted artist herself.

3. She had extensive therapy, suffered from depression and ended
up dying in a mental institution.

Zelda and Scott Fitzgerald met toward the end of the Great War.
Each had a different memory of their first encounter. The man found
the woman attractive and smart, but he was disturbed by the way she
constantly flirted with other men. His first impression of her was a
mixed one.

The woman, on the other hand, found the man charismatic and
talented with a dazzling mind. Zelda was the kind of woman who had
to love a man's brain before she could fall for him.

They got married in April 1920, carried by the winds of mutual
attraction and passion. When asked by a journalist what his greatest
ambition in life was, Scott Fitzgerald said it was to write the best novel
that ever was and to stay in love with his beloved wife forever. Yet from
the very start, they saw each other as potential rivals. The fact that both
had a tendency to take to the bottle at the sight of the slightest distress
did not help their marriage. In time, their disagreements grew more
violent and hurtful.

Alcohol, cigarettes, night life . . . They were no strangers to life in
the fast lane. But perhaps their greatest addiction was to their love.
Zelda and Scott adored, fought and marred each other in a roller-
coaster relationship. They were aware of each other's weaknesses and
knew how to hurt. One moment they would scream war cries and the
next they would jump into the car and drive dangerously fast on sharp-
curved roads. They loved to challenge fate. Being a creative, famous,
high-flying and self-destructive couple, they became the focus of the
media. Unsurprisingly, not everything written about them was true.
There was much gossip and speculation, and few reporters had the
time or the will to separate the facts from the lies.

In the years that followed, Scott Fitzgerald became increasingly
famous, swiftly climbing up the glass staircase of the literary pantheon.
Strikingly, the characters he wrote about and the themes he tackled
were often inspired by Zelda. Some of his characters spoke just like

Zelda. Did he "steal" ideas from his wife? Did he pilfer parts of her writing? From time to time Zelda would mockingly talk about how entries in the diaries she kept at home would end up in her husband's novels—sometimes entire paragraphs. In a review she wrote of *The Beautiful and Damned* for the *New York Tribune,* she made this insinuation public: "It seems to me that on one page I recognized a portion of an old diary of mine which mysteriously disappeared shortly after my marriage, and also scraps of letters which, though considerably edited, sound to me vaguely familiar. In fact, Mr. Fitzgerald—I believe that is how he spells his name—seems to believe that plagiarism begins at home."★

Perhaps every writer is a pickpocket of some sort, stealing inspiration from real life. Like magpies that can't resist making off with shiny objects, authors flap their wings across the boundless sky looking for themes to write about. And when they find one, they snatch it up. Whichever way we see it, the extent of the "literary patent" between Scott and Zelda Fitzgerald has not been fully resolved even today.

Fame and recognition brought little happiness for Scott Fitzgerald. Surrounded by women who admired him, critics who applauded him and reporters who saw in his every move juicy material to write about, he began drinking heavily. When not thinking about his next novel, he was shutting his mind off to the world; when not writing, he was imbibing, sometimes falling asleep in random places. Zelda was at least as unhappy as he was. They couldn't make each other happy, but they could not possibly let each other go their own separate ways. Like two kites whose strings had intertwined, they kept twisting and turning in each other's arms.

The friendship that grew between Scott Fitzgerald and Ernest Hemingway during this time is something that bemuses literary historians. The two of them were inseparable for a while—two bohemian writers who would pass out together. It was the kind of friendship that

---

★ Jackson R. Bryer and Cathy W. Barks, eds., *Dear Scott, Dearest Zelda* (New York: St. Martin's Press: 2002), xxviii.

did not sit well with Zelda. She found Hemingway too macho, his ego too inflated. She believed he wasn't a good companion for her husband. In time, the friendship fell apart.

Zelda's jealousy was legendary. In fit after fit of envy, she burned her clothes, destroyed her possessions and even damaged her surroundings. Once at a crowded, chic party, she took off the jewelry she was wearing and threw it into hot water in an attempt to make "jewel soup." She was often blinded by rage. Another night, after she noticed her husband paying lavish attention to the famous Isadora Duncan, she made a scene by throwing herself down a set of marble stairs. When they picked her up off the floor, she was covered in blood.

They had one daughter whom they both loved dearly—Scottie, who was born in October 1921 and was given to the care of a nanny. While she was still partly anesthetized, Zelda murmured, "I hope it is beautiful and a fool—a beautiful little fool." The same expression would be repeated in *The Great Gatsby* when Daisy talked about her own daughter. As always, life inspired fiction.

After Scottie, Zelda had three abortions. As much as she loved her daughter, she did not want to have another child, at least not so soon. The baby neither slowed down their lifestyle nor tempered their arguments. In the later stages of their marriage, Zelda always searched for something she could do that would be outside the realm of her husband's interests. For a while she tried taking ballet classes. Her husband scorned her interest, calling it a waste of time. In the end ballet couldn't make Zelda happy.*

That was when she started to feel jealous—not of another woman this time, but of her husband's writing. More and more often she tried to distract him during the hours he was working on his fiction. It was obvious to everyone but them that they could not stay in the same house any longer. Scott Fitzgerald wanted to keep his wife at home. He was worried that if she went out alone, she would flirt or even find a lover—just to get back at him, to relieve the pain in her heart.

---

* For a good biography see Nancy Mitford's *Zelda* (New York: Harper, 1983).

Rumi likens the mind to a guesthouse. Every morning we have a new, unexpected visitor, sometimes in the form of joy, sometimes dressed up as sorrow. For Zelda Fitzgerald her guesthouse entertained all kinds of unpleasant guests: Mr. Anxiety, Miss Panic Attack, Mrs. Resentment, Sir Bitterness . . .

Finally, in June 1930, after months that included a nervous breakdown, hallucinations and an attempted suicide, she was diagnosed with schizophrenia and taken to a hospital. She spent the rest of her eighteen years under psychiatric care. There is a letter she wrote to Scott shortly afterward that says a lot about not only her psychology at the time but also her vivacious and tempestuous style: "No matter what happens, I still know in my heart that it is a Godless, dirty game: that love is bitter and all there is, and that the rest is for the emotional beggars of the earth. . . ."*

Nonetheless, staying at the clinic seemed somehow to have triggered her productivity. She wrote constantly during this period—diaries, stories, letters. Not only did she make beautiful paintings, but she also wrote a semiautobiographical novel, *Save Me the Waltz*. In utmost sincerity she wrote about the fun-loving, inventive, but also hardworking Southern belle she had been, and the inner transformation that came with marriage. She also elaborated on the two conflicting sides of her personality: one independent and carefree, the other in need of love and security.

As soon as she finished the novel Zelda sent it to Scott's publisher. Her husband had not seen it yet and when he found out, he was furious. At the time he was working on *Tender Is the Night*. As they had made use of similar material (the story of Zelda's mental illness and the years they had spent together in Paris and on the Riviera), the two books largely overlapped. A great fight ensued, with marital and artistic repercussions, at the end of which Zelda agreed to revise her manuscript. When the book came out it was not well received by literary

---

* Jackson R. Bryer and Cathy W. Barks, eds., *Dear Scott, Dearest Zelda* (New York: St. Martin's Press: 2002), xxviii.

critics, selling only a limited number of copies. Demoralized, Zelda did not publish another novel.

Her husband rented houses near the various clinics she resided in so that he could still be close to her while he was writing. They spent the following years seeing each other only on visiting days, between pills and doctors and treatments. He died in 1940 from a heart attack. Eight years later a fire erupted in a mental institution in Asheville, North Carolina. Among the patients who lost their lives in that fire was Zelda Fitzgerald.

Faulkner once said that a writer's obituary should be simple. "He wrote books, then he died." But what about a woman writer like Zelda Fitzgerald: She sat on the edge, danced herself to heartbreak, painted the world in stunning colors, raised a daughter, loved with great passion, wrote stories, then she died.

Scott and Zelda left a huge unanswered question behind: If they hadn't worn each other thin, would they have lived longer, and produced greater works? I don't know. Some days I feel like it would have made a big difference if they had made life easier on each other; then other days I suspect the effortlessness of daily life wouldn't have mattered at all. The outcome would have been the same.

Zelda Fitzgerald was not a "normal" woman who conformed to conventional gender roles. Neither modesty nor passivity was her cup of tea. But if she had been the opposite, if she had been capable of living a more settled and secure life, would she have written better books, more books? Would she have been remembered more highly today?

As I write this now I suspect the opposite is true. Maybe through their constant wars and ups and downs, and their daring to swerve miles away from a conventional marriage, Zelda and Scott Fitzgerald were able to write, love and live to the best of their ability.

Brain Tree

The Center for Women's Studies at Mount Holyoke College is situated in a large, beige, three-story typical New England house, in which I occupy one room on the first floor that has a separate entrance. The second floor houses the offices of the faculty and other fellows as well. The walls and ceilings are so thin I can easily hear their conversations, and more than likely they can hear me shouting at my finger-women—explaining in part why I catch some of the faculty looking at me, at times, with concern.

Connecting my room with the center is a door that is so flimsy, the first time I cook cauliflower in my kitchen, the entire department stinks for days. The smell seeps through the cardboardlike door into every nook and cranny. I try preparing other simple but less smelly recipes—always with the same outcome. In a place where everyone drinks organic, fair-trade, antioxidant herbal teas, even the aroma of my Turkish coffee is too much. And so, I abandon the kitchen altogether, and stick to fruit, crackers and water.

In the evenings, when everybody leaves the building, I remain. There is something creepy about being alone in such a big house that suddenly becomes so quiet and dark. At night, when I try to sleep, I find myself disconcerted.

But not tonight. This evening in my nutshell of a bathroom, in the faint glimmer coming through the open window, I watch snowflakes fall from the deep sky onto Mount Holyoke's campus. The blanket of snow makes the world seem like a different planet, and I sit here feeling calmer and more composed than I have been in months.

The bathroom may not be the most appropriate place to observe a landscape this romantic, but it is the only place in the entire building where I can have a cigarette—without the others, and, most important, the fire alarms detecting my smoke. The healthy-life-happy-minded feminists may forgive me for my cauliflower, but I don't think they will pardon me for my Marlboro Lights.

But necessity is the mother of invention. Shortly after I arrived here, I set up a mini ironing board in the bathroom as a desk and closed the lid of a storage bin, making it as comfortable as an armchair by tossing a cushion onto it. This is where I write my newspaper column and stories. I lock myself in here, and eat red apples for breakfast, lunch and dinner, smoking to my heart's content.

So on this snowy night, I am here again, looking out the window as I write, when a loud scream yanks me out of my reverie:

"Help! Help! There's a thief!"

I put the cigarette out, leave the bathroom and check the clock by the corner of the bed. It reads 3:08. I grab the African mask on the wall and dash forward without thinking about what I am doing. Not that I am made of hero material. If I am brave at this moment it is precisely because I don't have a clue what is going on. And there is no time to stop and be frightened.

"There is a thief on the roof! Help!"

Now I recognize the voice. It is Miss Highbrowed Cynic who is screaming. I find her perched on top of a vase like a wingless chicka-dee, hiding among Christmas flowers, her face as pale as a ghost.

"What is it? Why are you yelling?"

"I just got back from the library. I was walking alone in the dark and then I saw it! Her! Someone is walking on the roof!"

"Maybe it is one of the other finger-women."

"No, it can't be. All three of them are here, don't you see?"

I flick a glance over my shoulder. It is true. Having rushed out of bed, they are all lined up behind me—Dame Dervish in her long nightgown, Milady Ambitious Chekhovian in her dark green commando pajamas, Little Miss Practical in her comfortable sweatpants. Straining our ears, we listen to the strange sounds echoing from somewhere else in the house.

"Yo, let's call the police," says Little Miss Practical. The day we moved here she wrote down the numbers for police, fire and ambulance on a piece of paper and stuck it on the fridge.

"Wait, don't rush. Let me go and take a look," says Dame Dervish.

But Milady Ambitious Chekhovian doesn't approve. "No way, you are the last person to do this."

"And why is that?" Dame Dervish asks calmly.

"I know you. Whoever you see on the roof, you'll say, 'God must have sent us this thief for a reason,' and you'll end up inviting the thug for dinner! You are too soft-hearted for the job. It's best if I go."

She has a point, I admit. Milady Ambitious Chekhovian has always been the bravest of the Choir of Discordant Voices. But since she masterminded a coup d'état, her audacity has tripled.

"All right, you go, then," I say.

Fully focused on her mission, she grabs a plastic fork as a weapon and goes off into the dark.

Milady Ambitious Chekhovian has no sooner disappeared than a commotion erupts on the roof, piercing the night's stillness. The squirrels inhabiting the trees around the center stick their heads out of their holes, trying to understand what is going on. A few of them jump down and vanish.

We hear Milady Ambitious Chekhovian's voice crack as she shouts at someone. The perceptible alarm in her tone is quickly replaced by anger and aversion. Whoever the other person is, she doesn't seem to quarrel, doesn't retort.

Ten minutes later Milady Ambitious Chekhovian comes back downstairs and attempts to stab a tangerine with her fork, fuming and furious. We all watch the fork break into two pieces.

"What is it? What happened?" I ask.

"See for yourself," she says. Then she turns toward the door, almost hissing. "Are you coming or not?"

Slowly, shyly, as if willing herself to disappear into the thick night, a finger-woman walks in. I recognize her immediately. It is Mama Rice Pudding.

"Hello there!" I pick her up and place her on my palm.

"You two know each other?" Milady Ambitious Chekhovian asks.

"Well, hmm . . . We've . . . m-met once," I stutter.

"Oh, yeah? When was that?" Miss Highbrowed Cynic asks, frowning. "And how come we don't know about it?"

Deciding that the best defense is a good offense, I snap: "In fact, I should be asking that question. In all this time, why didn't you ever tell me about Mama Rice Pudding?"

Milady Ambitious Chekhovian briefly considers the notion. "What do you think would have happened if we told you? What good would it have brought?"

"I have a right to know that I have a maternal side," I insist.

"Great, just what we needed," says Miss Highbrowed Cynic, grumbling to herself. "We crossed an entire ocean to get rid of this sticky miss. Alas, she found us here as well!"

Suddenly it dawns on me. Does my leaving Istanbul in such a hurry have anything to do with this?

"Wait a minute, hold on," I say. "Is this why you brought me all the way here to America?"

Miss Highbrowed Cynic and Milady Ambitious Chekhovian cast guilty looks at each other.

"Time for some real talk! Let the cat out of the bag!" says Little Miss Practical, shrugging nonchalantly.

"Okay, it might as well come out," says Milady Ambitious Chekhovian. She turns to me, her eyes blazing with fire. "I don't know if you recall, but sometime ago you were traveling on a steamboat and this plump woman with two sons sat beside you."

Of course I remember. I nod my head.

"Well, you might not have realized it, but you were profoundly moved by your encounter with that woman. She was young and pregnant with her third child. When you looked at her you lamented the opportunities you lost. You almost wanted to be her. If I hadn't acted at once and made you write "The Manifesto of a Single Girl," God forbid, you were going to get trapped in your dreams of motherhood."

"So I wrote that manifesto because of you?"

"Yes, of course," says Milady Ambitious Chekhovian, as she paces up and down. "I thought that would be the end of the story. But when Mama Rice Pudding noticed you were curiously watching pregnant women and mothers with their babies, she decided it was high time for her to come out of hiding and introduce herself. We tried to reason with her, and then we threatened her. But she didn't budge. She was going to upset the status quo, so we performed a military takeover. We forced you to leave Istanbul, but apparently Miss Nuisance followed us here!"

"But, if she is a member of the Choir of Discordant Voices, she should have an equal say in all matters," I venture.

"Thanks, but no thanks. We can't let that happen," Miss Highbrowed Cynic says, rubbing her temples as if on the verge of a migraine.

"We are not a democracy, okay? We were always a monarchy, and now we are a tight military regime," roars Milady Ambitious Chekhovian. A spark flickers in her eye as she turns to her chum. "Let's have an emergency meeting."

As the chairpersons of the High Military Council's executive committee, Milady Ambitious Chekhovian and Miss Highbrowed Cynic move to a corner, whispering in fierce tones. After what seems like an eternity, they walk back, their footsteps echoing their determination, their faces grim.

"Follow us outside," says Milady Ambitious Chekhovian.

"Where on earth are we going at this hour?"

"Move!" she scolds me, and then calls out to the others: "All of you! On the double!"

At three-thirty in the morning, under the watchful gaze of the braver squirrels, we march in single file in the snow. Our teeth chattering, our fingertips numb, we pass by the library and the dormitories.

"How serene the universe seems tonight," mumbles Dame Dervish as she takes a deep breath.

How she's able to find something positive to say even under the most stressful circumstances is a mystery to me. I pick her up and put her inside my sweater so she doesn't catch a cold. We move along in this fashion until we arrive under a massive tree.

"What is this?" I ask.

Miss Highbrowed Cynic delivers the answer: "I discovered this tree when we first arrived here. On sunny days, it's a perfect place to read. I would have much preferred to show it to you in the daylight, but I need to do it now. Pay attention to the tree trunk. What does it look like?"

Oddly enough, a mammoth balloonlike lump bulges out of the tree's thick trunk. It looks like a giant shriveled-up prune or a huge wrinkled walnut with ridges. Or else—

Miss Highbrowed Cynic gives me a sidelong glance. "Tell me, what does that mass resemble from afar?"

"Well, I don't know. . . . It's almost like . . . like a brain. . . ." I say.

"Bingo! It is a Brain Tree," says Miss Highbrowed Cynic.

"So tonight we have all gathered under the Brain Tree," Milady Ambitious Chekhovian says, launching into a speech. She has climbed onto a branch, where she pouts like a dictator assessing his people's intelligence before starting to lecture them.

"This is a historic moment," she bellows. "The time is ripe to make a choice once and for all." She points an accusing finger at Mama Rice Pudding. "Do you want to be like her? A forlorn housewife? Or would you rather live your life like a majestic arboreal brain?"

I can't take my eyes from the tree. In the velvety dark of the night, surrounded by all this snow, the tree looks fearsome and impressive.

"Please don't listen to them," whispers Mama Rice Pudding as she clings to my legs. Tears have formed in her eyes. So fragile she is. So little I know about her. I've seen her only twice while the others have been with me for years.

"We can make a great team, you and I," says Mama Rice Pudding.

"I'm sorry," I say.

A strong wind blows in fitful gusts, swirling the flakes. I feel like I'm on the set of *Doctor Zhivago*. This is not Russia and there isn't the slightest possibility of a Bolshevik revolution on this campus, but there are still profound emotional changes under way.

Finally, I muster the courage to answer. "If I have to make a choice, I'll certainly choose the Brain Tree."

"But you made me a promise!" Mama Rice Pudding bursts forth.

"I'm sorry," I say again, unable to meet her eyes.

Milady Ambitious Chekhovian jumps down from her branch and Miss Highbrowed Cynic grins at her, shouting, "Give me five!"

Partners in crime. They do such a complicated high five, with their arms and fingers passing through each other's, that we all watch with awe.

When the show is over Dame Dervish sighs heavily, Little Miss Practical takes off her glasses and cleans them nervously, Mama Rice Pudding cries silently.

"Now you have to repeat after me," says Milady Ambitious Chekhovian. *"I've traveled wide, I've traveled far—"*

I do. On the snow-covered Mount Holyoke campus, under that breathtaking Brain Tree, I swear these words to myself:

"I've traveled wide, I've traveled far, and I've placed writing at the center of my life. At last I've reached a decision between Body and Brain. From now on I want to be only, and only, Brain. No longer will the Body hold sway over me. I have no want for womanhood, housework, wife work, maternal instincts or giving birth. I want to be a writer, and that is all I want to pursue."

In this moment, one of the many things I realize is that this is a turning point in my life, a sharp one. While I veer fast, I don't know what awaits me around the corner.

"May the Body rot and may the Brain glow. May the ink flow through my pen like oceans to nourish the novels that shall grow within."

I repeat this oath three times. When it is over, I feel numb inside, almost anesthetized. Perhaps it is because of the cold. Perhaps the gravity of what I have just uttered has started to sink in.

A Mystery Called Brain

Before two weeks have passed my body starts to show signs of change. First my hair, then the skin on my face and hands, dries out. I lose weight. My stomach flattens. Then, one day, I realize I have stopped menstruating. I don't get my flow the next month, or the one after that. At first I don't pay any attention to it—in fact, I am even relieved to be rid of womanhood. Wouldn't it be liberating to free myself of femininity and sexuality, and become a walking brain? I feel like a crazy scientist who is experimenting with all kinds of unknown substances in his murky laboratory—except I am experimenting on myself. Not that I seem to be turning into a green, giant, humanoid monster. But I am transforming into an antisocial, asexual, introverted novelist, who, perhaps, is no less scary than the Incredible Hulk.

In late May, I am perusing the magazines in the waiting room of the Women's Health Center while waiting for the kind, lanky gynecologist who has done all sorts of hormonal tests on me. Finally, the nurse calls me in.

"Here is an interesting case," says the doctor as I walk into his office. "Feeling any better?"

"The same," I say.

"Well, well, let's see what we have here. . . ." says the doctor, inspecting the test results from behind his glasses. "Your hormone levels have come back fine, and so have the thyroid tests."

"You are normal," says the nurse next to him, as if she could not quite believe this.

"But, then, why don't I menstruate anymore?"

"Under these circumstances there is only one answer," the doctor responds. "Your brain has given your body the command not to."

"Is that possible?" I ask incredulously.

"Oh, yes, it is very possible," announces the doctor, squinting slightly, as if he were trying to peer into my soul. "You have to discuss this with your brain. I would, but I don't know its language."

"It'll take us some time to learn Turkish," says the nurse with a wink.

They chuckle in perfect synchronization—in the way that only people who have worked closely together for many years can manage. I, in the meantime, wait silently, unsure what to say.

"Could you tell me what you do for a living?" asks the doctor.

"I am a writer."

"Ah, I see," he says with brightened interest. "What kind of books do you write?"

This is a question I'd rather avoid. I don't know exactly how to categorize my books, and I am not sure I even want to. In fact, this happens to be a thorny question for almost any writer who doesn't produce within established genres, such as "romance" or "crime." Fortunately, the doctor is less interested in my answer than in an idea that has just occurred to him.

"Think of your brain as a riveting, suspenseful detective novel," he says.

"Okay," I say.

Then he lowers his voice as if revealing a terrible secret. "Your brain has kidnapped your body. . . ."

"Really?"

"Yeah. Now all you need to do is to tell it to stop. You can do this, believe me."

"I am sorry, I lost the thread here. Is my brain a detective novel or the detective himself or the villain?"

He leans back, and heaves a deep, deep sigh. That's when I realize, as nice a person as he is, the doctor is not good with metaphors. He tried to clarify things with a figure of speech, and ended up only complicating them more.

I don't go looking for other doctors. Neither do I tell anyone about the strange diagnosis I have received. But I visit the Brain Tree regularly, searching for stoic serenity it cannot grant me. Caressing the sturdy, old roots that rise out of the ground, observing the leaves on its infinite branches, I renew my vow and watch my womanhood perish day by day.

Every morning I go to the library with Miss Highbrowed Cynic. We are as thick as thieves now. Everything progresses the way she and Milady Ambitious Chekhovian had planned. I'm always reading, always researching. Many a night I stay until the wee hours, hunched over books in an area flanked by two collections: English political philosophy and Russian literature. Whenever my eyelids droop, I take a nap on the brown leather couch that is situated between the two long rows of bookcases.

In my spare time I go to panels, which are plentiful in a place such as this: "The Plight of Women in the Third World," "Feminism and Hip-Hop Culture," "Female Characters in Walt Disney: Does Mickey Mouse Oppress Minnie?" and so on. I attend all of them.

In the evenings, I sit in front of the computer and write down notes and compose journal entries far into the night. I don't socialize anymore, I don't go to parties and I avoid brown-bag lunches, as strong as the urge is sometimes. I don't allow anything outside of writing and books to enter my life.

Mama Rice Pudding watches me from a distance with eyes that cannot hide their hurt. Whenever I try to communicate with her, she turns her head and stares into space, sitting as still as a marble statue. Some nights, in bed, I hear her crying.

One day a major Turkish newspaper does an interview with me about my life in America. I speak to the journalist on the phone for about forty minutes. As we are about to hang up he asks me about marriage and motherhood.

I tell him that I am miles away from both right now. It is a huge responsibility to bring children into this world, I say. But when I am old enough, that is, after many more novels, I could see myself becoming a foster mom or perhaps raising someone else's children, helping their education and so forth.

That weekend when the interview comes out, its title is as catchy as it can be: "I am Raring to Become a Stepmom!"

Next to the revelation, there is a picture of me taken in Istanbul standing in front of the Topkapı Palace. I am dressed head to toe in black, my hair a cuckoo's nest due to a strong wind, my face etched with a grave expression. When my image is juxtaposed with the words, I look like a black spider about to jump on any divorced man with kids.

I decide not to give any more interviews for a while.

Approximately at the same time, as if a muse has fallen from the sky onto my head, I begin to write a new novel. It is called *The Saint of Incipient Insanities*. The story has sorrow cloaked in humor and humor cloaked in sorrow. It is about a group of foreigners in America coming from very different cultural backgrounds and struggling, not always successfully, with an ongoing sense of estrangement. I write about "insiders" and "outsiders," about belonging and not belonging, feeling like a tree that is turned upside down and has its roots up in the air.

PART FOUR

Never Say Never

Sweet Love

There is a short, round Mexican cleaning lady, Rosario, who every morning at seven o'clock vacuums the northwest section of the library where I usually work all night. I can still dip into Spanish, albeit clumsily. Rosario loves hearing my funny pronunciation and correcting my mistakes. She also teaches me new words every day, blushing and giggling as I repeat them, because some of them are pretty lewd.

When I fall asleep on the leather couch only a few feet away from the John Stuart Mill collection, it is Rosario who wakes me up. She brings me coffee that is so heavy and black my heart pounds for about three minutes after I take a sip. Yet I never tell her to make it a bit weaker. I guess I like her.

"Why are you working so hard?" she asks me one day, pointing to my laptop and a stack of books.

"You work hard, too," I say, pointing to her vacuum cleaner and duster.

She nods. She knows I am right. Then she takes out her necklace and shows it to me. There are four rings on her silver pendant. When I ask her what they mean, she says, smiling from ear to ear, "One ring for each child."

She is a mother of four. That's why she works so hard. She wants them to have a better life than the one she has had.

"How about your husband?" I ask. *"Tu marido?"*

"Marido . . . puff," she says, as if she is talking about gunpowder.

I cannot figure out whether he has died or run away with someone else or never was. Oblivious to my confusion, Rosario smiles again and elbows me. "Children are a blessing," she says.

"I am happy for you."

She pats my shoulder with a touch so genuine and friendly, I drink two more cups of coffee with her, my heart racing.

"You are a good girl," she says to me.

"Some of me are," I say, thinking of my finger-women.

She finds that hilarious and laughs so hard she almost loses her balance. When she manages to get hold of herself, she says, "When you finish your book you don't need to send it to a publisher. There is an easier way."

"Really?" I ask, inching closer to her.

"Yup," she says, nodding. "Send it to Oprah. If she puts her stamp on your book you won't have to work so hard anymore."

"In America they stamp books?" I ask.

"*Sí, claro mujer!*" She rolls her eyes as if to add, "You don't know how crazy these Americans can get."

I thank her for the advice. Then I go back to my novel and she goes back to her work, walking her slow gait, dragging her vacuum cleaner and rolling a bucket of detergents and soaps beside her. She disappears among the aisles of hardcover books. Puff!

In the summer I visit Istanbul for a short while. I am here to pick up a few bits and pieces from my old apartment, to see my friends and my mother, to do some book readings and signings in the city and to seal a contract with my Turkish publisher for *The Saint of Incipient Insanities,* which I have just finished. Then in ten days, I will return to the States.

However, life is a naughty child who sneaks up from behind us while we draw our plans, making funny faces at us.

On my first evening back in Istanbul friends invite me to have a drink in Yakup, a well-known tavern that journalists, painters and writers have long frequented. Jet-lagged and slightly grumpy, I nevertheless agree to meet them.

When I enter the place, the sound of laughter and chattering greets me, along with a thick cloud of smoke. Either there is a chimney inside the tavern or everyone is puffing on at least two Havana cigars at the same time. It is quite a change of scenery after my sterile life at Mount Holyoke.

I walk up to my friends' table, where I know everyone—except a young man with dark, wavy hair and a dimpled smile sitting at the end. He introduces himself as Eyup. It doesn't occur to me that it happens to be the name of the prophet Job, of whom I have said not just a few critical things in the past. Once again in my life, the angels are pointing their milky-white fingers at me, giggling among themselves. Again, I am failing to foresee the irony.

I watch him throughout the evening, cautiously at first, then with growing curiosity. The more I listen to him the more I am convinced that he is the embodiment of everything I have excluded and pushed away from my life. Pure patience, pure balance, pure rationality, pure calmness, pure harmony. He is a natural-born fisherman.

I don't even think I like him. I simply and swiftly fall head over heels in love with him. But I am determined not to let anyone at the table, especially him, see that. In order to hide my feelings, I swing to the other extreme, constantly challenging him and frowning at his every comment.

Hours later, as always happens in Istanbul when a group of women and men consume more than a carafe of wine and twice as much of *rakı,* people start to talk about matters of the heart. Someone suggests that we take turns quoting the best maxims about love that we know.

One of my girlfriends volunteers to go first: "This one is from Shakespeare," she says with a touch of pride. "'Love all, trust a few.'"

The quote is well received. Everyone toasts.

"This one is from Albert Einstein," says someone else. "'Gravitation is not responsible for people falling in love.'"

We toast again.

His eyes sparkling, Eyup joins the game after a few rounds. "This one is from Mark Twain," he says. "'When you fish for love, bait with your heart, not your brain.'"

Everyone applauds. I frown. But I join the toast all the same.

Ten minutes later everyone at the table is looking at me, waiting for me to utter my quote. By now I have drunk more than my usual, and my head is swirling. I put my glass on the table with a kind of borrowed confidence and a bit more forcefully than I intended. I wag my finger in the air and say:

"'Have you ever been in love? Horrible, isn't it? It makes you so vulnerable. It opens your chest and it opens up your heart and it means someone can get inside you and mess you up.' How stupid!"

For one stunned moment nobody says a word. A few people cough as if they have something stuck in their throats and some others force a polite smile, but no one toasts.

"This one is from Neil Gaiman," I say, by way of explanation.

Again silence.

"*The Sandman* . . . *Stardust* . . . *The Graveyard Book* . . ." I add quickly. "You know, Neil Gaiman."

I lean back against the chair, take a deep breath and finish the quote: "'You build up a whole suit of armor, so that nothing can hurt you, then one stupid person, no different from any other stupid person, wanders into your stupid life.' . . . How stupid!"

Everyone is looking at me with something akin to scorn on their faces. I have spoiled the fun and changed the mood from one of drunken merriment to somber seriousness. We can always go back to buoyant love quotes but it won't be the same. Everyone at the table seems slightly confused and annoyed—except one person who regards me with an infinitely warm smile and winks at me like we share a secret.

Madame Onion

In my dream, I am walking in an opulent, vast garden. There are all sorts of flowers, plants and birds around, but I know I am not here for them. I keep walking, with a cane in my hand, until I reach a humongous tree. Its trunk is made of crystal, and leafy silver branches spring from its sides like Christmas ornaments. There are squirrels nibbling walnuts inside every hole in the tree. One of the holes resembles a cavernous mouth.

"You look so beautiful," I say, pleasantly surprised. "I thought it was winter. How did you manage to keep all your leaves?"

"Winter is over now," says the Brain Tree. "You can leave me be."

"But I took an oath, remember? I said my body should shrivel up so that my brain could blossom. If I don't keep my promise, God will be angry."

"No, He won't," says the Brain Tree. "You don't know Him."

"Do you? Have you seen Him?" I ask. "What does He look like?"

But the tree ignores my questions and says, "Everything expires. So has your oath. Even I am about to perish in a little while."

As if in response to his last words, the winds pick up speed and pound with invisible fists on the Brain Tree. That is when I realize that its branches are made of the thinnest glass. In front of my eyes, they shatter into hundreds of minuscule pieces.

"It doesn't hurt, don't worry!" the Brain Tree yells over the noise.

Trying not to cut myself on the shattered glass covering the ground,

I walk and cry, although I know I am not sad. I just can't help it. In this state I walk away from the Brain Tree.

When I turn back to look at it one more time, I am surprised to see that the mammoth tree has shrunk to the size of a bonsai.

This is the dream I have the first night I spend with Eyup.

Once the Brain Tree releases me, my body and I start mending fences. Again, I feel a speedy change commencing within—this time in the opposite direction. My skin becomes softer, my hair shinier. Now that I am in love, I decide to treat my body as best as I can. I begin frequenting The Body Shop, purchasing creams, powders and lotions I have never used before.

Then one afternoon, just as I am placing the products I've bought on a shelf in Eyup's bathroom, I notice something moving there. Aware of my stare, she quickly hides behind a jar of facial cream. In shock, I move the jar aside.

Approximately six inches in height, twenty ounces in weight, it is a finger-woman—though she resembles none of the others. Her honey-blond hair is loose and hangs down to her waist in waves. She has penciled a mole above her mouth and painted her lips such a bright red that it reminds me of a Chinese lantern on fire. Her arms are encased in skin-tight black gloves that reach up to her elbows. She is wearing solitaire rings of various colors over her gloved fingers and has squeezed into a crimson stretchy evening dress. Her breasts are popping out of the décolletage neckline, and her right leg—all the way to her hip—is exposed by a long slit in her dress. On her feet are pointy red stilettos with heels so high I wonder how she manages to walk in them.

Without sparing me so much as a glance, she picks up a cigarette holder. With practiced ennui, she attaches a cigarette to its tip. Then, fluttering her mascara-drenched lashes, she turns to me.

"Do you have a light, darling?" she asks.

My blood freezes. Who is this woman?

"No, I don't," I say, determined to keep communication with her to a minimum.

"That's okay, darling," she says. "Thanks anyway."

Opening her handbag, which looks like a tiny mother-of-pearl pillbox, she takes out a lighter and proceeds to light her cigarette. Then, pursing her lips, she starts to make perfect smoke rings and sends them, one after another, my way.

With my mouth agape, I watch this strange creature.

"You don't recognize me, right?" she says in a half-velvety, half-naughty voice, like Rita Hayworth in *Gilda*. "Of course, that is very normal. When did you ever recognize me?"

She leans forward, exposing the deep cleavage of her breasts. I avert my gaze, feeling uneasy. Has this woman no shame?

"But, darling, I am not a stranger. I am you. I'm a member of the Choir of Discordant Voices. You expressed the wish to make peace with your body and I gladly took that as an invitation. So here I am."

"But who exactly are you?" It is all I can come up with.

"My name is Blue Belle Bovary."

"That sounds so—" I say, looking for a word that won't offend her.

"Poetic?" she offers.

"Well, yeah. It alliterates, sort of," I say.

"Thank you, darling," she says with a wink. "My name is a tribute to Emma Bovary, the woman who did everything in her power to escape the banality and monotony of provincial life."

"Right . . . but as you may know, she is also a rather problematic character. I mean, if you consider cheating on your husband, telling endless lies and dying in agony by swallowing arsenic a problem."

"Don't worry," she says. "Better to live with passion than to die of boredom."

She opens her bag again, takes out a compact and deftly powders the tip of her nose. Then she throws a piercing glance in my direction. "I like wearing sensual perfumes, silk clothing, sexy underwear and satin nightgowns. *Enchanté,* darling."

I can feel my face grow hot. "Could you please stop calling me 'darling'?" I say, my voice quivering. "I don't and could never have an inner voice like you. There must be a mistake."

"Oh dear, you are doing that again! You want to cast me back down into the dark abyss of negligence," she says after taking a drag from her cigarette. "I scare the hell out of you, don't I?"

"Why would I be scared of you?" I ask.

"Otherwise why do you always pose like you do in photos? In every interview you give, you appear guarded and serious. Your face scrunched, your gaze dreamy and distant. The contemplative-writer pose. Ugh!"

"Hey, wait a minute," I say.

Yet even as I try to object, I remember an adept analysis once made by Erica Jong. She said it was not that hard today for women writers to finish or publish their works. The real difficulty for us was to be taken seriously. Jong believed that the biased attitude toward female writers became even more visible in literary reviews. "I have never seen a review of a woman writer in which her sex was not mentioned in some way." I knew this to be true. In Turkey, a female writer can publish as many books as she wants, and yet it always requires a long struggle and much more work for a woman to be taken seriously by the conventional literary establishment.

"Why not wear fire-red lipstick, flowery dresses, and show a bit of skin? Would your writing career decline? Would you be less a woman of letters? You're terrified of being a Body-Woman. Tell me, why are you so afraid of me, darling?"

Words desert me.

"Unlike you, I am a great fan of everything bodily and sensual. I adore the sweet pleasures bestowed on us mere mortals. After all, I am a Scorpio. Hedonism is my motto in life. I enjoy my womanhood," she raves on. "But because of those boorish Thumbelinas, I have been censored, silenced, suppressed!"

A wave of the purest panic rolls over me. I break into a sweat.

"Of course you're sweating," she says, as she cocks her head to one side. "You always dress up like Madame Onion, layer upon layer of clothing. If you wore something light and skimpy, you'd feel so much better."

Could she be right, I wonder. Maybe I did somehow turn myself into Madame Onion. A woman who refuses to draw attention to her Body because she wants to be respected for her Brain, who dresses up in layers when she goes out in public. I always hide myself behind clothes, using them like armor. And whenever I pose for an interview, I make sure I don't smile too much, in order to not be taken lightly in a male-dominated environment. I try to look damn serious, and, often, older than I am.

"Now, those novels of yours . . ." mutters Blue Belle Bovary as she smoothes on a papaya hand cream—like an odalisque in an Orientalist painting.

"What's with my novels?"

"Oh, nothing, it's just that sometimes I get the impression that you female writers can't write about sexuality as freely as male writers do. Your sex scenes are always short, almost nonexistent. You know how, in the old movies, when a couple was about to make love, the camera would drift off to the side? Well, that is precisely how you women write about sexuality. Your pens drift off the page when you run into a sex scene!"

"That's so not true," I protest. "There are plenty of women writers who write lavishly about eroticism and sexuality!"

"Yes, darling, but I'm not talking about romantic or erotic novels," she says. "Just because I said I like satin and desire doesn't mean I'm ignorant. Obviously I'm aware that most of the writers in these genres are women. But that is hardly the topic. I'm not talking about those kinds of books."

Standing up, she flicks her hair with a quick toss of her head. "I'm talking about highbrow literature here. No offense, darling, but the number of women novelists who can write bluntly about sexuality is slim to none."

"There must be a way," I say, still not fully convinced.

"Oh, there is," she says with an impish smile. "Female novelists can write freely about sex only under three conditions."

"Which are?"

"The first condition is lesbianism. If the woman writer is lesbian and open about it, what does she have to fear? Lesbian writers tend to be better at writing about the body than your lot."

While Blue Belle Bovary continues with her monologue, I find myself growing increasingly captive to her silky voice and exaggerated gestures. It is too late to wonder where this conversation is going. Instead I ask, "And why do you think that is?"

"Probably because since they are already stigmatized, they can speak about sensitive subjects without fear of stigma. This makes them more interesting and sincere."

Of this I know a good example. The American writer Rita Mae Brown's groundbreaking novel *Rubyfruit Jungle* came out in the 1970s and challenged the mainstream society's approach to not only sex and sexuality but also lesbianism. Another example is *Tipping the Velvet* by the British novelist Sarah Waters, who calls her books "lesbo historical romps."

"The second condition, darling, is age. When you are an 'old woman writer' in the eyes of society, you are free to write about sex as much as you want. Old women are thought to be above nature. They can talk about sexuality to their heart's content and it will be called wisdom."

Alexandra Kollontai comes to mind—Russian revolutionary, social theorist, writer. Though she wrote passionately all her life, criticizing bourgeois moral values, celebrating love and sexuality as positive forces in life, in her older age she expressed herself even more unreservedly about such topics. Kollontai defended the economic, social and sexual emancipation of women—views that did not make her popular among the ruling elite. She developed her theory on nonpossessive love and sexuality in her novel *Red Love* and a controversial essay titled "Make Way for the Winged Eros," which was bitterly criticized by the leading figures of the Communist regime.

In a charmingly honest and compelling essay for *The New York Times*, Barbara Kingsolver says she used to write the shortest sex scenes ever—

mostly by means of a space break. However, after two children and reaching the age forty, she dared to write an "unchaste novel," breaking free.

"And the third condition?" I ask.

"Or else, you have to be reckless—ready to be the talk of the town, to be grain for the gossip mills. You have to be brazen enough so as not to care what people will think of you when they read your passages on sex."

I think of what Erica Jong did in *Fear of Flying*. Once she said to a journalist that she had accepted fear as an inseparable part of life, especially the fear of change. But this acknowledgment had not held her back: "I have gone ahead despite the pounding in the heart that says: Turn back."

Blue Belle Bovary pauses in case I have anything to add, and when she sees that I don't, she goes on, just as fervently.

"As for you, I am sorry to say you don't fulfill any of these conditions. Seriously, darling, you are in some kind of a fix. You never write openly about the body. Of course, I am the one who bears the brunt. My entire existence is censored!"

She could have a point. But there is something she doesn't recognize. It's not only me or us female writers who as a matter of self-protection shy away from the depiction of graphic sexuality in our books. The same goes for female academics, female reporters, female politicians and those women who tread into the business world. We all are a little desexualized, a little defeminized. We can't carry our bodies comfortably in a society that is so bent against women. In order to be a "brain" in the public realm, we control our "bodies."

I remember Halide Edip Adivar—Ottoman Turkish feminist, political activist and novelist, the diva of Turkish literature. Though she passionately believed in gender equality and worked to improve women's lives, Adivar often reiterated the good-woman/bad-woman dichotomy in her novels and desexualized the former. Her female characters were intelligent, strong-willed and so modest they did not undress even in front of their husbands. Rabia—the leading protagonist in her novel *The Clown and His Daughter*—changed into her nightgown inside the closet, and then came to bed where her husband awaited her.

In traditional Muslim society, where Rabia serves as an ideal woman, women can meet our bodies only inside closets or behind closed doors. The same impulse is reflected in our storytelling. More often than we care to admit, we women writers, especially those of us from non-Western backgrounds, are uncomfortable about writing on sexuality.

Could I ever be like Blue Belle Bovary? Could I wear ostentatious lipstick, teeny-tiny skirts and low-cut necklines like she does? Could I flip my hair as if I were in a shampoo commercial? Probably not. Two steps forward, and one of my heels would surely get stuck in a crack and break. I would never make it.

"Have you ever tried being sexy, darling?" she asks, as if she has read my thoughts.

It is a provocative question, when you come to think of it.

That same evening I ask Eyup to meet me for dinner at an elegant fish restaurant by the Bosphorus. I have never been there before, but it was highly recommended by a friend who called the place "as chic as Kate Moss."

Eyup goes there at seven P.M. and starts to wait for me. Actually, I, too, am at the restaurant, except I am hiding in the bathroom, trying to muster the courage to walk out.

How did I end up here, in hiding? I went to a hairdresser this afternoon and had my hair dyed, my nails manicured and my eyebrows plucked. It was fun for the first ten minutes, but then I got so bored I could have run out with a towel on my head and my hands dripping soapy water. There are very few things to read at a salon, only hairstyle magazines that contain hundreds of photos but roughly only twenty words.

Yet I made it. And here I am, my hair nicely shaped, my face shining under layers of makeup, and though I did not dare to wear the crimson dress Blue Belle Bovary was wearing, I managed to get into a tight, long gown—black, of course—with a feather boa.

Thirty-five minutes later I walk out of the ladies' room, not because I am ready but because there is an increasing number of women coming in and going out of the restroom, all of whom stop and eye me with a curiosity they don't bother to hide. So I leave my shelter and, trying not to trip on the hem of my dress or break my four-inch heels, ask the waiter to take me to the table where Eyup is waiting patiently, having eaten three rolls of bread and half of the butter.

Under the inquiring eyes of the customers, the waiter and I cross the restaurant from one end to the other, he marching steadily, me hobbling behind, totally out of sync but with the same unnaturally serious expression carved on our faces.

Eyup looks up and sees me coming. His eyes pop open, his jaw slightly drops as if he has just witnessed wizardry.

"I warn you, my self-confidence is pretty low now, so please don't say anything bad," I say as soon as I sit.

"I wasn't going to—" he says, suppressing a smile.

I feel the need to explain a little bit. "I am trying to resolve my internal conflicts, you know. I need to bury the hatchet and sign a cease-fire with my body."

He bites his bottom lip but can't help it, a chuckle escapes. "Is that why you are dressed up like this?"

That is when it occurs to me to look at the other customers more carefully. Though it is an elegant restaurant to be sure, posh and pricey, it is clear to me and everyone else that I am overdressed. I look like a wannabe actress who lost her way on the red carpet.

"Maybe I should ask for a shawl or—" I mumble, desperately needing something to hide my cleavage, and these silly feathers. I eye the tablecloth—but it wouldn't do. It's much too thick, too white.

"Don't worry," Eyup says. "Just sit back. Take a deep breath. I hear the butter isn't bad."

That's what I do. I forget all my internal struggles, those I know well and those I am yet to see, and enjoy the moment. It is the best butter I have ever tasted.

In Praise of Selfishness

Ayn Rand is one of those rare female writers who has dedicated readers all over the globe, whose fame is of the lasting kind. In addition to being a novelist, she was also an essayist, a playwright, a screenwriter and a philosopher. Since the 1940s numerous developments have contributed to the proliferation of her philosophy worldwide, the recent financial crisis being one of them. She is among the most loved and most hated writers in the literary world.

Born in 1905 in St. Petersburg to a Russian Jewish couple, Alisa Zinov'yevna Rosenbaum was a smart, gifted child. She had little interest in the world of her girlfriends and female relatives, preferring reading books to playing with dolls or worrying about her looks. In 1926, after graduating from the University of Petrograd with a degree in history, she moved to the United States with little money in her pocket and an urgent need to reinvent herself. She never returned to her country and never saw her family again. As if cutting a ravel of yarn, she thrust aside the past in no uncertain terms. Shortly after, she renamed herself, taking her surname from the typewriter she used—Remington Rand. "Ayn Rand" was the name she gave herself, the name with which she was reborn in the New World.

Rand was a passionate anticommunist, but, then, she was passionate about all her views. She married an actor named Charles Francis O'Connor and wrote many low-budget Hollywood screenplays. Though her first semiautobiographical novel, *We the Living,* had attracted considerable attention, her real breakthrough came in 1943 with her best-selling novel *The Fountainhead,* which took her seven years to write. Her magnum opus was *Atlas Shrugged,* a science-fiction romance and a novel of ideas. It was here that she introduced what she saw as a new moral philosophy—the morality of rational self-interest.

Not a great fan of Kant, she called him "the most evil man in mankind's history." Her response to those who accused her of caricaturizing the fountainhead of Western philosophy was even harsher: "I didn't caricature Kant. Nobody can do that. He did it himself."

In time her name became synonymous with individualism, capitalism and rationalism. Firmly believing that a person had to choose his values by using his reason, she defended the individual's rights against the community and the state, and opposed all sorts of governmental interference (hence her popularity today among those who oppose bank bailouts).

"No man can use his brain to think for another," Ayn Rand was fond of saying. "All functions of the body and spirit are private. Therefore they cannot be shared or transferred." Strikingly, she regarded "reason" not only as the basis for our individual choices but also as the foundation of love between opposite sexes. Even physical attraction, for her, was the working of the brain. Love, sex and desire might seem to be selfish if left untamed by society, but despite that, or perhaps precisely because of it, they rendered the human individual an object worthy of attraction and appreciation. As it was maintained in *The Fountainhead,* "To say 'I love you,' one must know first how to say the 'I.'"

Her views on female sexuality could be regarded as problematic, to say the least. On the one hand, she was one of the few female novelists who could write about carnal desires and sexual fetishism without self-censure. On the other hand, her tone was visibly discriminatory at times, and the "beautiful woman" in her works was often "blond, fair-skinned and long-legged"—the type of woman she was not and could never be. In almost all the sex scenes throughout her novels, there is a recurrent pattern: The woman first resists, the man insists, sometimes to the point of using physical force, and finally the woman surrenders.

Never a compliant personality, Ayn Rand loved to scandalize feminists with her views on women, especially her comments on how a female should admire her male. Ironically, such was not the pattern in her own marriage.

Increasingly over the years, Rand's husband, Frank O'Connor, was overshadowed by his wife's fame. Not an exceptionally talented actor or one who was popular with producers, he was often unemployed. From the moment they got married, the fact that she was the more famous and successful of the two was a burden on him. As if making fun of his predicament, he would often introduce himself as "Mr. Ayn Rand."

In 1951, the year after they moved to New York, Ayn Rand met a nineteen-year-old psychology student named Nathaniel Branden. He appreciated, admired and, perhaps, feared her. Such was his adoration that he founded an institution to spread her ideas far and wide. What started as an intellectual attraction soon turned physical. It was a kind of magnetic pull that intensified between a middle-aged, celebrated and intelligent woman and a young, ambitious and emotional man. Without hiding the situation from her husband, Rand gradually built a love triangle, situating herself right at the center. *Atlas Shrugged* was dedicated to both Branden and O'Connor.

Though it was a complicated scheme that made no one happy, it lasted fourteen years. When Ayn Rand turned sixty-one, Nathaniel left her for a young model. The famous writer who perceived even a sexual relationship fundamentally as an "intellectual exchange," could not possibly come to grips with her long-term lover's choice of "body" over "mind."

She never forgave him. Perhaps his renouncement of her philosophy hurt her more than the physical abandonment. In a bitter article in *The Objectivist,* she announced to everyone that they were on separate paths. They never saw each other again.

Ayn Rand was one of those female writers who chose, from the very start, not to have children. Just as children did not play a part in her life, they did not factor into her novels either.* She was criticized for not writing about children and not even trying to understand them, but there is nothing in her notes to make us think that she paid this any heed. The only children she ever wanted to have were her books.

She was a writer with scintillating ideas and a woman of spectacular contradictions—as is her legacy. It is no coincidence that even after her death, both those who admired her and those who disliked her have dug in their heels. Though she defended capitalism ardently, in her personal life she preferred to have relationships that bordered on totalitarianism. In theory she was on the side of individual freedom and critical thinking. But in reality, she absolutely hated being criticized; she cast out and held in contempt anyone who did not agree with her. She expected obedience and loyalty from her inner circle. Despite the fact that she was a headstrong woman, and that her novels were full of independent female characters, she argued that a woman had to surrender herself to her man. The fact that she did no such thing in her private life was a different matter.

Always a fighter, when she got cancer she didn't want anyone to know about it. She saw even her illness as a mistake that needed to be corrected. And she did "correct it," managing to beat the cancer. For her it was another victory of the brain over the body. A confirmation of her viewpoint.

But in 1982, she suddenly and unexpectedly died of a heart attack.

Today, literature enthusiasts from all around the world post their views on the Internet by asking questions such as "What kind of a psycho would I turn out to be if Ayn Rand had been my mother?" or "What would my life be like if I were married to Ayn Rand?"

Maybe they are right. Ayn Rand hadn't been born to be a mother

---

* In *Anthem* there is a couple with a child. But even in that novel, the real purpose for having a child is to create a new race and a different model of human being. When Ayn Rand wrote about the education of children it was almost always to show how a rational society of rational individuals would function.

or a wife. If she had been a mother she would very likely have been a dominant one, seeing each of her children as a different scientific experiment. But perhaps we are all badly mistaken. She may have found motherhood to be a "wonderfully intense intellectual excitement"— the way she described school and classes as a young girl in her diary. I am curious to know what she would have done when her child turned into a rebellious teenager.

It is equally plausible that early on she realized that in the mother-child relationship, the child always wins. Perhaps that was the real reason why she didn't want children. Ayn Rand liked to win.

Giving birth to books was enough for her.

When the Grand Bazaar Smiles

Exactly a year later we are sitting in a café at the Grand Bazaar, Eyup and I.

The finger-women are nowhere to be seen and I suspect each is shopping in a separate store. After Mount Holyoke I was a visiting scholar at the University of Michigan in Ann Arbor. I taught courses in women's studies, and slowly I started writing my new novel, *The Bastard of Istanbul*.

Now it is summer again. I am back in the city. We are sitting here, my love and I, between silver bracelets, smoke pipes, carpets and brass lamps that remind me of Aladdin's. A rumpus is going on around us. Young men pushing carts loaded with merchandise, old men playing backgammon, merchants haggling in every language known to humankind, tourists struggling to keep pushy sellers at bay, apprentices carrying tea glasses on silver trays, cats meowing in front of restaurants, children feeding the cats when their parents are not looking—everyone is in their own world.

Suddenly, Eyup holds my hand and asks, his voice raised over the din in the background, "Honey, I was just wondering. Are you still against marriage?"

"I certainly am," I say with conviction, but then add, "theoretically."

"And what exactly does *theoretically* mean?" he asks sweetly.

"It means, generally speaking. As an abstract idea. As a philosophical model—" I try to explain.

"In plain language, please?" he says, swirling the spoon in his tea glass.

"I mean, I am against human beings getting married, at least most of them, because they really shouldn't, but that said—"

"That said?" he repeats.

"I am not against *me* marrying *you,* for instance."

Eyup laughs—his laughter like a sword being pulled out of a silken sheath before the final thrust.

"I think you just made the most roundabout marriage proposal that a man has ever received from a woman," he says.

"Did I?"

He nods mischievously. "You can take it back, of course."

"But I don't," I say, because that is how I feel. "I am asking you to marry me."

The Grand Bazaar doubles up laughing at my endless contradictions, jingling its wind chimes, clinking its teaspoons and tinkling its bells. With a record such as mine, who am I to judge Ayn Rand's inconsistencies?

Eyup's eyes grow large and sympathetic. "It is a joke."

"But I am damn serious," I say and wait, hardly breathing.

His eyes rake my eyes for a long moment, as if searching for something, and then his face brightens, like the sun reflecting on a silver dome.

"And I gladly accept," he says. "I do."

Oscar Wilde once said, "Men marry because they are tired, women because they are curious." But if there is anyone who is tired here, most probably it is I. I've grown tired of my own biases. I've grown tired of failing to see the beauty in small things, of being against marriage and domestic life, of wearing myself thin, of carrying around suitcases from city to city and country to country.

But will I stop commuting when I tie the knot?

In English the word *matrimony* comes from the Latin word for "mother." The Turkish word for it, *evlilik,* is connected with "setting up a house." Laying down roots is a prerequisite for marriage.

"You know I have a problem staying in one place," I say guiltily.

"I noticed," Eyup says.

"Is this not a problem for you?" I ask, afraid to hear the answer.

"Honey, I stopped expecting anything normal from you the day you quoted Neil Gaiman as your motto on love," he says.

"I see."

He bows his head and adds in a softer tone, "We will do the best we can. You will be the nomad, I will be the settler. You will bring me magic fruits from lands afar, I will grow oranges for you in the backyard. We will find a balance."

I turn my head. Genuine kindness always makes my eyes tear, which I can hide, I think, but it is a different story with my nose, which reddens instantly. Eyup hands me a napkin and asks, "And since you are the worldwide traveler, tell me, where on earth would you like to say 'I do'?"

"Somewhere where brides are not expected to wear white," is my answer.

Using his teaspoon as a baton to emphasize his point, Eyup says, "That leaves us with three options: a nunnery, preferably medieval; a bar frequented by a gang of rockers on motorbikes; or the set for a movie on Johnny Cash. These are the places where you can wear a black bridal gown without anyone finding it odd."

I briefly consider each option, and then ask, "How about Berlin?"

"What about Berlin?"

"I have been offered a fellowship by the Institute for Advanced Study in Berlin. If I accept, I will be there for a while next year."

"Hmm, makes sense to me," he says, suddenly serious. "We will be like East and West Berlin, remarkably different and previously independent but now surprisingly united."

Little Women, Big Hearts

One of my favorite fictional female characters as a young girl was Jo in *Little Women*. Jo the writer. Jo the dreamer. Jo the romantic, adventuresome, idealist and independent sister. When her sister Amy burned her manuscript—her only copy—in an act of pure revenge, I was horrified. It took me a long time to forgive Amy—even though Jo herself wasn't that innocent; after all, she had not invited Amy to a play and almost drowned her while ice-skating. At any rate, the story of the four March sisters during the American Civil War was so unlike my life as the child of a Turkish single mother, and yet many things were familiar—absent father, struggling with financial ups and downs, nonconformity to gender roles. . . . That was the power of Louisa May Alcott's words, to create a universal saga shared by millions everywhere. It takes no little magic to "zoom" a story written in the late nineteenth century to readers across the globe more than a hundred years later.

A woman ahead of her time, a writer who held Goethe dear, Louisa May Alcott, too, favored Jo and was a bit like her: full of energy, ideas and motivation. The stories told in *Little Women* were highly reminiscent of her familial life as the second of four sisters. She keenly observed the people she met, absorbed the dialogues she heard and then incorporated them all in her stories. Always planning new books, living the plots in her head and scribbling whenever the inspiration struck, she was determined to earn her own money from writing.

"I never had a study," she once said. "Any paper and pen will do, and an old atlas on my knee is all I want."

When *Little Women* was published it brought its author fame and success beyond her modest expectations. Alcott wrote intensely, sometimes forgetting to eat or sleep. That her readers and critics wanted to see a sequel to the story must have both motivated and limited her. She had originally planned that Jo would not get married, earning her bread by the sweat of her own brow, but her publisher was of a different mind. Under constant pressure from him and others, a male character was introduced into Jo's life: Professor Bhaer. And the reader knew Jo was torn between two impulses—her sense of responsibility toward her family and her desire to nurture her individuality and freedom. "I'll try and be what he loves to call me, 'a little woman,' and not be rough and wild, but do my duty here instead of wanting to be somewhere else. . . ." Struggling with her family's expectations of her, Jo eventually chose marriage and domestic life instead of a career in writing—a drastic decision Alcott herself would have never made.

Alcott regarded the matrimonial institution with suspicion. It was clear to her that women who wanted to stand on their feet would have a hard time adapting to conjugal life. "Liberty is a better husband than love to many of us," she said, insinuating that sometimes the only way for a woman writer to find freedom was to remain a spinster.

Her sister May—a creative, prolific painter who had chosen to live abroad—was happily married. She seemed like a woman who had achieved it all—a successful career and a good marriage. Louisa Alcott compared her loneliness with her sister's fulfillment, saying, "she always had the cream of things and deserved it." Unfortunately, May died shortly after giving birth to a baby girl. Her last wish was to send the baby—named Louisa May after her aunt and nicknamed Lulu—to her Aunt Louisa to be raised by her.

So it was that Louisa Alcott, who never married, found herself raising the daughter of her sister. She gave her full love to this child and even wrote short stories for her, thus creating what later was to be named "Lulu's Library."

There is a wonderful passage in the second volume of the Little Women series, which was titled *Good Wives,* where Alcott describes Jo's, and I believe her own, urge to write fiction. I think it is one of the best descriptions ever written about the creative process and I can't help but smile each time I read it: "She did not think herself a genius by any means, but when the writing fit came on, she gave herself up to it with entire abandon, and led a blissful life, unconscious of want, care, or bad weather, while she sat safe and happy in an imaginary world, full of friends almost as real and dear to her as any in the flesh."★

Always a hardworking writer and a Chekhovian by nature, she said, "I don't want to live if I can't be of use." That's how she died, when she couldn't write anymore due to old age, in Boston in 1888.

Mary Ann Evans, born on November 22, 1819, was a shy, introspective and emotional child who loved to read and study. The story of her life is one of transformation—a journey that turned her into the restless, headstrong and outspoken writer known to everyone as George Eliot. When she was thirty-two years old, she fell in love with the philosopher and critic George Henry Lewes. He was a married man, but his was an "open marriage"—even by today's standards. His wife, Agnes, had an affair with another man, and when she bore his child, Lewes was happy to claim the baby as his own. Though the couple remained legally married, they had ceased to see each other as husband and wife. Mary Ann and George lived together. She adopted his sons as her own. It wasn't unheard-of in Victorian society for people to have relations outside of wedlock, but their openness about their love was simply scandalous.

At a time when women writers were few, she not only wrote fiction to her heart's content but also became the assistant editor of the *Westminster Review.* She called herself Marian Evans for a while, molding

★ Louisa May Alcott, *Good Wives* (Mont.: Kessinger Publishing, 2010), 29.

her name, seeing how it felt to have a masculine moniker. In her attempt to distance herself from the female novelists who produced romances, she decided that she needed a male pen name. To honor her love for Lewes, she adopted his name, George, and then picked out Eliot because it fit well with the first name.

In 1856 Lewes sent a story titled "The Sad Fortunes of the Reverend Amos Barton" to his publisher, claiming that it was written by a "clerical friend." The publisher wrote back saying he would publish the story and congratulating this new writer for being "worthy of the honors of print and pay." Thus began a new stage in Eliot's literary career. She wanted to remain incognito as long as she could, enjoying the advantages of being anonymous, and thereby unreachable. Her nom de plume enabled her to transcend Victorian gender roles, and carve for herself a greater zone of existence.

One evening at a party, Lewes read aloud a spellbinding story by Eliot and asked his guests to guess what kind of a person the author was. All of them came to the conclusion that the story was written by a man—a Cambridge man, well educated, a clergyman married with children. (Similar reactions were received when Eliot's stories were sent to other writers. Only Charles Dickens thought the author had to be a woman. Only he got it right.)

I love to imagine this scene: in a high-ceilinged apartment, a dozen or so guests sitting comfortably on cushioned sofas and armchairs, sipping their drinks, eyeing one another furtively as they listen to a story by an unknown author, their eyes rapt in the flames in the fireplace, their minds miles away as they try to guess the gender of the writer, and fail.

In her popular masterpiece *Middlemarch,* which Virginia Woolf famously described as "one of the only English novels written for grown-up people," Eliot created an impressive character named Dorothea. She is intelligent, passionate, generous and ambitious—in all probability a representation of the author herself. It is a constant disappointment to feminist scholars that neither Dorothea nor Eliot's other female characters ever achieved the sort of success or freedom that she enjoyed. But does a woman writer need to create fictional role models to inspire her female readers? Like all good storytellers, Eliot found pleasure in combining challenge and compassion. "If art does not enlarge men's sympathies it does nothing morally," she wrote. Contrary to the common belief, she wasn't someone who despised all things deemed to be womanly. Though she had masculine features, a cherished male pen name, a certain bias toward women writers and chutzpah that was, at the time, deemed fit for a man, she also enjoyed her femininity to the fullest. It was this unusual blend that mesmerized those who met her in person.

After the death of Lewes, she married a man twenty years her junior with whom she shared common intellectual ground. Like Zelda Fitzgerald she fell in love with brains first; like Ayn Rand she could be imposing in her private affairs. She died shortly afterward in 1880, at the age of sixty-one. She was buried in Highgate Cemetery in an area reserved for religious dissenters—even in death, not quite fitting in.

Louisa May Alcott and George Eliot, two contemporary women writers with a common passion for storytelling, one of them regarded as the voice of feminine writing, and the other known as a defeminized author—both equally unconventional in their ways. They remind me, across centuries and cultures, that there are other paths for a woman than conventional marriage and motherhood. Perhaps marriage is less a legal arrangement or social institution than a book awaiting interpretation. Every reader brings his or her own gaze to the text, and ends up reading the story differently.

One Blue, One Pink

Two years after saying "I do" in Berlin, I'm shaking like a leaf on the bathroom floor in Istanbul. The tiles on the walls are painted emerald and streaked with dark green ivies that suit your mood perfectly when you feel like a leaf.

I had spent the last year and a half teaching at the University of Arizona as a full-time tenure-track professor in Near Eastern studies. Moving from chilly Ann Arbor to sunny Tucson required a radical change in my wardrobe, which, thank God, consisted of two suitcases. During this entire time I had been commuting like crazy between Tucson and Istanbul, and now here I am, sitting with my back to the bathtub, taking deep breaths to calm my thumping heart.

In my hand there is a tiny object. It feels odd to attribute so much importance to an object this small and plastic, but that is how it is. On the back of the box it came in it reads: "If two lines appear on the screen it shows pregnancy. One single blue line indicates lack of it."

But at the moment I avoid looking at the screen, focusing instead on every other trivial detail, such as the date of expiration and the place of manufacture. It is made in China. That is why it cost me one-third of the price of the other home pregnancy test kits at the drugstore. I wonder how reliable it is. Doesn't it say in the newspapers that Chinese toys can cause allergies? How about Chinese test kits, could they give false positives?

More curious about the reliability of the product in my hand than my own physical condition, my gaze slides down to the small white screen. Relief. Oh, good. There is only one line. Blue. I wasn't ready for the second line. I can go now. But there is a nagging suspicion at the back of my mind, and something tells me not to hurry, not so soon. Then, just as I feared, taking its sweet time, the pink line appears.

Why doesn't the pink line come first and then the blue one? Or why don't they appear simultaneously? There would be less anticipation that way and far less apprehension. Have the Chinese manufacturers designed it this way to make it more exciting for women?

It takes me a few minutes to stop quarreling with the Chinese manufacturers and acknowledge my situation. Slowly but surely my mind recognizes what my heart has already accepted: I am pregnant.

Now what? I need to talk with someone but whom? The first thought that pops into my head is to consult with the finger-women. Yet I quickly abandon the idea. I can't tell them anything yet. Especially not Milady Ambitious Chekhovian, who, I fear, will tear the walls down. Nor Miss Highbrowed Cynic, I definitely can't tell her either. Even talking to Dame Dervish sounds like a lame idea. She will not give me advice to solve this predicament; instead she'll want me to figure it out on my own. But I am far too panicked for that.

Who can I speak to if I can't speak to them?

That's when I recall Mama Rice Pudding. She is the only one among the Thumbelinas who knows anything about babies and pregnancies. But where is she now? How is she doing? I haven't spoken to her since that night under the Brain Tree. I need to see her urgently. But will she talk to me? I'm sure she is still quite upset and will not respond if I send her an invitation. I guess I should go and find her.

Once again, I take a flickering candle and descend into the labyrinth of my soul. Again, I find it very confusing down here, where there are no road signs, no traffic lights. I don't know where Mama Rice Pudding lives and can't imagine what her house looks like.

After an hour of toiling I find her house. It is made out of a milk carton, complete with lace curtains and pots filled with tulips, carnations and hyacinths on its window ledge. I press the doorbell. It chirps a merry tune of singing birds.

"What do you want?" she asks when she opens the door and sees me.

She is wearing a rose-patterned dress and has her hair done up with multihued clips. She seems to have gained a bit more weight. On her feet are fuchsia-colored slippers with pompoms. She wears a red and white polka-dotted kitchen apron that has "Super Cook" written across the top. A divine smell wafts from inside the house. Something sweet and fruity.

"I want to apologize for breaking your heart," I say meekly. "I don't know how to make it up to you, and I fear that now it might be too late. It is just that there is something urgent we need to talk about. May I come inside?"

"Sorry," she says frostily. "I'm kind of in a rush and don't have time for you."

She looks over her shoulder toward her kitchen counter, as if she were about to slam the door in my face. Perhaps she is.

"I have food on the stove," she says. "I'm making beef kebab with artichokes. It is a special recipe that requires maximum attention. I'm also preparing strawberry marmalade. If it boils for too long the sugar will crystallize. I need to go back to my work."

"Wait, please."

Words get clogged in my throat, but I manage to utter an intelligible sentence: "Look, I don't know what to do and I'm scared. I need someone to talk to, but the other finger-women won't understand. Only you can help me."

"And why is that?" she asks, raising an eyebrow.

"Because I am pregnant."

The door springs wide open, a shriek of delight pierces the air and out runs Mama Rice Pudding, her face blossoming with life, her arms open wide. She jumps up and down with joy. I have never seen anyone receive news with so much glee, and for a second, I fear she has lost her mind.

"Congratulations!" she yells, staring at me wide-eyed, like a child at a circus.

"Listen to me, please. My mind is so confused I don't know what to do or how to feel. I guess I wasn't prepared for this, you know."

"Great! Fabulous! Oh, bless you!" she yells again. "Come on in, let me give you some food. You need to eat more now."

During the next hour I do nothing but gobble. Though she cannot convince me to eat meat, she makes me devour a generous slice of raspberry cheesecake, and then pushes into my mouth homemade pastries and spoonfuls of marmalade. When she is fully convinced that I cannot possibly eat another morsel she leans back, suddenly serious.

"Well, well. So this is the way of things," she says. "So you want my help?"

I don't like the change in her voice, but I nod all the same.

"All right, I will help you. But there is one condition."

"Which is?"

"There will be a change in the political regime. We are no longer living under martial law, is that understood? We are done with the coup d'état."

"Sure, of course," I say like a good sheep. "I have always wanted the Choir of Discordant Voices to move toward a full-fledged democracy. This will be the beginning of a new era."

"About that . . ." she says, suddenly having a coughing fit.

"Did something get stuck in your throat?"

Mama Rice Pudding gathers herself upright. "I need to make something very clear," she says. "I am not advocating democracy here. Actually, I want to go back to a monarchy again, except this time I will be the queen."

She must be joking. I'm about to scoff but something in her eyes stops me midway.

"Was there democracy when I was being oppressed?" she asks. "Why should I condone a democratic state now that I'm in charge? An eye for an eye, a tooth for a tooth. Time to hoot my toot!"

Suddenly I find her irritating, almost scary.

"Go and make me a golden crown," she says. "Those two crazies of yours are no longer in power. I'll have them rot in Alcatraz!"

"There is an Alcatraz inside me?" I ask.

"No, but I will build one," she roars. "Finally the tables have turned! *Je suis l'état!*★"

On my way back, I stop by Miss Highbrowed Cynic's house and break the news to her. She listens without a word, her face as pale as a white sheet. Together we go to Milady Ambitious Chekhovian's apartment and warn her about the upcoming takeover.

"You can't just get rid of us just like that," says Milady Ambitious Chekhovian, the strength in her voice missing.

"You can't do this to us," repeats Miss Highbrowed Cynic like a nervous parrot.

"There is nothing I can do," I remark. "This pregnancy has changed everything. As of this moment the coup is over."

First there was an oligarchy, then it was a coup d'état, inside me.

Now a monarchy has come to the Land of Me.

★ "I am the state!"

PART FIVE

Beautiful Surrender

Pregnancy Journal

Week 5

Today Mama Rice Pudding has ascended to the throne. She walks around with a crown on her head, and in her hand she carries a scepter no larger than a matchstick. To look taller, she has taken to wearing high heels. When she needs to go from one place to another, I carry her on a palanquin. The timid, rosy-cheeked woman I met on the plane has vanished. In her place is a tyrant.

Her Majesty the Queen's first act has been to create a new constitution. The first clause reads: "Motherhood is Holy and Honorable, and it should be treated as such." Unquestionable, untouchable, unchangeable.

As of now, even the tiniest criticism against marriage or motherhood will be punished by law. Simone de Beauvoir's books have been seized and burned in a huge bonfire. Sylvia Plath, Dorothy Parker, Anaïs Nin, Zelda Fitzgerald and Sevgi Soysal are strictly banned. I am not allowed to read any one of them during my pregnancy.

There is only one book Mama Rice Pudding allows me to keep nearby.

"Read *Little Women*. It will remind you of the importance of familial ties and thus prepare you for motherhood," she says.

"But I read that a long time ago," I complain.

"Just go over it again, then."

I understand that for Mama Rice Pudding there is no difference between reading a book and knitting a sweater. Just as you can knit the same pattern over and over, make the same recipe for years on end, you can also be content with a few books on your bookshelf and "go over them" again and again.

Week 6

This week I have learned that "morning sickness" need not be in the mornings. It can happen anytime.

"Mama Rice Pudding, I feel tired and sleepy all the time—as if I've been carrying a sack of stones," I say. "How will I bear it?"

She hits her scepter on the ground with a thud so loud that the earth trembles under my feet.

"You will bear it just like our mothers and grandmothers and great-grandmothers did. What of the peasant woman who gives birth in the fields after a hard day of work? She cuts the umbilical cord with any available instrument and without a single complaint goes back to hoeing the crop."

Do I look like a heroic peasant woman? I can't even tell barley from buckwheat, but I dare not remind her of this.

"Be grateful that you haven't come to this world as an elephant," says Mama the Queen. "If you were a female elephant you would be pregnant for twenty-two months! Thank your lucky stars!"

Sad for not being a peasant woman but happy for not being an elephant: That is the sum of my mood this week.

Week 8

I am not interested in food, only in snacks. And since most snacks are stuffed with calories, I am afraid I will end up like the plump woman on the steamboat.

In order to snack more healthily I do some shopping: low-fat biscuits, low-fat pretzels, low-fat milk, low-fat yogurt, low-fat cheese—and unsalted rice crackers. When I get home, Mama Rice Pudding jumps off her throne and inspects my grocery bag.

"What is this?"

"Nothing, just a few things to nibble on," I say.

She catapults my bag out the window.

"For shame! You should be embarrassed! No salt, no sugar, low fat, no fat. What is this? Are we running a weight-loss clinic here? Is that Blue Belle Bovary messing with your head? Don't you dare listen to that hussy!"

Befuddled and hurt, I consider how best—or whether—to answer her.

"Your only priority is to eat what is good for the child," she concludes. "So what if your figure changes from size eight to size twenty, who cares?"

My cheeks burn with guilt. Could she be right? Have I put my looks ahead of the health of my child? Her Majesty the Queen teaches me a deep human truth—that motherhood has a pen name: guilt.

Just to be rid of this guilt, I go and eat a huge box of hazelnut cookies. And I don't even like hazelnuts.

Week 12

On TV Christiane Amanpour interviews AIDS orphans in Africa. The CNN crew has ducked into an adobe hut, placed their cameras on strewn straw. The landscape is harsh, unforgiving. With a napkin in my hand, I watch and cry.

These days, all sorts of things bring me to tears. There is a pair of shoes—faded blue Converse sneakers—that dangles from the electric pole around the corner, and every time I pass by them I feel a sense of sorrow well up inside of me. I wonder who they belonged to. How did they end up there? Rain or shine, they are always there—by themselves, so vulnerable, so alone.

It isn't only the sneakers. Boys bullying one another at the playground, two stray cats fighting over a slice of meat in the garbage, the skinny Kurdish street vendor who sells chestnut kebabs with worms, the neighbor lady who beats her carpet out the window and showers the passersby with dust, the melting icebergs in Antarctica, the polluting of the atmosphere, the quagmire in Palestine, a piece of crushed bread on the ground. Everything, and anything, is so distressing. The world crumbles in my fingers like sandstone in the wind and my days are painted with melancholy.

On the evening news they show a dog—a terrier puppy with brown ears and a white body. It has a huge, dazzling bow around its neck. Its owner is a retired chemistry teacher. As the lady chemist plays the piano, the puppy sits at her heels and begins to howl along.

I watch the scene and my eyes fill with tears.

"Why are you crying again?" asks Eyup, his famous patience wearing slightly thin.

"Poor puppy," I say, sobbing.

"What is poor about that puppy? He is probably better fed than thousands of children who go to bed hungry every night."

"Thousands of children go to bed hungry every night," I repeat, on the verge of tears.

"Oh, God, I should never have opened my mouth," Eyup says softly.

He doesn't understand me. How can I make him see that I feel bad for the puppy? I feel bad for all terriers with dazzling bows around their necks. Our lust for baubles of fame, our inability to cope with mortality, our expulsion from the Garden of Eden—my lungs fill with the heaviness of being a mere human. I can't breathe.

Week 16

Mama Rice Pudding hands me a box of CDs. "Take these and listen to each of them at least three times," she commands.

I glance at the box and mumble, "But I don't really like opera."

"They aren't for you, they are for the baby," she says as she starts the CD player and turns it up full blast. A second later Georges Bizet's *The Pearl Fishers* pours into the room and out into the entire neighborhood.

The rug beater across the street pops her head out of her window and looks left and right trying to figure out where the deep male voice is coming from. Suddenly her face comes apart in terrible recognition that the music is coming from our apartment. Squinting her dark, piercing eyes, she peers through our window into my shivering soul.

"Could you please turn the volume down?" I implore Her Majesty.

"Why? The baby is getting her first taste of culture—and learning French. Do you know that babies can hear sounds while in the womb?"

She puts on another CD. We hear the sound of rain hammering a tin roof, followed by the bleating of goats and the tinkling of bells in the distance.

Aghast, I ask, "What is that?"

"The peaceful sounds of Mother Nature," says Mama Rice Pudding. "It is recorded specially for pregnant women. It has a soothing effect on them. A perfect nondrug sleep aid."

"I'm not having any problems falling asleep; actually I'm sleeping a lot," I say, trying to reason, trying to stay calm.

I don't know about the baby, but these sounds are starting to piss me off. "Birds chirping in an Australian rain forest seem like the perfect sleepless aid if you ask me."

"What do you want to listen to, then?" she asks.

"Punk, postpunk, industrial metal. This is the kind of music I always listened to while writing my novels. I could use a dose of Pearl Jam, Chumbawamba, Bad Religion—"

"No way," she says, scrunching up her face. "Forget all that vulgar noise. You are not making a novel. You are making a baby."

So the entire week, Kuzguncuk—one of Istanbul's most peaceful, oldest districts—reverberates with the sounds of cows mooing, ducks quacking, owls hooting and French arias.

Week 18

I don't cry as often anymore, but now everything smells strange. Like a hunting dog that's been released into the woods, with my nostrils flaring I spend the day trailing scents: a pinch of ginger in a huge pot of vegetable soup, the whiff of seaweed even when I am miles away from the shore, the odor of pickle juice on a store counter five blocks away. I walk around like Jean-Baptiste Grenouille in Patrick Suskind's *Perfume*.

Of all the scents there is one that makes my stomach turn and has me running in the opposite direction: coconut.

Who would have ever guessed that Istanbul smells of coconuts! It's like the city was built on a tropical island. Coconuts and their cloying aroma are ubiquitous: the sachets that dangle from the rearview mirrors in cabs, the liquid soaps used in public restrooms, the little white flakes that adorn the tops of bakery cakes, the heavy-scented candles decorating coffee shops and restaurants and the promotional cookies supermarkets give out to customers. When did Turkish people become so fond of coconut?

Istanbul is one large coconut cut in half. The Asian side is one half, the European side the other. I can't find anywhere to hide.

Week 20

We've found out the sex of the baby. It's going to be a girl.

I am happy. Eyup is happy. Mama Rice Pudding is thrilled.

"It is much easier to dress baby girls, and far more fun, too," she says, her eyes brimming.

Female babies are dressed in pale pink, dark pink and fuchsia, while male babies are dressed in dark blue, brown and aquamarine. For little girls you get Barbie dolls and tea sets; for boys, Kalashnikovs and trucks. I wonder if I can raise my daughter differently.

"What is the use of worrying your head over such useless things?" Mama Rice Pudding says when I share my thoughts with her. "Even if you dress your daughter in the color of sapphires or emeralds, the minute she starts school she will embrace pink anyway. She will want to dress up the way her friends and all her favorite characters do. Barbie has a pink house, Dora the Explorer has pink shorts, and Hello

Kitty is actually Hello Pink! Why are you trying to swim against the current?"

That same night in my dream I am swimming in a river as pink as cotton candy. I never see colors in my dreams, at least not to my recollection. I find it exciting to have a Technicolor dream, even if it is in pink.

Week 21

I secretly go to see Miss Highbrowed Cynic. There she is, as always, in a city as bustling with ideas as New York, behind an ornamented iron door, her walls still covered with posters of Che Guevara and Marlon Brando. She is wearing another one of her fringy hippie dresses. A necklace with large blue and purple beads hangs around her neck.

"Your necklace is pretty," I say.

"Do you like it? It was made by the villagers living on the outskirts of Machu Picchu. I bought it to support the locals against the juggernaut of global capitalism."

I can't help but smile. I've missed Miss Highbrowed Cynic—the only finger-woman I know who can go from talking about a simple necklace to analyzing corporate globalization in one breath.

"So, how's the pregnancy going?" she asks.

"Good, I saw the baby in an ultrasound. It's a wonderful feeling."

"Hmm," says Miss Highbrowed Cynic.

"But I feel a little empty inside. I'm always sleeping, crying, eating or smelling coconuts." My voice quivers slightly. "The truth is, I long for the depth of our conversations."

Miss Highbrowed Cynic looks down at her feet as if they are culpable for the situation.

"You and I used to talk about novels, movies, exhibitions and political philosophy. You would bitch about everything, chuck dirt at everyone, criticize cultural hegemony. . . . I've been disconnected from books. Except for *Little Women,* that is."

Miss Highbrowed Cynic lights a cigarette, but seeing my face, she puts it out immediately. She remembers I have quit smoking.

"Did you really miss me?" she asks.

"And how!"

"I missed you, too. We would read together for hours and gossip about other writers. It was fun. We don't get to do that anymore."

She weighs something in her head and then suddenly gives me a wink. "Come, let's read Sevgi Soysal."

"But I can't. She's on the forbidden-authors list," I say uncertainly.

Miss Highbrowed Cynic flushes scarlet with rage. "You've got to be kidding," she bellows. "That mama-woman doesn't know her limits. No one can ban a book."

I agree.

Opening a random page, Miss Highbrowed Cynic reads, and I listen to the lullaby of her voice.

Tante Rosa believed that the day would come where an apple would be an apple, that a father would be a father, that a war would be a war, that the truth would be the truth, that a lie would be a lie, that love would be love, that to be fed up would be to be fed up, that rebelling would be rebelling, that silence would be silence, that an injustice would be an injustice, that order would be order and that a marriage would be a marriage.

Week 22

I don't know how Her Majesty the Queen found out that I had visited Miss Highbrowed Cynic, but she did. Contrary to my fear, she doesn't throw a fit.

"So you missed reading books," she says with a sigh, as if the thought has tired her. Then she pulls out a box from inside her coat.

"What is this?" I ask.

"I bought you a present," she answers. "I thought you might enjoy this."

When I open the package a book falls out: *My Baby and Me*. Apparently it has been read first by Mama Rice Pudding. Some sentences are underlined, some chapters are starred: "Preparing the Baby's Room," "Fabulous Mashed Food Recipes." I thank her and put it down. I'll read it sometime.

My lack of enthusiasm doesn't escape Mama Rice Pudding.

"All right," she concedes. "I might have overreacted when I banned your books and burned all the paper and pens in the house."

I remain silent.

"You are someone who is used to expressing herself through writing. So I have a suggestion for you. Why don't you write to your baby?"

Smiling, I nod. That is the best advice I've ever gotten from Her Highness.

Week 25

Dear Baby (Since I don't know your name yet, I hope you don't mind me referring to you like this.),

This is the first letter I am writing you. I once read that some traditional tribes sustain the belief that babies got to pick their parents. I had laughed at the idea, but now it seems plausible. I imagine you sitting in the sky with angels, skimming through a huge, leather-bound catalog that contains photographs of potential mothers. Under each photograph there is a short description. The angels turn the pages with utmost patience. You look at all the candidates with a buyer's eye.

"Not this one," you say. "No, not this one either—"

Doctors, engineers, housewives and businesswomen pass before your eyes. Even though there are many highly eligible candidates, women who do their jobs well and are very accomplished, you ignore them.

Just then the angel turns another page and my picture pops up. It is not a very good photo of me, my hair is a mess—again—and my makeup is slapdash. I'm wearing my onion-clothes. Under my picture is a description: *Head pickled, chaotic personality, prone to moments of irrationality, has yet to find herself, is actively searching for answers. Loves telling stories. Writer. Columnist. Litterateur.*

Pointing your tiny little finger at my face you remark, "This one could be fun. Let me take a closer look at her."

I don't know why you ended up picking me out of all the potential mothers in the universe. Maybe you are a crazy kind of girl. You find the idea of a perfect mother boring. Or you already know me better than I know myself. Maybe you see the potential in me. Maybe you want to help me overcome my shortcomings. You can be my guide, my best teacher.

Like I said, I don't know why you chose me, but I want you to know that I am honored. I hope I will never make you regret your decision and say, "Of all the moms in the universe, why did I pick this one!"

Your loving mom who looks forward to your arrival,

Elif

Week 28

Mama Rice Pudding insists that I go to prenatal yoga. She says I have to learn breathing techniques.

"I can breathe very well, don't worry," I say.

But she is persistent. She wants the birth to be as natural and wholesome as the ones she thinks our great-great-grandmothers had in the past. I don't point out that our ancestors were hardly poring over yoga sutras before going into labor.

Week 29

There are ten women in the yoga course. Nine of them have their bellies against their noses. Either they are close to the end of their term or this course makes you puff up like a hot-air balloon. Maybe in her attempt to teach us breathing techniques the instructor is filling us up with heated air.

The only woman in the room who isn't pregnant is our instructor: an athletic and joyful Brazilian with long, curly brunette hair. Her pearly-white smile greets me as she introduces me to the group.

"Let us welcome Elif and her baby into our circle of love," she says and closes her eyes, already drifting away.

"Hello," I say to the group, but their eyes, too, are shut.

"First we shall cleanse our chakras. We shall fortify our personal energies. Then we will practice the Pranayama breathing techniques. We will feel the rise from the Sushumna toward our head and then unite with Sahashara."

Having no idea what we are supposed to do but copying the others all the same, I sit cross-legged on the floor, close my eyes and try to concentrate on this new language.

"Now let us feel the aura that wraps our bodies like a warm glove," says the teacher. "Can you feel how delicate it is, almost silken?"

To my amazement, I can feel something, a new presence, except it doesn't quite gently cloak my body but rather harshly pokes at my shoulder.

"Let's all say 'nice to see you' to this soft energy of ours," continues the teacher.

"Nice to see you," I mumble.

"Same here," comes an immediate response that jolts me.

The voice is strangely familiar. Suspicious, I open one eye to find Milady Ambitious Chekhovian standing on my left shoulder, staring at me.

"What are you doing here?" I whisper fiercely.

"Oh, nothing. We haven't talked for a long time and I was curious as to what you were doing with your life."

"Well, here I am."

"You must have quite a bit of time on your hands to be bothering with this nonsense," she says. "The last time I left you, you were writing novels. And now look at you."

I don't know what to say to that and wait for her next sentence.

"Come on, you should be writing fiction right now. Stories, ideas, plots, the world of imagination . . . They are all waiting for you. What are you doing here opening chakras, mumbling Indian words you can't even pronounce? Oh, I wish you had listened to me when I asked you to get your tubes tied."

Meanwhile, the teacher says zealously: "*Yoga* means 'to unite' in the Sanskrit language. Our aim is to ensure the unity of the body, the mind and the soul."

Milady Ambitious Chekhovian snorts. "How about the unity of the finger-women? We are suffering under the worst monarchy."

"Oh, please, give me a break," I say. "Your military regime was even worse."

"And now we are going to enter the realm within, where we will meditate on our heartbeat," says the teacher, "and become One with the universe."

"I'm leaving," says Milady Ambitious Chekhovian. "You stay and become One with whomever you want for 250 lira a session."

Oblivious to my attempts to say something, she jumps on the window ledge, gives a commander's salute and leaves. I close my eyes and sit still but it's no use. I can't give myself over to the class anymore. Perhaps Milady Ambitious Chekhovian is right. Let alone uniting with the universe, I cannot even unite with the Thumbelinas inside.

Week 32

I go out shopping with Mama Rice Pudding and spend hours in maternity stores. I never knew there was an entire fashion industry for babies, with hip and trendy clothes lines. They're so cute and so expensive, especially when you realize that every designer item will be worn for only about a few weeks, not to mention constantly puked, drooled and peed on.

I wonder how many of these baby products we really need. Plastic ducks that quack in the tub, tummy warmers made of organic merino wool, eco-friendly bathrobes for the summer, eco-friendly bathrobes for the winter, special chimes to attach to strollers, nontoxic brushes to clean the ducks in the tub, dinosaur-shaped door stoppers to keep the doors from slamming shut, glow-in-the-dark stickers in the shapes of planets and stars for the ceiling of the nursery—

All this endless bric-a-brac attracts Mama Rice Pudding like a magnet. She runs from one store to another with my credit card in her hand, determined to spend every cent I have on pink, cutesy baby things. She's so lost in the hysteria of shopping I want to run away from her. But where to? Can a pregnant woman steer clear of her maternal side?

Week 34

This week I learn what a huge topic a baby's intelligence is for an impending mother. Your Highness is obsessed with the matter. Omega-3 pills, fish oil capsules and some type of liquid that emits the vilest smell . . . She has been pushing all of these into my mouth with the belief that if I consume enough of them, the baby will be born with a high IQ.

"Caviar is the best," she says. "If a pregnant woman eats two spoonfuls of black caviar every day, chances are the baby will be born a genius."

"According to your theory the people around the Caspian Sea must be fricking brilliant," I say.

She waves off my sarcasm as if shooing a nagging fly. "You just do what I say," she orders.

I don't understand the obsession with IQ. And it is not only Mama Rice Pudding. In the doctors' waiting rooms, on TV programs, in blogs and Web sites, in the newspapers, everywhere and all the time, pregnant women are looking for ways to increase their babies' intelligence score.

"Let's assume for a moment that this IQ-caviar theory is true," I venture.

"All right," Mama Rice Pudding says.

"Let's say that Turkish mothers have created this 'superintelligent baby.' What then? The child is born, and when he is old enough to walk and talk it is clear that he is supergifted. Good at music, painting, sculpture, art or mathematics. He loves to read, too, devouring the classics at the age of five."

"What are you trying to say?" Mama Rice Pudding asks suspiciously.

"My point is, what will happen to these fish-egg babies in an environment that does not reward individual differences and unusual talents? What kind of irony is it to desire a clever baby, but not be able to acknowledge a creative child?"

Mama Rice Pudding bangs her scepter furiously.

"Enough! I know where all of this whining and bellyaching is coming from," she says. "You've been talking to Miss Highbrowed Cynic, haven't you? You are meeting with her behind my back, aren't you?"

Blushing up to my ears, I stop and say no more.

Week 36

It's true. I have been continuing my visits with Miss Highbrowed Cynic on the sly. We draw the curtains, lock the doors and talk about books—just like we used to do in the good old days. Like proper intellectuals we grumble and grouse about everyone else, holding our heads high, feeling like the brightest bulbs in the crystal chandelier of society. I double over with laughter when Miss Highbrowed Cynic throws a bedsheet over her shoulders and takes up a green bean for a scepter; she does a fantastic imitation.

One day, out of the blue, she says, "Did you ever wonder why mothers use the pronoun *we* when addressing their kids?"

"What do you mean?"

"Check it out. They have this funny way of talking. 'Did *we* get dirty?' they say. 'Did *we* get thirsty?' 'Did *we* pee in our pants?'"

I crane my neck forward and listen carefully.

"If the child falls down, the mother starts, 'Oh, honey, did *we* fall down? Nothing happened, it doesn't hurt!' How does she know if it hurts or not? It isn't she who fell down, it's the kid!"

"Yeah, you're right," I say.

"The child has a separate body from his mother's, and as such, he is a different ontological being. Many mothers simply cannot accept this."

"That is so true," I say agreeably.

Suddenly her tone mellows. "Just be yourself," she says. "Don't let Mama Rice Pudding turn you into one of those snow globe moms."

"What is a snow globe mom?"

"You know, those half-hysterical ones who speak to their kids in a high-pitched-toy-frog voice even when they are no longer babies? Who want to breast-feed until the child goes off to college? They've lost their minds with motherhood. They live in a vacuum. Their universe is a snow globe. Colorful and cute inside, no doubt, but overprotective and airless. Don't you become one of—" She leaves the sentence hanging.

"Who? Me? Never!" I say self-assuredly.

"There is a thin line between motherhood and fascism," she declares.

"Trust me," I say. "I won't ever force food into my child's mouth. If she doesn't want to eat, she won't eat. I'll give her plenty of space and freedom from the start. You'll see what a democratic mom I will be."

"Good," exclaims Miss Highbrowed Cynic. "That's my big Self."

Week 38

This week I learned that a pregnant woman's body belongs not to her but to all women.

The other day when I was grocery shopping, an old lady I had never seen before came over and checked my shopping cart.

"Oh, you are buying eggplants," she said with a look of sympathetic horror on her face.

"Yeah," I said cautiously.

"But there is nicotine in them," she said, and turned to the apprentice, as if he were responsible for this terrible mistake. "How can you give her eggplants? Take them back."

The grocer's apprentice nodded, accepting the lady's authority. Without consulting me, he took the eggplants out of my cart.

"Give her broccoli instead," said the old lady.

Again the apprentice did as he was told.

"And some spinach. It is very healthy. Oh, don't forget pepper. Whatever you cook, always put green pepper in it."

Into my cart went a package of spinach and half a pound of green peppers.

"Are you done with my shopping? May I go now?" I asked.

They both grinned at me.

It is the same when I go to the neighborhood pool. All the women feel the need to say something, anything, to help me through another day of gestation.

"Be careful. The floor is quite slippery," says one.

"Better stay in the shade," cautions another woman.

"Make sure you don't dive belly first," says the one next to her.

"Don't swallow chlorine," adds someone else.

On the street, in the bus, on the boat, in cafés and restaurants, complete strangers give me advice. If one of them happens to be eating something, she immediately offers half her food to me.

No matter how many times I say "no, thank you," they insist until I give in. So I walk around munching on other people's sandwiches and cakes. It doesn't matter that I've never met these women or that I'll never see them again. Where there is pregnancy there is no formality. Where there is no formality there is no privacy.

Week 39.5

A wave of tranquillity has come over me. Currents of air gently stir the haze of clouds near the horizon and the tulips of Istanbul sway in full bloom, purple, red and yellow. Suddenly the world is an exquisite place and life is heavenly. I am smiling so much that the muscles around my mouth have slackened.

As I pass by the electric pole today I realize the Converse trainers are no longer there. Someone must have taken them down. How great is that! How lovely the weather, how kind the people, how blue the sky. What a wonderful world!

"It is called happiness hormone," says Mama Rice Pudding. "It is released when a woman nears the time of birth."

For the first time in my life it dawns upon me how much power hormones have on us. I have always thought of myself as one thinking, choosing and creating individual. But how much of our lives and relationships, behaviors and choices, are guided by hormones? If they are capable of boosting up one's morale, can they also do the opposite, propel one deep into gloom? But life is too beautiful to contemplate such unsettling matters, and I simply don't.

Week 41

Panic! The time has come and I am terrified. Her Majesty the Queen is doing everything she can to calm me down, but it is no use. There's only one finger-woman who can help me right now. I need to speak to her.

My belly at my chin, careful not to slip, I descend the stairway to the basement of my soul. There, in a city as spiritual as Mount Athos, beyond a wooden door, I find Dame Dervish, sitting cross-legged on a grape leaf. On her feet are cerulean sandals, around her neck a silver Hu.

"Dame Dervish, may we talk?"

"Of course," she says. "Words are gifts from one human to another."

"Okay, do you remember the time I felt grateful for not being an elephant? Now I wish I were one."

Seeing the expression on her face, I decide to follow a different tack. "I'm not ready for this birth; I don't know what to do. Nine months is too short."

"First, calm down," she says tenderly.

"But what am I going to do?"

"Nothing," she says.

"Nothing?"

"You are so used to doing something all the time, not to have to do anything terrifies you. But it is, in fact, calming to do nothing. Don't worry, your body knows what to do, as do the baby and the universe. All you have to do is just surrender."

Surrender is not a great word with me, so I bite my lip and sigh.

"Do you know that the Sufis believe the world is a mother's womb?" she asks. "We are all babies in a womb. When the time comes we have to leave the world. We know this but we don't want to leave. We fear that when we die we will cease to exist. But death is actually a birth. If we could only understand this we wouldn't be scared of anything."

Imagining the world as one big womb and the billions of us human beings, of all races and religions, waiting to be born into another life has a calming effect on my nerves.

"Dame Dervish," I say. "How I've missed you."

"I've missed you as well," she says. "Now go and surrender. The rest will come of its own accord."

Two days later, early in the morning, I wake Eyup up and we calmly head to the hospital. All of the breathing practices, prenatal yoga, black caviar, broccoli salads and even *Little Women* lose their significance as I surrender.

Books and Babies

Likening children to books is not a common metaphor in the world of literature, but likening books to children surely is. Jane Austen considered her novels as her children and spoke of her heroines as "my Emma," "my Fanny" or "my Elinor." When George Eliot talked about her books, she referred to them as her children. Likewise, Virginia Woolf's diaries teem with references to writing as a maternal experience. While examples abound, I find it intriguing that it is always female writers who employ this metaphor. I have never heard of a male writer regarding his novels as his children.

As widely held as the metaphor might appear, there is one crucial difference between babies and books that should not go unnoticed. Human babies are quite exceptional in the amount and intensity of care that they require immediately after being born. Helpless and toothless, the infant is fully dependent on his or her mother for a long time.

Books, however, aren't like that. They can stand on their own feet starting from birth—that is, from their publication date—and they can instantly swim, just like newborn sea turtles: excitedly, doggedly, unsteadily—from the warm sands of publishing houses toward the vast, blue waters of readers.

Or perhaps novels resemble baby ducklings. As soon as they open their eyes to the world, they take whomever they see first to be their mothers. Instead of the authors, "the mothers" may be their editors, their translators or, yes, their loving readers. If indeed that is the case, once the books are born, their authors do not really need to keep an eye on them or discuss them; just like books do not need to give interviews, pose for photographers or tour around. It is we writers and poets who crave the recognition and the praise. Otherwise, books are in no need of being nursed by their authors.

One woman writer who jeered at the egos and ambitions looming in the world of art and culture was the legendary Dorothy Parker. Five feet tall and slight, her physical presence may not have been overwhelming, but the words that poured forth from her pen still astonish and amuse readers today. In her capacity as the "most renowned lady wit in America," the sharp-tongued critic for *Vanity Fair* and *The New Yorker* wrote about a wide range of topics without hiding her claws. She was the most taciturn member of the famous Algonquin Round Table and yet she remains the most renowned of them all.

Having a special knack for loving the wrong kind of men, ever-impossible men, she suffered from several unhappy affairs, depressions, miscarriages and an abortion. But perhaps none of her relationships left a deeper mark on her life than her on-again, off-again marriage to the actor and playwright Alan Campbell. Like two planets orbiting around the same path but never really meeting, they tired each other out endlessly—until the day in 1963 when Campbell committed suicide. Parker herself survived several suicide attempts throughout the years—each episode, perhaps, worsening her addiction to alcohol.

As a fierce advocate of gender equality and civil rights, Parker was critical of the dominant social roles of her era. In her poems, short stories and essays, she questioned all sorts of clichés and taboos. One of her earlier poems summarizes her take on life.

> If I abstain from fun and such,
> I'll probably amount to much;
> But I shall stay the way I am,
> Because I do not give a damn.

Her close friendships with Dashiell Hammett and Lillian Hellman have been a favorite topic among literary historians. Years later, when asked if there was ever any competition between the two women writers, Hellman replied, "Never." Theirs was a dependent relationship, of which she claimed, "I think between men and women there should be dependency, even between friends. . . . Independent natures aren't worried about dependency." In the paranoia of the early 1950s, it didn't take long for them to make their way onto the famous Hollywood blacklist. Not that they cared much. They were creative and self-destructive; they were members of a generation that drank, quarreled, argued and laughed abundantly; and they died either too early or too depressed.

Parker was not a great fan of romantic love, domestic life or motherhood. When she spotted a mother who fussed over her child in public, she didn't waste any opportunity to pass judgment on the scene. To her, motherhood seemed like some kind of entrapment and perpetual unhappiness. Her mind was corrosive, her mood volatile, her sarcasm legendary and her dark eyes brimful of mischief—almost up until the moment that she died of a heart attack at the age of seventy-three, alone in a hotel room.

If ever there was a voice in the world of literature throbbing with rage, compassion, justice and love—all at the same time, all with the same vigor—it was Audre Lorde's. She was a soul with many talents and multiple roles: poet, writer, black, woman, lesbian, activist, cancer survivor, educator and mother of two children. Early on she had changed her name from Audrey to Audre not only because she liked the symmetry with her last name but also because she simply could. She loved re-creating herself again and again, remolding her heart and her destiny, like two pieces of soft dough. In a ceremony held before her death she was given yet another name, Gamba Adisa—"Warrior: She Who Makes Her Meaning Lucid."

At times, she was her own mother, and at times, her own daughter. She saw herself as a link in an endless chain, as part of a "continuum of women." Bridging differences across the boundaries, challenging racism, sexism and homophobia, Lorde encouraged what she saw as "the transformation of silence into language." Through words we understood ourselves and each other, and brought out the inner wisdom that existed in each and every one of us. Connecting was one of the things she did best—writer and reader, white and black, sister and sister. "I am who I am, doing what I came to do, acting upon you like a drug or chisel to remind you of your me-ness, as I discover you in myself."★

In her autobiographical novel, *Zami: A New Spelling of My Name*, Lorde took a closer look at her childhood in Harlem and her coming-of-age as a black lesbian feminist. She said she had always wanted to be both man and woman, adding into her personality the strongest and richest qualities of both her mother and her father. Her writing was suffused with the belief that the synthesis between seeming opposites was perhaps what made us ourselves. In every woman there were masculine traits and in every man, the feminine. As such, treating the two sexes as if they were mutually exclusive was a big deception and a step away from understanding humanness in all its complexity and fullness.

Strikingly, motherhood is redefined in Lorde's work and glorified without being sanctified. It is divine but there is nothing sacred about it. Lorde believed that there was a black mother in all of us, whether we were mothers or not. Men, too, had this quality inside, although quite often they chose not to deal with it. Lorde's metaphor of the black mother was the voice of intuition, creativity and unbridled passion. "The white fathers told us 'I think, therefore I am,' and the Black mother within each of us—the poet—whispers in our dream, 'I feel, therefore I can be free.'"

Lorde did not reject rationality or empiricism outright, but wanted to make it clear, once and for all, how limiting each was in grasping the world. Too much analytical thinking and worship of abstract theory did not sit well with her. Her connection with language and her hand on the pulse of the universe was unashamedly sensual. She regarded selfhood—and, therefore, womanhood and motherhood—

★ Audre Lorde, *Sister Outsider: Essays, Speeches* (Berkeley: Crossing Press, 2007), 12.

as essentially multilayered. Thus she refused to be pigeonholed into any single and static category. She was always many things at once, and after her death, she remains so.

If Audre Lorde were alive today and we had met, she would probably have laughed at my six finger-women and then brought out her own numerous finger-women so that they could all dance together under a warm summer rain.

Sandra Cisneros is an eloquent writer and an outspoken scholar who calls herself "nobody's mother and nobody's wife." She has always talked candidly and courageously about the difficulties—and beauties—of being a single woman from a patriarchal background and a writer on the border of two cultures, Mexican and American. She says, "I think writers are always split between living their life and watching themselves live it."

Born in Chicago in 1954, the only daughter in a family of six sons, Cisneros closely observed the making of manhood and how painful it could be for those who did not fit into given gender roles. Though she grew up in a crowded, noisy house, she received a lot of love from both parents and was given her own space. "I am the product of a fierce woman who was brave enough to raise her daughter in a nontraditional way," she says.

Cisneros says she wants to tell the kind of stories that do not get told. *The House on Mango Street* is the riveting story of Esperanza, a Mexican-American girl growing up in the Hispanic quarter of Chicago. The book deals openly with machismo, chauvinism and the struggle of a woman of color to find her own voice. Esperanza soon discovers that writing heals her wounds, frees her soul. It helps her to develop her natural talents, find out who she really is and resist all kinds of indoctrination that limit her choices in life due to her gender, culture or class.

Questioning both Mexican and American constructions of femininity, Cisneros wants to explore alternative models of womanhood. Her views on marriage and motherhood have always been controversial. In an interview she says in many ways she still feels like a child. And precisely because of this, because she is still one of *them,* she doesn't pick up children and fuss over them. That is not what one child does to another. Cisneros explains how throughout her twenties and thirties she put off marrying and starting a family in order to focus on her writing and work. When she reached her forties, however, she felt like she had to get married soon, not because she wanted to but because her father wanted her to. It took her some more years to realize she didn't need to do this—a realization that brought her to a final decision: She would not get married. When asked why she chose not to start a family of her own, her response is intriguing: "My writing is my child and I don't want anything to come between us."

Dorothy Parker, Audre Lorde and Sandra Cisneros—women who refused to identify female creativity with reproduction and pursued their writing with passion. We learn from them to look with a new perspective into the making of womanhood, sisterhood and manhood, respectively. Reading their works wakes up our souls, pierces the shell of our daily habits. Learning more about their lives makes us realize that the cultural predispositions that have been bred in each and every one of us since early childhood are neither incontestable nor unchangeable. True, the three of them led different personal lives and came from diverse backgrounds. But there is one thing they have in common: They did not take gender roles and barriers for granted. They questioned the established norms and, most important, changed the world by changing themselves first.

A Sea without a Shore

The baby is sleeping in the crib. Whoever came up with the expression "to sleep like a baby" doesn't know what he is talking about. Babies doze in bits and pieces, waking every so often as if to check whether you are still there and the birth were not only a dream.

As for me, I don't sleep at all. The second I close my eyes, unpleasant thoughts and discomforting images barrage my brain. Who knew that my head was such an arsenal of anxieties? I haven't been able to sleep properly for days. Around my eyes there are circles as dark beige and round as the *simits*★ of Istanbul. Never had it entered my mind that my heart could hold so bleak an anguish.

I am wearing a long, lavender nightgown with sporadic shapes across the breast line. One of the shoulder straps has snapped and been tied into a hasty knot. But because one strap is now shorter than the other, the neckline—from a distance—looks sloped, giving the impression that I am sliding to one side, like a sinking ship. Perhaps I am. As for the shapes on the gown, though they seem to be the creation of a crazy fashion designer, they are in fact breast milk and puke stains.

It has been seven weeks since I gave birth.

I want to be a brilliant, perfect mother but I end up doing everything wrong. I am all thumbs when it comes to changing diapers, burping the baby or figuring out how to end bouts of hiccups. My

---

★ *Simit* is a popular street food made with dough and sesame.

self-confidence has become a scoop of ice cream melting fast under the duress of motherhood. It would have helped if Eyup were by my side, but he has gone to serve his compulsory military duty. For the next six months he will get military training in a small division in North Cyprus, and I will be on my own.

Five nights a week a television channel shows reruns of *Wheel of Fortune* for those who cannot sleep. Two blond women in skimpy miniskirts and glittery tops turn the letters on the manually operated puzzle board. I sit and watch. The letters spell D_ PR_ _ _ ION, but I refuse to read it aloud.

Meanwhile, a giant wheel of fortune is spinning inside my brain, flashing its gaudy bulbs. I apportion my daily tasks into slots of different colors and give points to each, except they are all negative.

Causing the baby to puke by lifting her up too fast from the crib	-15 points
Yelling at people, taking your own mistakes out on others	-25 points
Feeling unusually untalented	-30 points
Panicking when the baby cries and crying with her	-50 points
Not stopping crying even after the baby has quieted down	-70 points

At the end of each day, I add up my points, always ending in the red. My record of motherhood so far resembles a plummeting stock-exchange index. I have a deep suspicion that other women were told to spend years preparing themselves for the transition that comes with the birth of a baby, and I missed the memo. How am I—who could not even manage womanhood naturally and effortlessly—now going to manage motherhood?

I know I need help but it never occurs to me to ask for it.

I think of Doris Lessing—a remarkable writer and pursuer of ideas. Born in Persia in 1919, the Nobel laureate spent her childhood on a farm in Southern Rhodesia (Zimbabwe). She was raised by a domineering mother and sent to a Catholic school, where she was taught to be a proper and pious lady. She remembers much of her colonial childhood today as a time with "little joy and much sadness." Lessing dropped out of school when she turned thirteen, ran away from her home and from her mother two years later and basically had to raise herself.

She was a girl-woman who mothered herself.

When she turned nineteen, Lessing got married and had two children, a son and a daughter—a revolutionary experience that she talks about in great detail in her two-volume autobiography, *Under My Skin* and *Walking in the Shade*. She writes candidly about the conflicting feelings she had during this period—a longing to spend more time with other new mothers, talking about babies and mashed food, and an equally strong desire to run away from them all. Lessing is highly critical of the ways in which many capable women seem to change after giving birth. She believes such women are happily domesticated for a while, but then sooner or later they start getting restless, demanding and even neurotic. "There is no boredom like that of an intelligent young woman who spends all day with a very small child," she says. Looking back at the early years of motherhood, she is surprised to see how hard she worked and how tired she was all the time. "I wonder how I did it. I swear young mothers are equipped with some sort of juice or hormone that enables them to bear it."★

The triple role of housekeeper, mother and wife did not make Lessing happy. In 1943 she left her husband and two children to get married to Gottfried Lessing, a Communist activist. They had a son, Peter. The marriage ended in 1949. By this time she was unable to bear life in Rhodesia, particularly the racism of the white ruling class. Taking her son, some money and many ghosts with her, she moved back to Britain. It was a big, painful decision and one that required her to leave her two children with her first ex-husband. She came to England with the manuscript of her first novel, *The Grass Is Singing*.

★ Moyra Davey, ed., *Mother Reader: Essential Writings on Motherhood* (New York: Seven Stories Press, 2001), 11.

The book was published a year later and henceforth Lessing dedicated herself fully to writing.

A cauldron boils in my mind. What if I fail to become a good mother and a good wife? I do not want to betray myself or to pretend to be someone I am not. What scares me most is the possibility of an adverse chemical reaction between authorship and domestic responsibilities. Novelists are self-enamored people who do not like to draw attention to that fact. Mothers, on the other hand, are supposed to be selfless creatures—at least for a while—who give more than they take. Perhaps I am worrying too much, but worrying comes with thinking.

How can I tell my brain not to think?

Eyup calls whenever he can between field exercises. The line is always crackly and there is stomping and marching, shouting and yelling, in the background, which is the complete opposite of my life in Istanbul, where I watch Baby TV and listen to the rain fall on the begonias.

"Hello, sweetheart," Eyup says.

"Hi there," I say. "How's it going, my love?"

"I lost eight pounds," he says, "but I'm surviving. We do a hundred push-ups, a hundred lift-ups and run two miles every morning. I now have biceps like Chuck Norris and my face is so tanned from exposure to the sun that I would stand out even in a dark alley."

I smile—as if he could see me.

"I've missed you sorely," he says, his voice wavering a little.

"I've missed you, too."

"What were you doing when I phoned?"

"I was putting ten droplets of gripe water onto a spoon for the baby's hiccups and thinking about Doris Lessing."

"Does it help?"

"Not really, perhaps it makes it worse."

"Which one? Gripe water or Doris Lessing?"

"Both," I say.

There is a brief silence at the end of the line. Then, softly, Eyup says,

"Honey, you are thinking too much. That makes things harder for you."

"What do you mean?"

"Many people do not constantly analyze and reanalyze every little thing, you know, they just go along with the daily routine," he remarks. "Like when you know you have to do a hundred push-ups, you just accept and do it."

"You want me to start doing push-ups?" I ask.

"Come on, you know what I mean," he says with a gentle laugh. "Can't you do without thinking for a while?"

"I don't know," I say. "Let me think about that."

Why Are We Depressed When We Want to Be Happy?

The next day in the evening, the Choir of Discordant Voices begins to yammer inside me. I ask all of them the same question: How is it possible to feel so down when I am, in fact, happy and grateful?

1. "Yo, it's 'cause of the hormones," says Little Miss Practical. "Everything will be just fine. We can run a few tests and see what the problem is. Take some happy pills. You know what they call them: 'bottled smiles.' The mighty hand of Western science will fix the problem in a jiffy. Call the doctor and ask for help. Let them solve this. Be practical!"

She could be right. I should call my doctor. But my pride—or vanity—won't let me do it. I don't want anyone to feel sorry for me or make assumptions about my sanity. My doctor has always been friendly and fatherly, and we have a superb relationship; I don't want him to see me in my freak-on-wheels moment.

"Let me pull myself together first, then I'll talk to him," I say.

So I make a plan: I will go to see a professional when I am much better and no longer need to go to see a professional.

2. "Forget about doctors and pills. What you need is books," prompts Miss Highbrowed Cynic. "You feel demoralized because you are not reading enough. You have missed the intellectual

world. You have missed me. All this baby food and diaper
changing have numbed your brain. You need to reactivate your
intellect, that's all."

She could be right. My mind might settle into some kind of order
if I start reading novels again. If I focus on other people's stories, I'll
stop running in circles around my own. Proust will save me.

But there is something I can't confess to Miss Highbrowed Cynic.
I have started to suspect that in the months following birth a new
mother's brain doesn't work like it used to. I couldn't read even if I
wanted to. Forget Proust, I can't even focus on a tomato soup recipe.

3. "You don't need books, what you need is to take that horrible
nightgown off and put on something sexy," suggests Blue Belle
Bovary. "If only you paid a little attention to your appearance it
would push that depression right out the door. Let me take you to
a hairdresser. Don't you know that the first thing women should
do when they are down is to change their hair? A new cut and a
new color will cure the deepest melancholy, darling."

She could be right. I might feel better after a visit to the hairdresser,
and from there, to the shopping mall. But I just don't feel like it. Quite
to the contrary, I want to cling more firmly to my oily hair, my pallid
skin, my tattered clothes. In a world that feels increasingly foreign,
only this nightgown is familiar and comforting.

4. "Pure nonsense," objects Milady Ambitious Chekhovian. "The
only reason why you are down in the dumps is because you are
producing below your full capacity. I have to get you out of here
immediately. Let's arrange a book tour for you. We need to get
back to work."

She could be right. If there was a literary festival or a book signing
now, I could possibly ditch this gloomy mood. It is always a morale

boost to meet my readers, listen to their sincere comments, answer their questions and do more readings. But I have little, if any, ambition or desire these days. How can I sign books when my hands are tucked into my armpits for warmth all the time? As Jane Smiley beautifully shows in her *13 Ways of Looking at the Novel,* there is a difference between the novelist as a literary person and the novelist as a literary persona.

Smiley says the literary persona is always a more mature personality, more polished and worked upon and with a different set of duties and responsibilities. It is shaped by three major inspirations—literature, life and language—and is therefore not fully in the author's control.

If Smiley is right, and I think she is, then the gap between my literary persona and me as a living person has never been wider. There is a huge postpartum canyon stretching between the two sides now.

5. "What Milady says is sheer gibberish!" snorts Mama Rice Pudding. "You're feeling this way because you are not focused enough on being a mother, that's all. This is the time when you have to put everything else aside, all that artistic and literary gobbledygook, and be a full-time mom. Only then will you come out of this depression."

She could be right. Spending time with my lovely daughter makes me feel good, elated and blessed. Perhaps I should close myself off to the outside world and just be a mom from now on. Perhaps I am depressed because I haven't fully enacted that decision yet.

But there is something I can't explain to Mama Rice Pudding, something that I know she would never understand: In a society where motherhood is regarded as the best thing that can happen to a woman and with an upbringing that tells us to settle for nothing less than excellence, how can I not compare myself to other mothers? And when I weigh myself against other moms, how can I not be envious of their accomplishments and ashamed of my deficiencies? I am not proud of feeling this way but this is what I experience deep down. It is not my love for my baby that I doubt. Love is there, pure and tender, enveloping my soul in its pearly glow. It is my talents as a mother that I find lacking.

6. "Try to see this as a test," says Dame Dervish. "God likes to try us from time to time. He does so through failure and vulnerability sometimes, success and power at other times, and believe me, we don't always know which case is worse. But remember one thing: Where there is difficulty there follows ease."

She could be right. I must not forget that this is a temporary phase and probably some good will come out of it, though I cannot see that now. Later on when I look back with hindsight, I will judge things from a different and brighter perspective.

But there are some things I cannot reveal to Dame Dervish. I know there are thousands of people out there who try hard to have children, who put themselves through all sorts of medical procedures, make huge sacrifices and suffer endless frustrations, individually and as a couple, and yet still cannot reach their goal. I know how appreciative I should be, and I am, but my embarrassment for not being happy enough, thankful enough or good enough is so profound, I cannot even talk to God anymore.

All I know is that after a period of oligarchy and a short interval of military rule, this monarchy, too, has come to an end. Now there is only anarchy in the Land of Me.

The Celestial Eye

When I was a little girl, maybe six or seven years old, I stayed with my paternal grandmother for a few weeks in Smyrna. The idea was to make sure I got to see my father and spend quality time with him, but I ended up seeing more of my grandma than my dad. She was a stern woman who wore large glasses that magnified her eyes and spoke in sharp, curt sentences that usually boiled down to "Do that! Don't do this!" She often talked about the fires of hell, which she described in vivid and frightful detail. To her, Allah was an unblinking Celestial Eye that saw everything I did and recorded every single one of my sins, even the ones I only thought about.

I came back from her house with a glowing imagery of blazing flames and boiling cauldrons, and the idea of God as an austere father frowning down at His creation. I don't know if this experience had any role in my choices later on, but as soon as I was old enough to know what the word *agnostic* meant—that is, around the time I was seventeen years old—I decided I was going to be one. I have never felt close to atheism—for I found it too arrogant in its outright rejection of God—but agnosticism seemed befitting of people who were perpetually bewildered about things, including religion. For an atheist, faith is not a very important matter. For an agnostic, however, it is. An atheist is sure of his convictions, and speaks in sentences that end with a full stop. An agnostic puts only a comma at the end of his remarks, to be continued. . . . He will keep pondering, wondering, doubting. That is why he is an agnostic.

I went to college to major in international relations. At the time, I was a rebellious young woman who liked to wrap several shawls of "-isms" around her shoulders: I was a leftist, feminist, nihilist, environmentalist, anarcho-pacifist. . . . Though taking questions of faith seriously, I wasn't interested in any specific religion, and the difference between "religiosity" and "spirituality" was lost on me. Nevertheless, having also spent several years of my childhood with my maternal grandmother, I had a feeling there was more to this universe than I could take in with my five limited senses. But the truth is, I wasn't interested in *understanding* the world. I wanted only to *change* it.

Then one day Dame Dervish came into my life. She introduced herself as my spiritual side and explained to me that the Creator was not a nucleus of "fear," but a Fountain of Limitless Love. A kind of wonder possessed me. At first, her very presence in my life was more intriguing than anything she said. Around her was an aura of light and calmness, like the moonlight shining on a gently rolling sea. Motivated by her, I started to read about Sufism. One book led to another. The more I read the more I unlearned. Because that is what Sufism does to you, it makes you "erase" what you know and what you are so sure of. Then you start thinking again. Not with your mind this time, but with your heart.

Of all the Sufi poets and philosophers that I read about during those years there were two that moved me deeply: Rumi and his legendary spiritual companion, Shams of Tabriz. Living in thirteenth-century Anatolia, in an age of deeply embedded bigotries and clashes, they had stood for a universal spirituality, opening their doors to people of all backgrounds equally. They spoke of love as the essence of life, their universal philosophy connecting all humanity across centuries, cultures and cities. As I kept reading the *Mathnawi,* Rumi's words began to tenderly remove the shawls I had always wrapped around myself, layer upon layer, as if I were always in need of some warmth coming from outside. I understood that no matter what I chose to be—"leftist," "feminist" or anything else—what I most needed was an intimate connection with the light inside me. The light of Truth that exists inside all of us.

Thus began my interest in Sufism and spirituality. Over the years it would ebb and flow. Sometimes it was more vivid and visible, at other times it receded to the background, faint and dusky, like the remains of a candle still burning, but at no stage in my life did it ever disappear.

Then why is it that now, after having devoured so many books on spirituality and religious philosophy, after having been through thick and thin with Dame Dervish, I once again feel like that timid girl in Smyrna? These days I cannot raise my eyes to the sky for fear that God might be looking down at me with his brows drawn over his eyes. Is that what depression is about—the sinking feeling that your connection to God is broken and you are left to float on your own in a liquid black space, like an astronaut who has been cut loose from his spaceship and all that linked him to Earth?

PART SIX

Dark Sweetness

The pen puts its head down
To give a dark sweetness to the page.

—Rumi

A Djinni in the Room

One morning in November when I wake up, I sense a strange presence in the room. The baby is two months old and is sleeping better now. There is a dusky light penetrating through the curtains, a whispery sound in the background and a perfumed smell in the air. I shiver as if being pushed into a Murakami novel where everything is surreal.

There is a creature in the corner—not human, not animal, not like anything I have seen before. He is as dark gray as storm clouds, as tall as a tower, as elusive as a will-o'-the-wisp. He has a long, black ponytail, though he has dyed a clump of it white and let it hang across his face. A diamond the size of a hazelnut glitters on one ear. His face is small, his goatee is tiny, but his fiery eyes appear enormous behind his metal-rimmed spectacles. One second he stretches up, his head reaching the ceiling; the next he widens, spreading from one end of the room to the other. Like thick cigar smoke he drifts in the air. In his hand he carries a beautiful cane and on his head is a silk top hat.

I immediately recognize him as one of the djinn my maternal grandmother warned me against in my childhood. I don't know anything about their sexual orientation, but this one seems gay to me.

"Who are you?" I ask fretfully.

"Ah, but don't you recognize me?" he says, chivalrous and poised, as if he were a brave knight and I, a damsel in distress.

"No, what do you want?"

"Please, *cheri*," he says snippily. "Have you never heard of the djinni who haunts new mothers?"

I give a sobbing breath and my face gets hot. "My grandma says there is a djinni named Alkarısı, known to molest women who have recently given birth."

He cracks a laugh. "The times are changing fast, *cheri*. Alkarısı is so old-school. She retired long ago, that minx. Today nobody knows about her anymore. She wouldn't make it to the top ten."

I am surprised to hear the djinn have a top ten list, but instead of asking about this, I remark, "I didn't know you guys could age."

Taking a napkin from his pocket, he begins to wipe his glasses. "Of course we do age, though we haven't lost our minds over Botox creams, like your kind. At least not yet—"

I look at him more closely, only now suspecting that he might not be as young as he looks.

Putting his glasses back on, he continues: "Of course, we don't age as quickly as you poor sons of Adam and daughters of Eve. Your ten years are approximately"—he makes some calculations in his head—"equal to 112 years in djinn time. So a hundred-year-old djinni is just a kid where we come from. As for Alkarısı, how should I put it? Her name is synonymous with *nostalgia*."

"Do djinn have nostalgia?"

"Not us, you guys do! Don't you ever watch Disney movies? They use us as decor. I mean, what is that thing about the djinni in a lamp? We are living in the twenty-first century, hello! No one hangs out in lamps anymore!"

"Do djinn find Disney movies politically incorrect?" I ask, mesmerized.

"You, too, would feel the same way if your kind were portrayed as pudgy-bellied, five-chinned, blue ogres with baggy trousers and fezzes on their heads," he flares. "Don't you see we've all adjusted to the times? I go to the gym four days a week and I don't have an extra ounce of fat on my body."

"Who are you, for God's sake?!"

Like a good gentleman he tips his hat and bows to me with a roguish smile. "My sincere apologies if I forgot to introduce myself. I am your obedient servant, the Djinni of Postpartum Depression. Otherwise known as Lord Poton."

I feel a chill go down my spine. "What do you want?" I ask, although I am not sure I want to hear the answer.

"What do I want?" he prompts. "It is a good question because, as it happens, my wish is your command."

"Hmm, shouldn't it be the other way round?"

"As I said, forget those clichés. Let's get to know each other better."

Lord Poton is such a shifty being that I don't immediately realize how creepy he can be. For the first couple of days I watch him more out of curiosity than worry. Little do I realize that he is settling in during that time, making himself at home. Then one day, he produces a lockbox.

"What is that?"

"It's my gift to you," he says, grinning. "Don't you always complain about how your finger-women tire you out with their endless quarrels?"

"Yes, but—" I say tentatively.

"Good, I will lock them all away so that they won't bother you anymore."

"Wait a minute," I object. "I want no such thing."

But he doesn't listen to me. "My wish is your command, remember," he whispers, as if to himself. Then he stretches out his manicured nails and pulls the members of the Choir of Discordant Voices out of me, one by one.

The first to get caught is Milady Ambitious Chekhovian.

"What do you think you are doing, mister?" she admonishes him as he holds her by the nape of her neck and forces her into the box. "I have important things to do! Let go of me!"

Next comes Little Miss Practical. I would have expected her to follow the course of least resistance and surrender, but apparently she finds swearing more practical. Smoldering with anger, she yells, "Yo, who do you think you are? You moron! Get your hands off me!"

"Please don't bother, I will go where I need to go," says Dame Dervish as she walks with dignity into the box.

"Poton, darling, why the rush? Why don't we talk first tête-à-tête? Just the two of us. May I call you Potie?" says Blue Belle Bovary, pouting her lips, tilting her head to one side, trying to use her feminine wiles to get herself off the hook. Despite her best efforts, she, too, is sent into the box.

"But I have lentil soup on the stove, you cannot arrest me now," begs Mama Rice Pudding.

Finally comes Miss Highbrowed Cynic. "You call yourself 'Lord' and you think you represent the black sun of melancholy. But you seem to have forgotten that that sun is not solely a destructive force. As Julia Kristeva said, 'melancholy is amorous passion's somber lining.'"

"Ughh?" asks Lord Poton, sounding seriously confused, but he tucks her into the box anyhow.

So it is that all six members of the Choir of Discordant Voices find themselves trapped in a lockbox. The silence in the house is disconcerting.

"At last we are rid of the Thumbelinas!" says Lord Poton, the sweetness in his tone contradicting the sharpness of his glance. "They are all gone."

"Yeah, they are," I say.

"From now on there will be no one around to yammer at you. You will hear only my voice. Isn't that great?"

I try to join his laughter, but it just doesn't pass through my throat.

Quickly I assess the new situation: centralization of authority under a dictator, the suppression of alternate voices via violence, systematic usage of propaganda, absolute obedience to the leader . . . All the signs are here. Political scientists have widely analyzed the connection between fascism and economic depression. In my case, there is a connection between fascism and psychological depression.

Now I know that after oligarchy and martial law, after monarchy and anarchy, the days of fascism have arrived.

Womanhood as an Incomplete Narrative

Today Lou Andreas Salomé is less remembered as an author and intellectual in her own right than as the colorful and controversial woman behind several powerful men of letters. She is portrayed as the mysterious muse who inspired Rilke, Nietzsche and Freud to look more closely at womanhood and feminine creativity. Such descriptions, though no doubt intriguing, do not do justice to Salomé's vision or versatility. In her time she was a famous author, which makes it hard to understand why her novels have been so widely forgotten today. In addition to fiction and plays, she wrote contemplative essays on a wide spectrum of topics such as Russian art, religious philosophy, theater and eroticism.

Born and raised in St. Petersburg, Salomé grew up with five brothers and was much loved and pampered by her father. As a child she had a special gift for telling stories, though she found it difficult to abandon her imaginary characters afterward. She felt guilty for leaving them. This tendency to blame herself for things for which she was not responsible would continue to haunt her throughout her entire life.

Salomé arrived in Zurich in 1880, only nineteen years old. She was beautiful, brilliant and dauntless. Almost instantly she was drawn to the avant-garde circles where she met Europe's leading scholars and artists. With them she engaged in heated debates, surprising many with her self-confidence and zeal to learn. Women, in her eyes, could not be expected to just complement men, or be sidelined, silenced and strapped in housework and motherhood. A woman was an affirmative, inventive creator on her own—not an object to derive inspiration from, and thereby not necessarily a muse. Salomé believed that every attempt to control women would damage their natural, creative femininity.

Rilke adored her, seeing Salomé as the personification of sublime femininity. Inspired by her, he maintained that an artist, whether man or woman, had to bring out the feminine power within. Producing artwork was akin to childbearing, for through this process the artist gave birth to new ideas and visions. Rilke claimed that "one day . . . the woman will exist whose name will no longer signify merely the opposite of masculinity, but rather something in itself, something thought of in terms not of completion and limitation, but rather of life and existence."

Yet it was rather ironic that it was Salomé who later convinced Rilke to modify his name on the grounds that it sounded "too effeminate." The "Rene" in his name was changed to "Rainer," though Rilke didn't give up "Maria." Thus he became Rainer Maria Rilke.

Salomé had a long affair with the author Paul Ree, and later got married to the linguistic scholar Carl Friedrich Andreas. Being a married woman didn't seem to change her critical views on bourgeois marriage. She openly flirted with men, all of whom happened to be intellectuals or connoisseurs of the arts. The fact that she was married and had many lovers makes it difficult to understand how it was that she remained a virgin for long years. Her marriage was unconsummated. The powerful, independent writer and thinker was either scared of sexuality or unwilling to lose herself in an Other.

Nietzsche once said, "For the woman the man is a means: the end is always the child." As compelling as it sounds, the statement did not apply to Lou Andreas Salomé. Not that she did not want to have children. She did. She even proclaimed motherhood as the highest calling for a woman. Her own childlessness was a source of regret and sorrow for her and she talked candidly, sometimes mordantly, about it. She interpreted the bond between the mother and the child as one that truly connected the Self to the Other.

Yet she also loved men. Those she treasured she did not see as a means to an end. In her eyes, each was a world unto himself. Like a housewife who took a special satisfaction in ironing out the wrinkles in a shirt, she patiently strived to smooth down the flaws in their personalities. She was an intuitive, insightful and controversial writer with strong opinions. Those who loved her—mostly men—loved her deeply; those who hated her—mostly women—did so with the same intensity.

Marguerite Duras—the diva of French literature according to many—was born in Saigon in 1914. Her parents were both teachers there, working for the French government. She lost her father at an early age, after which her mother remained in Indochina with her three children. The family did not have an easy life and there were financial problems deepened by quarrels and domestic violence. When Marguerite was a teenager she started having an affair with a wealthy Chinese man, a relationship she wrote extensively about in both her fiction and her memoirs.

At the age of seventeen she went to France, where she got married and wrote novels, plays, movie scripts, short stories and essays. She moved deftly between these different genres. When she wrote *The Sea Wall,* which was based on her childhood in Indochina, she and her mother had a huge quarrel about the way she had depicted her family. "Some people will find the book embarrassing," she said. "That doesn't bother me. I have nothing left to lose. Not even my sense of decency."* There is a scene in her memoirs where her mother reads the book for the first time upstairs and the writer waits anxiously for her approval downstairs. When she comes downstairs her mother's face is stern, showing her dislike. She accuses Marguerite of distorting the truth and playing to the gallery of readers; Marguerite, in turn, defends her book and her right to blur fact and fiction.

If the past is a foreign land, Duras visited it often, coming back with

---

* Laure Adler, *Marguerite Duras: A Life* (Paris: Editions Gallimard, 2000), 217.

different memories of the same events. "No other reason impels me to write of these memories, except that instinct to unearth," she said. Her interpretation of the story originally told in *The Lover,* which was based on her affair as a teenager with a Chinese man twelve years her senior, subsequently changed from book to book. Though prolific and generous with her craft, Duras was a writer who did not shy from exploring the same themes over and over. After the turmoil of 1968, her writing took on a more political overtone. In tandem with the spirit of the period, the title of one of her books reads *Destroy, She Said.*

She lost her first child, carrying the loss and pain with her all through her life. She had a second child—a turning point after which she started running at breakneck speed from one task to another. Juggling motherhood, housework and writing books during the day, she would drink and socialize at night. She didn't want to miss anything. Her marriage faltered under several pressures. She and her husband split but did not really separate—still spending time together, seeing to their son's education. She had several other love affairs later on; she was a woman who could do neither without loving men nor without writing books.

Her passion for writing was commendable, yet her personality was overshadowed by self-obsession and self-absorption to the point of narcissism. She liked to be adored and praised, and retained a competitive, possessive spirit until the end. She did not speak to several members of her family and was widely criticized by critics and fellow writers for her egomania. Several times throughout her life, she lapsed into bouts of guilt, self-pity and alcoholism.

Rebecca West was a novelist, literary critic, travel writer and journalist. Born in 1892 as Cecily Isabel Fairfield, she adopted her nom de plume from a play by Ibsen, *Rosmersholm.* She began her writing career as a columnist for a suffragist weekly. As a young woman she embraced radical feminist and socialist views. Though she revised her views over the years, her concern for social justice and equality lasted a lifetime. In 1913 she met the famous science fiction writer H. G. Wells after writing an acerbic review of his novel *Marriage*. They fell in love, though Wells was twenty-six years her senior, and married. Their affair lasted ten years, and in 1914 their son, and her only child, Anthony, was born.

Striving as a single mother from then on, West started to write critical essays for various newspapers and magazines. She became one of the leading intellectuals of the time and a prolific novelist. Yet, in her private life, she was not always happy or successful. The relationship with Wells suffered from repeated ups and downs and she had several other affairs. In some ways she was like Lou Andreas Salomé, a sharp-witted woman in male intellectual and artistic circles, friend and lover.

Her relationship with her son was strained to the breaking point in later years. Anthony West, a gifted author himself, wrote a biography of his father that became very popular but made his mother very unhappy. Rebecca West accused her son of distorting reality, sharing private memories and, especially, unfairly degrading her as a bad mother. She sued him in order to prevent the publication of his semi-autobiographical novel *Heritage*. Perhaps what hurt her most was that she had raised him on her own while his father had been absent for most of the time and yet Anthony had written more favorably about his father than his mother. There were mutual accusations and the wounds were never fully healed. When Rebecca West died in 1983 her son was not with her. After her death, Anthony West published his *Heritage* and his tone toward his late mother remained critical, bitter.

Simone de Beauvoir once said a "woman is not a completed reality, but rather a becoming, and it is in her becoming that . . . her possibilities should be defined." Lou Andreas Salomé, Marguerite Duras and Rebecca West, three headstrong women with different stories but similarly stormy lives, similarly dealing with issues of body, love and femininity, were women "becoming."

Just like all of us.

Stranger in the Mirror

There should be a law forbidding people who are going through a depression to come anywhere near a mirror. They should be prevented, for their own good, from seeing their reflections until they are way out of their gloom. If for some reason a depressed person *must* look into a mirror, he or she ought to do so fleetingly. Mirrors are the worst objects you can have around when your self-esteem has hit rock bottom and there are dark clouds hovering above your soul.

Yet here I was, alone in the room, looking into a mirror for what felt like an eternity. It was a round mirror with budding and flowering roses carved in its silver frame and a reflection of a young woman staring back. Her hair was unwashed, her body was that of a rag doll and her eyes were immensely sad. Never lifting my gaze off her, I scrutinized this familiar stranger with a curiosity that verged on anger. As she was new to me, I couldn't help wanting to know more about her. I was furious with her, too, because somehow she had replaced me. Of one thing I was sure: The woman in the mirror was sinking, and if she sank deeper, she would take me down with her.

In some parts of Turkey, elderly women believe that mirrors are not, and have never been, simple decorative objects. That is why they adorn not the fronts but the backs of mirrors and then hang them on the walls with their backs facing out. If and when a mirror has to be turned around, it is covered with a dark cloth—preferably black or red velvet. You move the cloth aside to take a peek at yourself when combing your hair or applying kohl, then you pull it back down. The surface of a mirror is thought to be too dangerous to leave exposed in the open for too long. It is an old Eastern tradition nowadays mostly forgotten, but there are still many grandmothers who see in every mirror a gateway to the unknown. If you look into a mirror for too long, there is a chance that the gate might suddenly open and suck you inside.

Around the globe there are several words that function like common currency. East or West, wherever you go, the words sound more or less the same in every language and culture. *Television* and *telephone* are the most well-known examples; *Internet* is yet another. And so is *depression*.

As common as the word *depression* is across languages, there are still noteworthy cultural differences. In Turkish, for instance, one says "I am *at* depression" instead of "I am depressed." The word is used as if depression were less a state of mind than a specific area, a dark corridor with only a weak lightbulb to illuminate the place. The person who is depressed is thought to be not "here," but in that "other space," separated by glass walls.

Not only are the depressed in a different place but their relationship to time is also warped. Depression recognizes only one time slot—the past—and only one manner of speech: "If only." People who are depressed have very little contact with the present moment. They live persistently in their memories, resurrecting all that has come and gone. Like a hamster on a wheel or a snake that has swallowed its tail, they are stuck in a roundabout of gloom.

That, pretty much, was my state of mind in the weeks that followed. Something had ripped inside of me, something I could not quite put my finger on, and through that opening in my soul all the anxieties and worries I had accumulated throughout the years were now pouring out in an unstoppable flood.

But what really made it worse was that I could not write anymore.

I was eight years old when I started writing fiction. My mother came home one evening with a turquoise notebook and asked me if I would like to keep a personal journal. In retrospect, I think she was slightly worried about my sanity. I was constantly telling stories, which was good, except that I told these to imaginary friends, which was not so good. So my mother thought it could do me good to write down my day-to-day experiences and emotions.

What she didn't know was that I then thought my life was terribly boring. So the last thing I wanted to do was to write about myself. Instead I began writing about people other than me and things that never really happened. Thus began my lifelong passion for writing fiction, which from the very beginning I saw not so much as an autobiographical manifestation as a transcendental journey into other lives, other possibilities.

Now, however, I felt as if illiterate. Words that had been my lifelong companions abandoned me and dissolved into soggy letters, like noodles in alphabet soup.

Gradually, my condition became apparent to those around me.

Some people said, "You must be having a writer's block or something. No big deal, it happens to everyone. It will pass."

Others said, "It's because you went through some pretty stressful days. You were brought to trial due to the words uttered by characters in your novel *The Bastard of Istanbul*. Being pregnant at the time, it was a taxing experience and took its toll."

My maternal grandmother said, "Your depression must be the doing of the evil eye. May those malicious eyes close!"

A spiritual master I visited said, "Whatever the reason, you need to embrace your despair and remember, God never burdens us with more than we can bear."

Finally, a doctor I consulted said, "Welcome to postpartum depression. Let's start with two Cipralex a day and see how it goes. If you experience any mood changes down the road, you should immediately report them to me."

"Thank you, Doc," I said, putting the pills in my shirt pocket.

Cipralex, Xanax, Prozac . . . The trouble was, if I started taking them, my milk would have been affected, and I wanted to breast-feed.

That same afternoon, back at home, I thought hard about this dilemma and decided to give my Cipralex pills to the pink cyclamen in the kitchen. One in the morning and one in the evening, on an empty stomach. Every second day, the fuchsia in the sitting room got its share of Xanax. Four times a week, I put Prozac into the gardenia's soil and watered it to make it easier for the plant to gulp the pill down.

A month hadn't passed when the cyclamen turned a color so dark it was almost purple and the fuchsia's leaves went numb, unable to feel anything. The gardenia was perhaps the one that was most deeply transformed. What a blissful flower she had turned into—jovial and buoyant, cracking jokes, giggling from dawn to dusk.

My mood, on the other hand, remained the same.

Lord Poton and His Family

Today it is a well-known fact that many new mothers go through an emotional turbulence in the early stages of motherhood. Yet only a few actually get to meet Lord Poton. Most women come across his young, innocent nephew, and then there are a small number of women who, unfortunately, run into his nasty uncle.

1. Baby Blues (Poton's nephew)

Baby Blues is a low-key emotional imbalance that may occur immediately after the delivery. A harmless and frequent visitor to maternity wards, Poton's nephew is not regarded as a serious problem.

2. Postnatal Psychosis (Poton's uncle)

This is the most dangerous and alarming psychological transformation that a new mother can go through. Those who come into contact with Lord Poton's uncle can end up harming themselves, their children and their surroundings. It requires long-term and serious medical therapy to be rid of him.

3. Postpartum Depression (Lord Poton)

As the lord of the djinn, he is estimated to appear to one out of ten new mothers. Usually he pays his first visit within four to six weeks after the delivery. He looks simple and innocuous at first, but gradually reveals his true colors.

Months into my depression, I began to read extensively on the subject, dying to learn the reason behind my condition, if there was one. I had stopped asking why this didn't happen to other women. Now I wanted to understand why it happened to me. Thus I frequented Web sites, gathered brochures, devoured books and medical reports. Curiosity of this sort was pointless perhaps and yet it was essential for me to be able to move on.

As I researched I understood that it was not only "unhappy" or "unfulfilled" women who suffered from postpartum depression. New mothers of every class, status, religion and temperament were susceptible to it. There were no golden formulas to explain each and every case. Yet, there were a number of causes that triggered the process, such as previous experience with depression, physical health issues during pregnancy, ongoing marital, financial or social problems, lack of cooperation of close relatives and friends, a sudden change in surroundings and so on.

It is not easy to detect the symptoms for postpartum depression, as Lord Poton is highly skillful in reinventing himself. But the following are good signs: lack of energy, excessive sensitivity and irritability, feeling guilty or inadequate, inability to focus, forgetfulness, a fear of hurting yourself or the baby, irregular sleep patterns, lack of appetite, lack of sexual drive, antisocial behavior (closeting yourself in the house, avoiding people and even close friends), lack of interest in physical appearance, an ongoing indifference toward the rest of the world . . .

The truth is, as women of flesh and bones, as the granddaughters of Eve, we all experience ups and downs every now and then, particularly at a time as challenging and stressful as the arrival of a new baby. So, more than the symptoms per se, it is how strongly and persistently we suffer from them that matters.

Dissatisfied with the information I gathered, I decided to prepare my own pop quiz for new mothers.

Lord Poton and You

HOW LIKELY WILL YOU TWO MEET?

How did you feel after you checked out of the hospital and came back home?

A. Like a baby bounced out of his bath. I wish we had stayed a bit longer at the hospital. The nurses were cool and comforting, and were constantly checking on us. When we came home I realized I didn't even know how to hold the baby properly.

B. I felt like a fish out of water, but figured that was normal. Isn't it?

C. I felt terrific, ready for a new beginning! Good thing I had made the baby's room ready. Pink and lavender with unicorn murals. I painted every unicorn myself.

What is your clearest memory of the day of delivery?

A. The pain! And the stress I felt as we entered the operating room. How can I wipe off my mind the sight of masked doctors and nurses?

B. Oh, the moment I held the baby in my arms. It was an incredible feeling. I cried and cried. I still cry when I think about it.

C. The flowers and chocolates sent by our friends and relatives! They were fabulous and those teddy bears were so cute!

Think about how you've been eating lately.

A. I feed the baby but I neglect myself. I don't have much of an appetite anyway.

B. I have been eating regularly, though now that I think about it, I'm not sure how regularly.

C. My appetite is so huge I can eat three breakfasts a day. Don't blame me! Blame Rosita, our cook. Oh, those *biscochitos*! How am I going to shed the extra pounds?

Think about how you've been sleeping lately.

A. What sleep! Listening to make sure the baby is breathing properly, I stay awake all night, every night.

B. I sleep fine, I guess. Well, some nights I sleep better than others.

C. I'm like Sleeping Beauty. When the baby cries my husband gets up to check. Isn't he adorable?

Do you see any differences in yourself since the birth?

A. Better to ask me, "What has stayed the same?" My life has changed, I have changed, everything has changed.

B. I am not my usual self but I'm not sure in what way exactly.

C. Well, I'm fatter than I was before the pregnancy, if that's what you are trying to get at. But I'm much thinner than I was during the pregnancy! So there you go!

A romantic movie that you've watched before is showing on TV. When it gets to a heartbreaking scene, how do you feel?

A. Heartbroken, of course. I cry at pretty much everything these days.

B. Since I've seen the movie before it won't affect me that much, I guess. But you never know.

C. Why on earth would I sit and watch a movie I've seen before when there are plenty of new movies out there?

After giving birth how did you feel toward your husband?

A. I had to go through all the pain, and the guy became a dad, just like that. And then he goes and buys her overalls that have "Daddy's Girl!" written all over. I'm the one who changes diapers, but the baby still gets to be "Daddy's girl." I should have been born a man!

B. I think I feel some distance toward him, but I don't know why.

C. He took me out the other night. We were like high school sweethearts. We even popped a bottle of champagne.

When your doctor comes to mind, how do you feel?

A. Resentment! I'm mad at him. He could have done an epidural.

B. I wonder what it feels like to bring so many babies into the world and see so many women going through the miracle of birth. Must be nice, right? . . . Right?

C. My doctor is the sweetest guy. So the other day I asked him, "Will I be able to wear a bikini this summer?" He said, "Oh, sure, and you will make a few heads turn!" Isn't he charming?

Do you feel energetic during the day?

A. I don't feel like doing much. What's the point anyway?

B. Sometimes my knees feel like rubber. They turn into jelly for a moment and then the feeling passes.

C. Oh, and how! I exercise like crazy. I even hired a fitness trainer. He is Italian!

Who did you argue with last?

A. Oh, just about everyone: my mother, who so favors my husband; my neighbor, who was being testy at a ridiculously early hour; my sisters, who have taken to asking stupid questions over the phone; my mother-in-law, who is trying to control my life; and my husband, who is always on her side.

B. I don't argue with people. I'm always accommodating. Always.

C. I don't fight, honey. I make love.

When was the last time you got together with your close friends?

A. Two months ago? Maybe more? I am not in the mood to socialize these days.

B. Friends and family come to visit, bless them. I have no control over who is coming, who is going.

C. The other day the girls threw me a baby shower; we had so much fun. I had to go off my diet, of course. How could I resist those cupcakes?

How at peace are you with your body and sexuality?

A. My husband and I sleep in different rooms. I won't be the least bit surprised if we soon start living in separate houses or even on separate continents.

B. We still sleep in the same bed, but I'd rather sleep with the baby. I don't say that though. I wouldn't want to hurt his feelings.

C. Oh, you mean hanky-panky? Oh, yeah, like bunny rabbits.

What do you think about this test?

A. A waste of time.

B. I don't know, I didn't fully concentrate on it.

C. It was fun. Not a problem!

The Evaluation Key

If your answers were overwhelmingly A: You've not only met Lord Poton but you may already consider him your best friend. Call your doctor immediately and get help.

If your answers were overwhelmingly B: Your self-esteem is not at its highest and you show signs of passive-aggressive behavior. Be on guard. Lord Poton may knock on your door at any moment.

If your answers were overwhelmingly C: You don't have to ever worry. Depression to you is like Earth compared to Jupiter. In all likelihood, you will never cross paths with Lord Poton.

Writer-Mothers and Their Children

Alice Walker is one of the leading and most outspoken figures among contemporary American women writers. She has an international following and her work has been translated into more than twenty languages. The youngest of eight children, she was born in Georgia to a family of farmers. Her childhood was not a privileged one. Yet her mother was determined to give her children the same opportunities that white children had and did everything in her power to make sure they had a good education. Alice started school at the age of four. When she was eight years old she suffered an eye injury that was to have a profound impact on the course of her life and, perhaps, her writing. Though she forgave the brother who caused her a permanent loss of sight in her right eye, she became timid and withdrawn in the face of the teasing and bullying of other children. From those days on she retained a fondness for solitude and a passion for storytelling, weaving together both oral and written traditions.

In the turbulent early 1960s in the South, Walker followed her heart and married a white lawyer. At a time of rampant racism and xenophobia, they were the only interracial couple in the circles in which they moved. They had one daughter, Rebecca. Becoming a mother was a significant turning point in Alice Walker's life. She felt more fully connected not only with her own mother but also, perhaps, with mothers around the world—those whom she would never meet. Later on, in an essay called "In Search of Our Mothers' Gardens" she wrote, "For these grandmothers and mothers of ours were not Saints, but Artists; driven to a numb and bleeding madness by the springs of creativity in them for which there was no release." Elsewhere she said that her novels carried the kind of thoughts and feelings that she felt her ancestors wanted to pass on to the new generations.

The marriage ended in divorce, after which Walker refused to walk down the aisle again. Her views on matrimony and domestic life have been critical ever since. In an essay entitled "A Writer Because of, Not in Spite of, Her Children," Walker questions the conventional ideas about art and creativity in the Western world. She says the dominant culture draws a boundary between the duties of child rearing and the area of creativity. She sees the institution of marriage as a patriarchal construct unsuitable for an independent, free-spirited writer like herself. She playfully adds, "Besides, I like being courted."

Her most acclaimed novel, *The Color Purple,* vividly testifies that Walker is an author who deals head-on with misogyny and racism. Throughout her life she has worked for a better world where there would be equality and freedom regardless of sex, class or race. In her youth she was active in the civil rights movement and the women's movement. Interestingly, she has resisted the term *feminism,* criticizing it for being indifferent to the problems of women of color. Instead she suggested using a term she coined: womanism. She said womanist was to feminist as purple was to lavender.

More recently she has taken up criticizing the Bush administration's policy in Iraq, drawing the attention of the media to Iraqi mothers and children. She has also traveled to Gaza, meeting with NGOs and the people of Palestine and Israel, bridging cultural differences. She has always been openly political.

In the last few years Alice Walker's private life has been brought to the fore due to a controversy that rose between the writer and her daughter. Rebecca has made several disparaging remarks about her mother, accusing her of forgetting her own child while trying to save the children of others. She says that as a child and teenager she was constantly neglected while her activist mother was running from one event to another. She did not have an easy youth, using drugs and having affairs with both men and women by the age of thirteen. A year later, she became pregnant. She wrote extensively about her ups and downs in her autobiography, *Black, White and Jewish*. After giving birth to a son she wrote a second memoir about the experience and how she came to choose motherhood after a period of hesitation and doubt. Rebecca believes feminism has deceived many women and has even betrayed an entire generation of women into childlessness.

It is a complicated story. One that has two very different sides, like all mother-daughter stories tend to have. For me, it is interesting to see how such a successful, outspoken writer and empathetic mother like Alice Walker could become so estranged from her daughter. Did she experience an existential clash between her life as a mother and her life as an author? Is this a personal story, incited by specific circumstances, that rests between the two of them? Or does it indicate something more universal that can happen to anyone at any time?

Inasmuch as I love reading Toni Morrison, I must say I also love listening to her. She has an androgynous raspy voice, as if speaking to us from beyond invisible barriers, beyond the ghosts of past generations. She is the kind of person to whom you could listen attentively even if she were reciting a recipe for pumpkin pie. You would sit spellbound, just the same.

The critic Barbara Christian calls the kind of realism found in Morrison's work "fantastic earthy realism." Morrison doesn't introduce the past in one swoop; she delivers it in bits and pieces, expecting us to work along with her. She wants the readers to be actively engaged in constructing the story, rather than sitting by passively. The past for her is a mesmerizing jigsaw puzzle that is painful to put together, but it must be done. She writes with rage and melancholy, but also with compassion and love. In one of her most acclaimed books, *Beloved*, which tells the riveting tale of the fugitive slave Sethe, motherhood is examined against the background of slavery. At the end of the novel, Sethe murders her own baby daughter rather than see her become a slave and suffer like she has.

Morrison's women are brave and epic, yet there is nothing overtly heroic about them. It is this combination of the extraordinary with the ordinary in her fictional characters that makes her work remarkable. The kind of motherhood she depicts is based on an elated love that is, at its heart, transformative and healing. Nevertheless, mother and child do not live in a social vacuum, and a woman's performance as a mother is not immune to the ills and sins of the world in which she tries to survive.

Morrison married young to an architecture student. It wasn't an easy marriage, and after having two sons the couple split. She worked as a book editor to support her family. This was the time when she started writing her acclaimed novel *The Bluest Eye*. It was difficult for her to write after work—she felt she was not very bright or witty or inventive after the sun went down. Her habit of getting up very early, formed when her children were young, became her choice. In interviews about that period she admits with modesty that she found it difficult to call herself a writer, preferring instead to say "I am a mother who writes" or "I am an editor who writes."

Her sons once said that they did not particularly enjoy growing up with a mother who wrote for a living. When asked about the reason for this, Morrison gives a candid and wise answer: "Who does? I wouldn't. Writers are not *there*." Morrison says writers like, need and value vagueness. Yet the same vagueness that is crucial for literature and creativity can be burdensome for the children of writers.

Morrison is a writer before everything else. She says her friends understand this and accept her the way she is. Real friends do. Sometimes she even needs to give priority to her writing over her children. There is a wonderful memory she shares that I find very moving. When she was working on *Song of Solomon,* she told her younger son—who was ten years old at the time—that this would not be a fun summer for him because she would be working all the time. She asked him to please bear with her, which he reluctantly but kindly did. Morrison says her son still calls that period of their life "a terrible summer."

Both Alice Walker and Toni Morrison value the richness found in oral storytelling, which has been passed down from grandmothers to granddaughters. Whenever they face great obstacles they are inspired by the many courageous women of earlier generations, and they inspire us to care about untold stories and silenced subjects, past and present. Although motherhood is precious for both, in their fiction they refrain from depicting it as a sacred identity. They talk openly about the conflicts of motherhood, including the hardships they have personally experienced. Numerous defeats, weaknesses and losses shape the women in their stories; sometimes they carry hearts so bruised that it hurts to read about them. Yet these female characters are fighters. They are survivors. It is their passionate struggles—not the losing or winning—that make them who they are.

A Crystal Heart

By late December, Istanbul had adopted a Christmasy look, bright and colorful, and I had tried a few cures to no avail. On the electric pole where the sneakers had hung, there was now a single string of lights, pale green and flimsy. I watched them blink weakly at night, as if they had long given up fighting the dark.

During this time I went to a psychiatrist—a smart woman who had a habit of biting her thumbnail when distracted—but I didn't have much faith in the treatment, and when there is no faith, there is little success. The side effects of the antidepressants she prescribed ranged from an itch in my hands (although this may well have been caused by my desire to write again) to dry mouth and a red rash on my face. It is an endless irony that as beneficial as antidepressants may be for some people, for others their side effects can generate even more depression. I went to therapy, too, but after each session my problems felt amplified rather than diminished. I briefly tried a support group, but being an introvert by nature, I couldn't get used to the idea of talking about my private life to a circle of strangers. As soon as words slipped out of my mouth, they felt unreal, almost illusory.

I didn't know anymore how much of my depression was due to hormones or outside forces, how much of it was self-imposed or culturally imposed. Depressions happen to us against our will and without our knowledge, but then, slowly and furtively, they may turn into a river in which we willingly paddle. There was a nagging fear at the back of my mind that I could be suffering from *The Magic Mountain* syndrome. In Thomas Mann's novel, his hero, Hans Castorp, goes to a sanitarium to visit a friend who suffers from tuberculosis. During the visit he develops similar symptoms and ends up staying seven years in the same sanitarium. Mann believed that sickness opens up a set of new possibilities for human beings and facilitates moral growth.

Likewise I had embraced depression to the point of seeing it as a permanent condition and looking at life through its blurry lenses. I urgently had to go back to writing to find my way out of this quagmire. I had to put my thoughts on paper, but the words wouldn't flow. I couldn't write for eight months.

Eight months might seem like nothing; for me, however, it felt like an eternity. During that time, postpartum depression became an inseparable part of my life. Wherever I went, whatever I did, Lord Poton followed me like an avid stalker. His presence was tiring, and yet he never took things to the extremes. He didn't eradicate you, but he turned you into something less than human, an empty shell of your former self. Perhaps he didn't stop you from eating and drinking altogether, but he took all the pleasure out of it. Perhaps he didn't destroy all your reserves of strength, but he drained them enough that you felt stuck between deep sleep and wakefulness, like a doomed somnambulant.

Before I knew it, literature turned into a distant and forbidden land with bulky guards protecting its boundaries. Worried that I would never be allowed in again, I wondered if writing was like riding a bike—something you didn't really ever forget once you learned how to do it. Or was it like learning Arabic or Korean? The kind of skill that abandoned you, little by little, if you were out of practice for long.

First, I convinced myself that I had forgotten how to write.

Then I started suspecting that writing had forgotten me.

Writing novels—composing stories, creating and destroying characters—is a game favored by those who refuse to grow up. Even though the game takes place on paper, the possibility of playing it over and over again helps you forget your own mortality. "The spoken word perishes, the written word remains." Or so we like to think. It gives comfort against the fleetingness of life. A novelist believes, somewhere deep down inside, that she or he is immortal.

And faith is an important part of being a writer. You come to believe so intensely in the stories you create that the outside world at times will seem dull and inconsequential. When your friends call, when some important matter arises, when your husband wants to go out to dinner, when social responsibilities weigh down on your shoulders, you will find an excuse to get out of each. Everything will be "secondary"—only for writing will you find the time.

The novelist is, and has to be, selfish. Motherhood is based on "giving."

While the novelist is an introvert—at least for the duration of writing her novel—a mother is, by definition, an extrovert. The novelist builds a tiny room in the depths of her mind and locks the door so that no one can get in. There she hides her secrets and ambitions from all prying eyes. As for the mother, all her doors and windows must be wide open morning and night, summer and winter. Her children can enter through whichever entrance they choose, and roam around as they please. She has no secret corner.

When your child falls and scrapes his knees or comes home with his tonsils swollen or lies in bed with fever or when he performs as SpongeBob SquarePants in the school play, you cannot say, "Okay, well, I am writing a new chapter just now. Can you please check back with me next month?"

Betty Friedan—writer, activist, feminist—firmly believed that we needed a broader definition of success than the one largely held by modern society. We had to reframe family values in order to change the system in which every suburban mother struggled on her own, thinking there was something intrinsically wrong with her when she experienced the slightest sense of failure. Friedan herself wrote groundbreaking books and raised three children. "People's priorities—men's and women's alike—should be affirming life, enhancing life, not greed," she said.

All kinds of depression deepen when we forget to enhance life. Perhaps the most persistent question we ask ourselves at times like these is, Why? Why is this happening to me? Why not to others, why me? Saint Teresa of Avila once said, "Our soul is like a castle created out of a single diamond or some other similarly clear crystal." The trouble is we women sometimes fear the crystal is irreparably fractured when it is not, and we think it is our fault when it is not.

My maternal grandmother was married at the age of fifteen to an army officer she had seen for only two minutes (my grandfather knocked on her door pretending to be looking for an address, and she opened the door and gave him directions, similarly pretending). My mother married a philosophy student at the age of twenty, when she was still in college and could not be dissuaded from marrying so young.

One woman had an arranged marriage in Turkey in the 1930s, raised three kids and was fully dependent on her husband's ability to support her. The other married in a love marriage of her choice, got divorced, graduated from college (she finished her degree after the divorce), raised her kid and was economically independent. Although my grandmother was bound by traditional gender roles and my mother was the emancipated one, interestingly, when it came to surviving the vicissitudes of womanhood (like postpartum blues, menopause, etc.), there were times when my grandmother was better prepared. From one generation to the next some valuable information was lost along the way: that at different stages in her life a woman could need, would need, the help of her sisters, blood or not. As for my generation, we are so carried away with the propaganda that we can do anything and everything we want, our feet don't always touch the ground. Perhaps we forget how to ask for help when we need it most.

Today, we do not speak or write much about the face of motherhood that has been left in the shadows. Instead, we thrive on two dominant teachings: the traditional view that says motherhood is our most sacred and significant obligation and we should give up everything else for this duty; and the "modern" women's magazine view that portrays the quintessential "superwoman" who has a career, husband and children and is able to satisfy everyone's needs at home and at work.

As different as these two views seem to be, they have one thing in common: They both focus solely on what they want to see, disregarding the complexity and intensity of motherhood, and the way in which it transforms a woman and her crystal heart.

Farewell to a Djinni

Katherine Mansfield once remarked in that captivating voice of hers, "True to oneself! Which self? Which of my many—well really, that's what it looks like it's coming to—hundreds of selves? For what with complexes and repressions and reactions and vibrations and reflections, there are moments when I feel I am nothing but the small clerk of some hotel without a proprietor."*

As the small clerk of my own hotel, I wish I could say that, in the end, using my willpower, self-control or wits, I defeated Lord Poton. I wish I could claim that I beat him with my own strength by cooking up a grand scheme, tricking him into oblivion. But it didn't happen like that.

This is not to say that none of the treatments had any effect. I'm sure some of them did. But the end to my postpartum depression came more of its own accord, with the completion of some inner cycle. Only when the time was right, when I was "right," did I get out of that dark, airless rabbit hole. Just as a day takes twenty-four hours and a week takes seven days, just as a butterfly knows when to leave its cocoon and a seed knows when to spring into a flower, just as we go through stages of development, just as everything and everyone in this universe has a "use by" date, so does postpartum depression.

---

* Patricia L. Moran, *Word of Mouth: Body Language in Katherine Mansfield and Virginia Woolf* (Charlottesville: University Press of Virginia, 1996).

There are two ways to regard this matter:

The Pessimist: "If one cannot come out of depression before the time is ripe, there is nothing I can do about it."

The Optimist: "If one cannot come out of depression before the time is ripe, there is nothing depression can do to me."

If you are leaning toward the Pessimist's approach, then chances are you are in the first stages of postpartum depression. If you are leaning toward the Optimist's, then congratulations, you are nearing the exit. Every woman requires a varying amount of time to complete the cycle. For some it takes a few weeks, for others more than a year. But no matter how complex or dizzying it seems to be, every labyrinth has a way out.

All you have to do is walk toward it.

Lord Poton: There is something different about you this morning. A sparkle in your eyes that wasn't there before.

Me: Really? Could be. I had a strange dream last night.

Lord Poton: I hope it was a nightmare! Sorry, I have to say that. After all, I am a dastardly djinni. I can't wish you anything good, it's against the rules.

Me: That's okay. It was as intense as a nightmare anyway.

Lord Poton (*more interested now*): Oh, really? Tell me!

Me: Well, we were standing by a harbor, you and I. It turns out you were leaving on a ship that transports djinn from this realm into the next. It was a mammoth ship with lots of lights. The port was so crowded, hundreds of pregnant women were gathered there with their big bellies. Then you embarked and I sadly waved good-bye to you.

Lord Poton (*confused*): You were sad to see me go? Are you sure? You must have been jumping for joy. Why, I've destroyed your life.

Me: No, you haven't. It was me who has done this to myself.

Lord Poton (*even more confused*): Are you trying to tell me you're not mad or angry with me?

Me: I am not, actually. I think I needed to live through this depression to better reassemble the pieces. When I look at it this way, I owe you thanks.

As if I have smacked him in his face, Lord Poton flushes scarlet up to his ears and takes a step back.

Lord Poton (*his voice shaking*): No one has spoken to me like this before. I don't know what to say. (*His eyes fill with tears.*) Women hate me. Doctors, therapists, too. Oh, the terrible things they write about me! You have no idea how it feels to be insulted in brochures, books and Web sites.

Me: Listen, that ship in my dream had a name: *Aurora.* It means "dawn" in Spanish, *şafak* in Turkish.

Widening his slanting eyes, he looks at me blankly.

Me: Don't you understand? I am that ship. I was the one who brought you into the port of my life.

Lord Poton (*scratching his head*): Let's accept what you are saying for a moment. Why would you do such a thing?

Me: Because I thought I couldn't deal with my contradictory voices anymore. I've always found it hard to handle the Thumbelinas. If I agreed with one, I could never make it up to the others. If I loved one a little more, the others would begin to complain. It was always that way. I had been making do by leaning a little bit on one and then a little bit on another. But after I gave birth the system stopped functioning. I couldn't bear the plurality inside of me. Motherhood required oneness, steadiness and completeness, while I was split into six voices, if not more. I cracked under the pressure. That was when I called you.

That is when the strangest thing happens. There, in front of my eyes, Lord Poton starts to dissolve, like fog in the sunlight.

Lord Poton (*taking out his silk napkin and dabbing at his eyes*): I guess it is time for me to leave, then. I never thought I would get so emotional. (*He wipes his nose.*) I'm sorry—you took me by surprise is all.

Me: That's all right.

Lord Poton (*sniffling*): I guess I'll miss you. Will you write to me?

Me: I'll write *about* you. I'll write a book.

Lord Poton (*clapping his hands*): How exciting! I'm going to be famous!

A heavy silence descends, rushing into my ears like the wind through the leaves. I feel light, as if something has held me and lifted me up.

Lord Poton: Well, good-bye. But what will happen to the finger-women?

Me: I will take them out of the box. I'm going to give them each an equal say. The oligarchy has ended, and so have the coup d'état, monarchy, anarchy and fascism. It is finally time for a full-fledged democracy.

Lord Poton (*laughing*): Let me warn you, love, democracy is not a bed of roses.

Me: You might be right. But still, I'd prefer it to all other regimes.

PART SEVEN

Daybreak

The Calm after the Storm

One sunny day in August, when the plums in the garden had ripened to purple perfection, Eyup came back from the military, looking thinner and darker. He didn't say a word for a long time, only smiled. Then I heard him in the bathroom, talking lovingly to the shampoo bottles, perfumes and creams.

"You don't say hi to your wife, but you chat with your shaving cream?" I asked.

He laughed. "In the army one gets to miss even the tiniest luxuries in life and learns to be grateful for what he has on hand."

"Perhaps depression teaches us the same thing, too," I said. "I've learned to look around with new, appreciative eyes."

"I'm sorry I couldn't be with you," he murmured, pulling me toward him. Then he added pensively, "We could have handled this better."

"What do you mean?"

"Why didn't we ask for help from our families or friends while you were going through that turbulence? Why didn't we hire a nanny to help you? You tried to do everything alone. Why?"

I nodded. "I thought I could manage. I thought I could rock the baby to sleep, feed her healthy food and write my novels. It never occurred to me I wouldn't be able to do this alone. That was my strength and my weakness at the same time."

"From now on, we will do it together," he said tenderly.

"Good," I exclaimed. "Are you going to take care of the baby while I write?"

He paused, a trace of panic flickering in his eyes. "Let's start looking for a nanny."

We did. In ten days we found a nanny from Azerbaijan, a woman larger than life—huge breasts, teeth capped with gold, a loud voice and a hearty laugh. A bewildering combination of Mary Poppins, Xena the Warrior Princess and Impedimenta—the stout, matriarchal wife of Chief Vitalstatistix and the first lady of the village in Asterix the Gaul. A woman who could say the sweetest words in Turkish, talk a blue streak in Russian, and believed the main problem with Stalin was that he hadn't had a good nanny as a child. She taught us the basics about babies—how to burp them, rock them to sleep, feed them, and still have time for ourselves. She helped us greatly. We all helped one another.

The same month, there was the anniversary of a liberal newspaper's literature supplement. When I went to the place of celebration, I found a crowd of novelists, poets, critics, local and foreign reporters, photographers and academics drinking wine out of paper cups, nibbling cheese cubes and milling about garrulously. As in most social activities in Istanbul there was a thick, gray haze that swirled around in lazy spirals, the smoke of all those cigarettes, cigars and pipes hovering in the atmosphere. But we were on a terrace and the air beyond and above us was crisp, the sky a deep ocean blue.

It was there that, after all this time, I ran into Mrs. Adalet Agaoglu. She broke into a smile when she saw me.

"Do you remember the talk we had a while ago?" she said.

"How can I forget?" I said.

"I think you did the right thing by becoming a mother in the end," she said, holding my hand in her hand, my eyes in her stare.

I gently squeezed her hand, and offered humbly in return, "And I respect your decision not to become a mother so as to fully dedicate yourself to your writing."

After all, as even the smallest glimpse into the lives of women writers—East and West, past and present—keenly shows, every case is different. There is no single formula for motherhood and writing that suits us all. Instead, there are many paths on this literary journey, all leading to the same destination, each equally valuable. Just as every writer learns to develop his or her own unique style and is yet inspired by the works of others, as women, as human beings, we all elaborate our personal answers to universal questions and needs, heartened by one another's courage.

Later on, as I watched Mrs. Agaoglu walk away from the party and the evening come to a slow close, I realized the wheel of life had moved through one full turn.

Rule of the Thumbelinas by the Thumbelinas

I hold the lockbox tightly in my lap, listening. Not a sound. Not a peep. My heart pummels wildly. Are they all right? I have missed them so much my eyes water.

A little bit of twisting and the lock opens with a click.

"Please come out," I say.

Nothing moves for a full minute. Then, shielding their eyes from the sudden light, weary but otherwise in good shape, the finger-women start to emerge one by one.

"Finally, freedom!" says Mama Rice Pudding. "My back has gone stiff. What a terrible experience. No refrigerator, no microwave, no rice cooker. I couldn't even brew tea for months!"

Miss Highbrowed Cynic's head pops up next. Gathering the skirts of her hippie dress, she walks out, a haughty look on her small face.

"You speak for yourself. I'm pretty sure this existential torment we now left behind will generate an artistic breakthrough in me. The Greek philosophers thought melancholy wasn't necessarily a bad experience. According to Plato, for instance, melancholy could increase the quality of artistic production. . . ."

"Oh, give me a break," grumbles Milady Ambitious Chekhovian. With her tiny frame she struggles to climb atop the box and manages to sit herself on the lid, fixing her hair. "I can't believe how much precious time we lost inside this penitentiary. That djinni literally stole eight months of our life! Oh, the things we could have achieved in all that time."

"Yo, is that ogre gone?" asks Little Miss Practical as she gets out and glances around.

"Yes, don't worry. He has gone," I say.

Little Miss Practical smiles, something of her old mischief twinkling in the depths of her eyes. "Wait a sec. Did you rush here to release us first thing?"

"Yes, I did," I say. "Because I missed you very much."

"Did you miss me, too, darling?" asks Blue Belle Bovary, blowing me a kiss with her cherry-red lips. "Even me?"

"Also you," I say. "There is no 'even' about it. I missed all of you equally."

"What do you mean?" says Blue Belle Bovary. "You never treated us equally."

"You're right. It was a mistake and I apologize to all of you. From now on, I'm not going to censure any of you, you will all have an equal say. We are a democracy now."

"At long last," says Dame Dervish with a genuine smile. "That's what I wanted all along. That's fantastic!"

For the first time in my life, I realize, I see them as One—inseparable pieces of the same whole. When one is out in the cold, they all shiver. When one is hurt, they all bleed. When one is happy and fulfilled, all benefit from her bliss.

When Milady Ambitious Chekhovian and Miss Highbrowed Cynic launched a coup d'état that long-ago night, it was because I wanted to suppress my maternal side. I wasn't ready to meet Mama Rice Pudding. And the oath I took under the Brain Tree was because I was not at peace with my body. I wasn't open to Blue Belle Bovary. Mama Rice Pudding's absolute monarchy during the pregnancy was a result of my belief that my other inner voices were not compatible with motherhood. At every turn, I would put one finger-woman on a pedestal at the expense of all the others.

I am all of them—with their faults and virtues, pluses and minuses, all their stories make up the book of me.

Hélène Cixous—scholar, essayist, literary critic, writer and one of the most original and critical voices of our times—says her text is written in white and black, in milk and night. Patriarchy, for her, does not exist outside the realm of aesthetics and poetics. She analyzes the Freudian approach that sees woman as "lack," replacing it with "woman as excess." She describes women's writing by using metaphors of childbirth, breast-feeding and allusions to the female body. "It is important to define a feminine practice of writing, and this is an importance that will remain, for this practice will never be theorized, enclosed, encoded—which doesn't mean that it doesn't exist."

For Cixous motherhood is a fulfilling experience, the most intense relationship that a human being has with another human being. Though she draws a line between the cultural and the biological, the latter is not insignificant for her. Female biology is an inspiration for her figurative way of writing. "I'm brimming over! My breasts are flowing. Milk. Ink. Nursing time. . . ." Cixous is a scholar who is both critical of and supportive toward women writers. She thinks instead of "undermining patriarchy from within," many female authors have chosen to write like men, repeating the same codes and stereotypes. She advocates a new writing based on the libidinal economy of the feminine, an *écriture féminine*, that is critical of logocentrism and phallocentrism and operates outside and under these terrains, like underground tunnels made by moles.

There is no social change without linguistic change. Women need to break their silence. They need to write. "We should write as we dream," she says.

Ursula K. Le Guin is one of my favorite women writers. When asked what she would be if she weren't a writer, she answered: dead. From the day she started writing at the age of five to the present she has never slowed down. Though always prolific and creative in several genres, she said writing was never easy. "The difficulty of trying to be responsible, hour after hour, day after day for maybe twenty years, for the well-being of children and the excellence of books, is immense: it involves an endless expense of energy and an impossible weighing of competing priorities." Despite the difficulties involved, she says the hand that rocks the cradle writes the book.

Placing the finger-women on my writing desk, I hug all six of them. Giggling, they hug me back.

Miss Highbrowed Cynic, Milady Ambitious Chekhovian, Little Miss Practical, Mama Rice Pudding, Dame Dervish, Blue Belle Bovary and voices that I have not yet met stand next to one another. No one tries to rule the others, no one is a dictator. No one is wearing a crown or carrying badges. Not anymore.

This is not to say that they agree on every issue. But by listening, not just talking, they are learning the art of coexistence. They now know that to exist freely and equally, they need one another, and that where even one voice is enslaved none can be free. Together we are learning how to live, write and love to the fullest by simply being all of who we are. Sometimes we manage this beautifully and artlessly; sometimes we fail ridiculously. When we fail we remember the moments of harmony and grace, and try again.

That, pretty much, is the pattern of my progress in life: Take a step forward, move on, fall down, stand up, go back to walking, trip over and fall down on my face again, pull myself up, keep walking . . .

Epilogue

The next year I finished my new novel, *The Forty Rules of Love,* which became a record best seller in Turkey. I went back to giving interviews, writing columns and essays, attending literary festivals and commuting between cultures like I always did. I stopped teaching at the University of Arizona, as it proved impossible to travel with a baby for so many hours. Instead we made a new beginning in London, spending half the year there, half the year in Istanbul. I learned to fuse a nomadic existence with the requirements of a settled life.

Our daughter's name is Shehrazad Zelda—the former from the charming storyteller of the East, the latter from Zelda Fitzgerald. Eighteen months later we had a son, Emir Zahir—the former from the old traditions of the East, the latter from a story by Borges, "The Zahir," and a book by Paulo Coelho, *The Zahir.*

In everything I wrote and did, I was, and still am, greatly, gratefully, inspired by Zelda and Zahir, and by the beauties and intensities of motherhood.

The second pregnancy was an easy one, and neither after the delivery nor in the months following it did I run into Lord Poton—or any of his relatives. I hear he is getting old and stiff with arthritis. Perhaps he will soon stop bugging new mothers altogether, preferring to spend his time shining his lamp.